MW00465731

Common Chinese Patterns *330*

汉语常用格式 *330* 例

陈　如　朱晓亚　编著

华语教学出版社
SINOLINGUA

First Edition 2010
Second Printing 2012

ISBN 978-7-80200-647-8
Copyright 2010 by Sinolingua
Published by Sinolingua
24 Baiwanzhuang Road, Beijing 100037, China
Tel: (86)10-68320585, 68997826
Fax: (86)10-68997826, 68326333
http://www.sinolingua.com.cn
E-mail: hyjx@sinolingua.com.cn
Printed by Beijing Mixing Printing Co., Ltd.

Printed in the People's Republic of China

In my early stages of Chinese language study as a student of the author Professor Chen Ru at Peking University, I found her to be one of the most inventive and yet practical and applied teachers of language I have ever encountered. Most American students in our early group that included United States Treasury Secretary Tim Geithner did not have a strong grasp of Chinese grammar, much less our own English language grammar. To compensate, Prof. Chen created imaginative examples of sentences that demonstrated the proper use of grammar patterns, and our studies advanced quickly. This compilation of 330 of the most common patterns inspires me with that same fun, creative and applied teaching approach that emphasizes contemporary usage in China that was so effective even 30 years ago. I am certain that this book will inspire a new cadre of students who will become as devoted to learning from Prof. Chen's teachings as I have in my life.

I still remember the Chinese saying 活到老, 学到老, 还有三分, 学不到. (One will study and live until old age, but there will still remain a portion that we will never learn.) After 30 years of Chinese study, the truth of this saying continues to haunt my study and teaching of the Chinese language. Even now as a teacher of Chinese at an Ivy League university, Dartmouth College, I sometimes struggle with Chinese phrase constructions, sometimes stopping in mid-sentence when I realize I have used the wrong word or phrase. In these moments I feel as if I have memorized a dictionary but skipped a line after each word and got all the definitions wrong. I have searched desperately for a practical book that enumerates the most common constructions and provides concrete and contemporary Chinese-specific examples of their use. In 2009, while directing Dartmouth's summer foreign study program in Beijing, I met with my dear teacher Prof. Chen Ru and asked her if such a book existed. Imagine my elation when she showed me the new manuscript co-authored by her and Ms. Zhu. It seems now that the "portion we will never learn" in our studies is indeed reachable.

As an author of five phrasebooks for Lonely Planet publications including *Mandarin* and the 16-language *Languages of the Silk Road*, and as someone who has studied 25 languages in my lifetime so far, I have found books such as this to be essential for the mastery of important language constructions, to boost a learner's language level with practical examples formatted in a repeated logical structure. Whether one is in the first years of Chinese study or an advanced learner, this text and reference grammar is an essential addition to your language toolkit. It will also prove invaluable to teachers. Though we may never fully master that 三分 portion of our Chinese studies, with this book it will get us ever within reach and we will come closer to fluid mastery of the Chinese language.

Dr. Justin Rudelson
Asian and Middle Eastern Languages and Literatures
Dartmouth College

我是在北京大学开始学汉语的，师从本书的作者陈如教授。她是我见过的最具创造性，又很注重实践的一位语言教师。我们这些刚开始学汉语的美国人，包括现任美国财政部部长蒂莫西·盖特纳，大多数都对汉语语法掌握得不好，自己的母语英文语法甚至更差。为弥补我们的不足，陈教授编写了很多充满想象力的例句，来诠释如何正确使用格式，我们的学习因而进步很快。她和朱晓亚老师编写的这本330个最常用的格式，让我想起那种强调实际运用、充满乐趣、创造性和实用性的教学方法。这种方法在30年前就是非常有效的。我相信，这本书肯定能激发起学习汉语者的兴趣，使他们像我一样从陈教授的教学中受益。

我还记得这样一句中国俗语：活到老，学到老，还有三分，学不到。经过30多年的汉语学习，这句话的意义仍然贯穿于我的汉语学习和教学中。虽然我已经是美国常春藤名校达特茅斯大学的汉语教师，有时候还是会弄不清汉语短语的结构，有时候还是会意识到自己用错了词汇或短语，话讲到半截只好停下来。这种时候，我会感觉自己就像背了一本字典，每个词却漏记了一行，结果把整个释义都弄错了。我到处寻找，想买一本实用的书，列举最常用的结构，并提供这些结构的具体而且符合中国实际的用法例句。2009年，我带队到北京举办达特茅斯夏季外语学习项目，见到了我敬爱的陈如教授，问起她是否有这样的书。可以想见，当陈老师拿出她和朱老师的书稿时，我有多么惊喜，好像那"学不到的三分"现在也触手可及了。

我作为作家参与编写过五本孤独星球出版社的常用语手册，其中包括《汉语》和16个语种的《丝绸之路上的语言》。我学习过25种语言，依我的经验，拥有这样一本书非常必要，它能教会学生掌握重要的语言结构，通过逻辑性的复现，采用实用的例句，帮助学生提高语言水平。无论是汉语初学者，还是高级程度学习者，这本书都是必不可少的工具书，对教师也将会非常有价值。也许在汉语学习中，我们永远不能完全掌握"学不到的三分"，但是有了这本书，我们能够更进一步，汉语能够掌握得更加熟练。

达特茅斯大学 亚洲和中东语言文学系 贾斯汀·卢德森博士

在学习汉语的过程中，学生一定会遇到这样的问题：听、读某个句子时，对其中所有的词语都能解释，却怎么也弄不明白句子的意思。为什么会这样呢？问题就在于，在汉语中存在着大量这样的语法现象：在一个句子中通过前后词语的搭配，形成一个固定的格式，从而表达相对稳定的含义。比如："爱～不～"，表示对对方的做法或选择不满，但表面上却无所谓的意思，而不是"喜欢什么不喜欢什么"的意思了。由于在形式上这些词语已经形成了定型的结构，人们就通俗地把它们叫做"格式"。我们编写这本书的目的，就是把汉语中日常习见的一些"格式"汇集在一起便于学生学习。

本书所列的"格式"主要有两类：一类是句子格式，如"不但～反而～"、"管～叫～"；一类是短语格式，如"有～无～"、"东～西～"、"大～大～"等。这两类是本书"格式"的主体部分。另外，我们还将教学中遇到的学生理解起来比较困难的，整体意义不等于每个词语意义相加之和的一些词汇、修辞方面的东西也纳入进来，这些条目不是严格意义上的"格式"，但是本书主要是从便于学生学习的角度出发，这些理解和使用的难点是我们在几十年的对外汉语教学过程中积累起来的，考虑到学生在学习过程中确实需要，我们也收录进来。

为了使学生学习得更快，理解得更准确，掌握得更熟练，我们为常用的330个"格式"编写了3300个实用例句。全书由注释、例句、对话和练习四部分组成。在注释部分，我们不求详尽、全面，而是选择每个格式常用的、高频的意思和用法做简明、扼要的解释。注释中提到的用法在例句和（或）对话部分都有对应，以便使学习者能较快地理解、掌握，对授课教师也会有参考和使用价值。例句部分有难有易，并适当出现一些常用成语或固定词组，以利于提高学习者的兴趣和文字阅读及表达能力。对话部分注意提高学习者的表述和应答能力，加强实用性。练习部分较容易完成，着重于让学习者学会对该格式的运用以提高学习者的成就感。

本书是一本学习用书，教师在备课的时候也可以参考。这种收词方式在以前出版的对外汉语教学类图书中还没有过，希望能起到抛砖引玉的作用。也正因为是一种新的尝试，所以错误难免，请多提意见。谢谢！

欢迎你来学"格式"，祝你学习汉语"更上一层楼"。

编　者
2009 年 9 月

When learning Chinese, you must have encountered the following problem: you understand all the words when listening to or reading a sentence, but still you do not understand the sentence. Why? The reason is that there are a large number of grammatical phenomena in the Chinese language, where some words are always used together with specific others, forming a set structure or collocation which has a specific meaning. For instance, 爱～不～ seems to offer a free choice, but it actually expresses dissatisfaction with the behavior or choice of the other person; it does not mean "to like something and dislike something" as it may appear to mean. Since these expressions are of a set structure, people usually call them 格式 (set patterns). We have compiled this book as a collection of common set patterns in the Chinese language to facilitate students' study.

There are two main categories of set patterns in this book: 1. set sentence structures, such as: 不但～反而～, 管～叫～; 2. set phrases, such as 有～无～, 东～西～, ～大～ etc. Besides, we have also included some phrases and rhetorical words that are very challenging for students to learn or that make literal sense. The latter ones can not be strictly called set patterns. However, considering we have noticed that over the decades of our Chinese teaching they are the most difficult points for foreign students to master, and are an essential addition to their language practice, we included them in the book.

To help the students learn these patterns faster, understand them more accurately and use them more skilfully, we have compiled 3,300 example sentences for the 330 patterns. Each pattern is presented in its own section comprised of four parts: Explanation, Examples, Dialogues and Exercises. We try to make the Explanation part as concise as possible and ensure that the usages mentioned in the Explanation part are the most commonly met and are all covered in the Examples and Dialogues parts, thus enabling learners to understand and master the expressions more quickly. This also makes this book a valuable resource for teachers' reference and use. Examples are designed to vary in their level of difficulty, and some are idioms or set phrases, so as to arouse the learners' interest and enhance their abilities to read and speak Chinese. Dialogues are more practical to enable learners to better communicate in Chinese. Exercises are made easy to enable students to use the patterns and enjoy a stronger sense of achievement.

This is a students' book and can also be a tool for teachers. As the word entries are the first of their kind, we hope to generate discussion. All comments and suggestions are welcome.

Welcome to the learning of 格式. We wish you great progress in learning Chinese.

From the Compilers
September 2009

目　录

X

解释 *Explanation*

分别用在同一个动词前，表示对对方的做法或选择不满，但表面上却表示无所谓。

Used before the same verb to express a free choice, but actually dissatisfaction with the behavior or choice of the other person.

例句 *Examples*

1. 道理我都讲清楚了，你爱听不听。

   I have made it clear. It's up to you whether to accept it or not.

2. 他爱生气不生气，反正我有意见就得提。

   Whether he is angry or not, I must voice my opinion.

3. 你爱复习不复习，不过考不好可不要怪别人。

   Whether you review or not is your business, but don't blame others when you do poorly in the exams.

4. 你爱说不说，以后你想说我还不想听了呢。

   Whether you speak or not is up to you, but don't expect me to listen next time.

对话 *Dialogues*

1. A：我不爱吃面条。

   I don't like the noodles.

   B：爱吃不吃，不吃就饿着吧。

   It's up to you. If you don't eat, stay hungry.

2. A：我不想去看电影了。

   I don't want to go to the cinema.

   B：爱去不去。你不去，我自己去。

   You make the decision. I will go by myself if you don't.

练习 *Exercises*

用"爱 ~ 不 ~"完成句子。Complete the sentences with the pattern.

1. A：我给你买的那件衣服，你怎么一直也不穿？

   B：那件衣服颜色太鲜艳了，我不好意思穿。

   A：你_____吧，我以后不会再给你买衣服了。

2. A：我朋友说这房子的房租太贵，不想租了。

   B：_____，我这房子想租的人多着呢。

爱 ~ 就 ~

解释 *Explanation*

表示愿意怎样就怎样，有时也略含不满意味。

Used to indicate "do as you wish", sometimes expressing slight dissatisfaction.

例句 *Examples*

1. 一个人生活可自由啦，爱干什么就干什么。

   It's so free living alone. You can do whatever you want.

2. 放假了，我爱几点起就几点起，太舒服了。

   The holidays have begun, so I can get up whenever I like. It's so comfortable!

3. 我这几天都在家，你爱哪天来就哪天来吧。

   I am at home these days. You can come whenever you want.

4. 父母都出差了，孩子在家爱打扑克就打扑克，爱看电视就看电视，没人管。

   The parents are on a business trip. Without their oversight, kids do whatever they like. If they want to play cards, they play cards, and if they want to watch TV, they watch TV.

对话 *Dialogues*

1. A: 妹妹正在床上躺着呢，她说累死了，不想吃饭了。

   My little sister is lying on her bed. She said she's so tired that she doesn't want to eat.

   B: 爱躺着就躺着吧。

   Let her lie down if she wants to.

2. A: 小王又在背后议论咱们了。

   Xiao Wang is gossiping about us again.

   B: 他爱怎么说就怎么说，别理他。

   Let him talk if he wants to. Don't worry about him.

练习 *Exercises*

用"爱 ~ 就 ~"完成句子。Complete the sentences with the pattern.

1. A: 你怎么跟那样的人交往呢？人品不好，又没脑子。

   B: _____，你管得着吗？

2. A: 妈妈，你说今天我穿哪件衣服去参加晚会？

   B: _____，随便。

汉语常用格式330例

解释 *Explanation*

表示"认为 A 是 B",或"把 A 变成 B"。"成/做"前用动词。

Used to indicate to regard A as B or to turn A into B. A verb is placed before 成 or 做.

例句 *Examples*

1. 看来政府要把社会医疗保险当成大事来抓。

   It seems the government will treat social medical insurance as a major issue.

2. 中国人把长城看做中国的象征。

   Chinese people regard the Great Wall as the symbol of China.

3. 我说怎么听不懂这个句子呢,原来我把"中国文字"听成"中国蚊子"了。

   I know why I did not understand the sentence. I mistook 中国文字 for 中国蚊子.

4. 做这个菜要费些工夫,首先得把所有的用料都切成细丝儿。

   It takes some time to cook this dish. First of all, you need to cut all ingredients into fine strips.

对话 *Dialogues*

1. A: 上午十点开会,你怎么下午四点才来?

   The meeting was held at 10:00 a. m. Why did you come at 4:00 p. m.?

   B: 咳,我把"十点"听成"四点"了。

   Well, I mistook 十点 for 四点.

2. A: 你不是说你喜欢我吗? 怎么又不愿意做我男朋友呢?

   Didn't you say you like me? Why don't you want to be my boyfriend?

   B: 我是把你当成妹妹那样喜欢啊。

   I regard you as a younger sister.

练习 *Exercises*

用"把 A ~ 成/做 B"完成句子。Complete the sentences with the pattern.

1. 从小就是刘阿姨照顾我,我_____。

2. 这两个双胞胎兄弟我总是认不清楚,常常_____。

把～当回事

解释 Explanation

表示重视某人或某事。

Used to indicate that attention is paid to somebody or something.

例句 Examples

1. 他太把自己当回事了,让别人产生了反感。

   He regards himself as a personage,which provokes dislike in others.

2. 你别太把比赛成绩当回事,友谊第一比赛第二嘛。

   Don't take scores too seriously. Friendship comes before competition.

3. 她总是说我不在乎她,其实我挺把她当回事的。

   She always says that I don't care about her. But actually I'm very concerned about her.

4. 她早就提醒我要注意这个问题,可是我没把她的话当回事。

   She reminded me of this problem long ago,but I didn't take her words seriously.

对话 Dialogues

1. A: 你说那些贪污腐败的人就不知道他们的行为是违法的吗?

   Do you think that those corrupt people don't know they have broken the law?

   B: 他们是钱迷心窍了,根本没把党纪国法当回事。

   They're obsessed with money,and think nothing of Party disciplines and the law of the country.

2. A: 我早餐吃得很简单,有时干脆不吃。

   I usually have simple breakfast. Sometimes I just skip it.

   B: 早餐是最重要的一餐,你怎么能不把它当回事呢?

   Breakfast is the most important meal of a day. How can you take no count of it?

练习 Exercises

用"把～当回事"完成句子。Complete the sentences with the pattern.

1. 那些闯红灯的人根本就没_____。

2. 身体最重要,你得_____,不能这么没日没夜地干。

解释 *Explanation*

表示处置,起加重语气的作用。用于口语。

Used in oral Chinese to add emphasis when dealing with something.

例句 *Examples*

1. 请把这些书给整理整理,太乱了。

   Please sort out these books. They are so messy.

2. 这次出差,我一定要把新技术给学到手。

   I must learn this new technology on this business trip.

3. 请马上把会议厅给打扫干净,有外宾来。

   Please clean the conference hall as soon as possible. Some foreign guests are coming to visit us.

4. 快考试了,我把学过的课文、生词都给复习了一遍。

   The exams are coming. I have gone over all the texts and new words.

对话 *Dialogues*

1. A：谁把我的抽屉给翻乱了?

   Who messed up my drawer?

   B：谁知道。反正不是我!

   Who knows! Not me, anyway!

2. A：你在中国待了两年,都去过什么地方啊?

   You have been in China for two years. Where have you been?

   B：我去过的地方可多了,几乎把中国南方著名的旅游景点都给玩遍了。

   Many places, including almost all the famous tourist attractions in South China.

练习 *Exercises*

用"把～给～"完成句子。Complete the sentences with the pattern.

1. A：你的嗓子怎么哑啦?

   B：我昨天看足球比赛太激动了,一直喊"加油!",_____。

2. A：明明,你为什么打弟弟?

   B：这是我最喜欢的一件生日礼物,可是弟弟_____。

~罢了

解释 *Explanation*

表示说话人认为仅此而已,没什么大不了的。

Used to express the speaker's belief that it's no big deal.

例句 *Examples*

1. 他也没什么了不起的,有几个钱罢了。

   He's no big potato. He just has some money.

2. 我开个玩笑罢了,谁知道他竟生气了。

   I was just kidding. Who would think he'd get so angry?

3. 我并不想买什么,随便逛逛罢了。

   I don't want to buy anything,just to window-shop.

4. 他说要出家当和尚,我看不会的,说说罢了。

   He said he would leave home to become a monk. I don't think so. He's just kidding.

对话 *Dialogues*

1. A: 他们老吵架,究竟是为了啥?

   Why are they always arguing?

   B: 没什么大事,无非是些鸡毛蒜皮的小事罢了。

   No big deal, it's just over trivial things.

2. A: 这件衣服我买上当了,越想越生气。

   I got screwed when I bought this dress. The more I think about it, the angrier I get.

   B: 也就是多花了几个钱罢了,别老想了。

   You only spent a bit more money. It's no big deal, so just forget about it.

练习 *Exercises*

用"~罢了"完成句子。Complete the sentences with the pattern.

1. A: 老李,真太麻烦你了,这两天我出差,孩子天天在你家吃饭。

   B: 说什么呀,＿＿＿＿＿＿＿＿＿＿＿＿,你太客气了。

2. A: 小王,你的英语说得这么好,真让人羡慕。

   B: 哪里,＿＿＿＿＿＿＿＿＿＿＿＿,复杂点儿的意思就不会表达了。

解释 *Explanation*

表示为某人某事花了时间、精力、物力、财力，但未获得预期的效果，或未得到应有的回报。

Used to indicate that somebody spent time, energy and physical and financial resources on something, but did not see the expected result or due reward.

例句 *Examples*

1. 你快说啊，别让我们白浪费时间。

   Say it! Don't let us spend time in vain.

2. 我调动工作的事情没办成，白忙乎了一场。

   I failed to get a transfer. My efforts were fruitless.

3. 我临走前真是白叮嘱你了，你一样都没照办。

   I warned you before I left, and you did not follow my instructions. My efforts were wasted.

4. 子女都在国外定居了，父母现在成了空巢老人，那孩子不是白养了。

   Some parents are now empty nesters as their children settle down abroad. They get no reward for bringing up children.

对话 *Dialogues*

1. A: 出国时你妈给你带了两大箱东西，都用上了吗？

   Did you use all the things in the two suitcases your mother let you take when going abroad?

   B: 说实话，有一些是白带了，还花了超重费。

   To tell you the truth, some of them are of no use, and I had to pay overweight charge.

2. A: 我没有看见你给我留的条儿啊。

   I didn't see the note you left for me.

   B: 啊？真是的，害得我白等了两个小时。

   What? So I waited for two hours in vain.

练习 *Exercises*

用"白 ~ （了）"完成句子。Complete the sentences with the pattern.

1. 今天的考试取消了，我＿＿＿＿＿＿＿＿＿＿＿＿＿＿＿＿＿＿。

2. 我吃得也不算少啊，可就是不长肉，＿＿＿＿＿＿＿＿＿＿＿＿＿＿＿＿＿＿。

白 ~（了）（2）

解释 *Explanation*

表示没有任何付出就得到了好处。

Used to show somebody gets benefits at no expense.

例句 *Examples*

1. 这款手机已经过时了，白送给我也不要。

   This kind of cell phone is so old. I wouldn't take it even if it were free.

2. 你们俩争得你死我活的，结果两败俱伤，让别人白捡了个便宜。

   You two fought tooth and nail and both suffered losses, letting others gaining advantage without making efforts.

3. 上次白吃了王叔叔家一顿，趁他家孩子过满月，咱们也送他们点儿什么吧。

   Last time Uncle Wang treated us to a meal though we sent no gift. Now that his child is one month old, we shall give him some gift.

4. 她把穿不下的衣服都送我了，白得了这么些漂亮衣服，我哪能不高兴。

   She gave me all the clothes she cannot wear. Of course I'm happy for getting so many pretty clothes for free.

对话 *Dialogues*

1. A：老潘真是太客气了，硬是不肯收房钱。

   Lao Pan is so hospitable that he refuses to take our rent.

   B：是啊，我们在他家白吃白住了一个月，真不好意思。

   Yes. We're so indebted for being freeloaders in his home for one month.

2. A：这些钱你拿去用吧。

   Take the money for your use.

   B：我不能白拿你的钱啊，我能为你做些什么呢？

   I cannot take your money for free. What can I do for you?

练习 *Exercises*

用"白 ~（了）"完成句子。Complete the sentences with the pattern.

1. 虽说是住在亲戚家，但也不能一直_____。

2. 拿人手软，吃人嘴软。千万别_____。

汉语常用格式330例

解释 *Explanation*

两个"半"各用在意思相反的单音节词前，表示两种性质或状态同时存在。

Used before two monosyllabic antonyms to indicate that two opposing qualities or states exist simultaneously.

例句 *Examples*

1. 酒吧里闪着半明半暗的烛光。

   Dim candlelight flickers in the bar.

2. 这段时间我老睡不好觉，总感觉是半睡半醒的。

   Recently I have not been able to sleep properly, so I am always half-asleep.

3. 虽然他说爱我，但我总觉得他的口气是半真半假的。

   Although he says he loves me, I always feel his tone is only half sincere.

4. 像夹杂着英文单词的白话一样，这些茶馆的设备、装潢都是半中半西的。

   Just like vernacular Chinese is mixed with English, the furniture and decorations in these teahouses is half Chinese and half Western.

对话 *Dialogues*

1. A: 为什么京剧的唱词那么难听懂？

   Why is Beijing Opera so difficult to understand?

   B: 因为京剧的唱词多是半文半白的。

   Because it uses semi-literary and semi-vernacular language.

2. A: 你完全相信他的话吗？

   Do you believe what he said?

   B: 不，我对他的话半信半疑。

   No, I'm not quite convinced.

练习 *Exercises*

选词填空。Choose the right phrases to fill in the blanks.

半公半私   半新半旧   半喜半忧   半开半关

1. A: 你儿子要去美国留学了，你一定很高兴吧。

   B: 我是_____。儿子能去哈佛读书我当然高兴，但是我也很担心，怕他照顾不好自己。

2. A: 你这次到北京来是公事还是私事？

   B: _____。我给单位采购些东西，也给我儿子联系个学校。

半～不～

解释 *Explanation*

表示某种中间状态，有时含厌恶、不满的意思。常与"的"一起用。

Used to show an intermediate state, sometimes carrying a sense of disgust and discontent, often used with 的.

例句 *Examples*

1. 几天没浇水，花都蔫儿了，半死不活的。
   The flower has not been watered for several days and is half-dead.
2. 第一次见面的时候，她穿着一件半新不旧的旗袍。
   When they first met, she wore a semi-new cheongsam.
3. 这个理论太深了，老师讲得也不太清楚，我们还是半懂不懂的。
   This theory is very profound, and the teacher didn't explain it clearly. As a result, we are still confused.
4. 南方梅雨季节时，衣服老干不透，有时穿的衣服都是半干不湿的。
   In the rainy season in southern China, clothes cannot get dry. Sometimes the clothes people wear are half-wet.

对话 *Dialogues*

1. A: 你碗里的饭怎么剩下这么多？
   Why did you leave over so much rice in the bowl?
   B: 这米饭半生不熟的，实在没法吃。
   It's half-cooked and I cannot eat.

2. A: 你看我这件衣服好看吗？
   Take a look. How does my dress look?
   B: 半长不短的，我觉得不怎么好看。
   It is neither long enough or short enough. I don't think it looks great.

练习 *Exercises*

用"半～不～"完成句子。Complete the sentences with the pattern.

1. A: 你刚来这里，还不习惯吃西餐吧？
   B: 是的，尤其是_____的牛排，上面还带着血。

2. A: 你儿子多大了？
   B: 十六七岁，正是_____的年纪，教育起来可真不容易。

解释 *Explanation*

表示程度极高、极深，含夸张语气。后面常跟形容词，句尾常带"了"。

Often used before an adjective to indicate a high degree, usually in an exaggerated tone. The sentence often ends with 了.

例句 *Examples*

1. 面试时，我甭提多紧张了。

   I'm so nervous when being interviewed.

2. 这本小说甭提多有意思了。

   This novel is so interesting.

3. 过年的时候，孩子们都回来了，家里别提多热闹了。

   During the Spring Festival all the children come back, and you can't imagine how happy and lively our family is.

4. 想解决这里的河水污染问题，别提多难了。

   It's so difficult to solve the problem of river pollution here.

对话 *Dialogues*

1. A: 你去过内蒙古大草原吗？

   Have you been to the Inner Mongolia grassland?

   B: 去过，蓝天白云连着草原，别提多美了。

   Yes, I have. The blue sky scattered with white clouds against the vast green grassland is so beautiful.

2. A: 假期过得怎么样？

   How was your holiday?

   B: 想吃就吃，想玩就玩，想睡就睡，甭提多自在了。

   I ate anytime I liked, had fun when I wanted and slept when I was tired. I feel so free.

练习 *Exercises*

用"甭/别提多 ~"完成句子。Complete the sentences with the pattern.

1. 这段时间又要上课，又要写论文，又要找工作，＿＿＿＿＿＿＿＿＿＿。

2. 今天老师表扬了我，爸爸也给我买了好多东西，我＿＿＿＿＿＿＿＿＿＿。

A 比 B ~ 得多

解释 *Explanation*

表示同类事物或情况相比较时，相差很大。A 比 B 程度高。"得" 前多用形容词做谓语。

Used to indicate a big difference between two observations. A is in a higher degree than B. An adjective is often used before 得 as the predicate.

例句 *Examples*

1. 我家比他家远得多。

   My home is much farther than his home.

2. 塑料碗比瓷碗轻得多。

   A plastic bowl is much lighter than a porcelain one.

3. 我认为健康比金钱重要得多。

   I believe health is much more important than money.

4. 郊外的空气比市内的好得多。

   The air in the suburbs is much better than that in the city.

对话 *Dialogues*

1. A：今年的收成怎么样?

   How was the harvest this year?

   B：比去年好得多。

   Much better than last year.

2. A：德国车质量真好。

   German cars are of good quality.

   B：可是，价钱也比国产的贵得多。

   However, they are much more expensive than domestically made ones.

练习 *Exercises*

用 "A 比 B ~ 得多" 完成句子。Complete the sentences with the pattern.

1. 最近我学习很努力，不像以前那样爱玩了，所以这次考试的成绩＿＿＿＿＿＿＿＿＿。

2. 我的房间有 20 平方米，他的只有 8 平方米，＿＿＿＿＿＿＿＿＿。

12

解释 *Explanation*

表示所指出的事物和其他事物相比程度是最高的。"比"后面多用表示任指的疑问代词，如"谁"、"什么"、"哪儿"、"哪"等。

Used to indicate what is talked about is of the highest degree, compared with others. An interrogative pronoun is often used after 比, such as 谁, 什么, 哪儿 and 哪.

例句 *Examples*

1. 中国人口比哪国都多。

   China's population is bigger than any other country.

2. 一个人的人品比什么都重要。

   A person's character is of utmost importance.

3. 出头露面的事他比谁都积极。

   He is more active than anyone else when it comes to taking the opportunity to appear in public.

4. 有人说杭州、苏州的姑娘比哪儿的都好看。

   Some people say girls in Hangzhou and Suzhou are more beautiful than those in any other places.

对话 *Dialogues*

1. A: 这个工作交给老赵行吗？

   Can I give the work to Lao Zhao?

   B: 当然行，他比谁都可靠。

   Yes, of course. He is more reliable than anyone else.

2. A: 这儿环境真好。

   The environment here is so good.

   B: 是，比哪儿都安静。

   Yes, it's quieter than anywhere else.

练习 *Exercises*

用"比 ~ 都 ~"改写下列句子。Rewrite the sentences with the pattern.

1. 这个房间是最敞亮的。→＿＿＿＿＿＿＿＿＿＿＿＿＿＿＿。

2. 他认为工作是最重要的。→＿＿＿＿＿＿＿＿＿＿＿＿＿＿。

A 比 B ~ 多了

解释 *Explanation*

表示经过比较，差别很大。A 比 B 程度高。"多"前多用形容词做谓语。

　Used in comparison to indicate a big difference between A and B. A is in a higher degree than B. An adjective is often used before 多 as the predicate.

例句 *Examples*

1. 他的个子比我高多了。

   He is much taller than me.

2. 有的人认为，藏文比汉字难写多了。

   Tibetan is much more difficult to write than Chinese according to some people.

3. 东北地区比南方冷多了。

   It is much colder in Northeast China than in southern areas.

4. 现在亚太地区的股市情况比早两年好多了。

   The stock market in the Asia Pacific is much better than two years ago.

对话 *Dialogues*

1. A：你怎么什么都听他的？

   How can you obey him on everything?

   B：谁都知道他的经验比我多多了。

   Everyone knows that he is much more experienced than I am.

2. A：这部电影怎么样？

   What do you think of this film?

   B：比上星期咱们看的有意思多了。

   It is much more interesting than the one we saw last week.

练习 *Exercises*

用"~比~多了"完成句子。Complete the sentences with the pattern.

1. 上次考试我只考了70分，这次考了95分，_____ 。

2. 这种冰箱功能、式样都好，不过价格太贵了，等打折时再买吧，_____

   _____。

解释 *Explanation*

表示两种程度都很高的事物相比，前者的程度更高更深。

Used to indicate that the former is higher in degree than the latter, though the two are both high in degree.

例句 *Examples*

1. 我相信将来一定会比现在更好。

   I am confident that the future will be much better than the present.

2. 我同意你的看法，人的内心比外表更重要。

   I agree with you. What's inside a person is more important than the appearance.

3. 他一米八二，够高的吧？可他弟弟比他还高呢！

   He is 1.82 meters tall. Is he tall enough? His younger brother is even taller than him!

4. 她虽然是个演员，可平时穿得比一般人还朴素。

   Although she is an actress, she is dressed even more plainly than average people.

对话 *Dialogues*

1. A: 中国的黄河可长啦，有 5464 公里。

   China's Yellow River is very long. It runs for 5,464 km.

   B: 可长江比它更长，6300 公里呢！

   But the Yangtze River is much longer. It's 6,300 km.

2. A: 这是我们单位的招待所。

   This is the guesthouse of our company.

   B: 哟，比一般的大饭店还豪华。

   Oh, it's more luxurious than some big hotels.

练习 *Exercises*

用 "~比~更/还~" 完成句子。Complete the sentences with the pattern.

1. A: 小丽和小云都是既漂亮又温柔的姑娘。

   B: 对，不过我觉得＿＿＿＿＿＿＿＿＿＿。

2. A: 我以为我是来得最晚的一个了，没想到＿＿＿＿＿＿＿＿＿＿。

   B: 真不好意思。我起晚了。

汉语常用格式330例

15

A 比起 B 来 ~/比起 B 来，A ~

解释 *Explanation*

表示 A 和 B 相比，强调 A。

Used to compare A with B and to emphasize A.

例句 *Examples*

1. 现在中国的各种法规比起过去来健全多了。

   Nowadays China's laws and regulations are more sound than those in the past.

2. 上下班时堵车堵得很厉害，骑自行车比起开车来还快呢。

   At rush hour, the traffic is terrible. Riding a bike is faster than driving a car.

3. 比起普通相机来，数码相机方便多了。

   Digital cameras are more convenient than ordinary ones.

4. 比起以前来，现在我们的居住环境好多了。

   Our living environment is much better than that in the past.

对话 *Dialogues*

1. A: 近几年来，你们国家的经济发展得很快。

   In recent years, your country's economy has developed rapidly.

   B: 对，不过比起发达国家来差距还不小。

   Yes, but it still lags far behind developed countries.

2. A: 我觉得学生应该经常听到鼓励而不是批评。

   I think that students should be frequently encouraged instead of criticized.

   B: 你说得对。鼓励比起批评来，效果更好。

   You're right. Encouragement gets better results than criticism.

练习 *Exercises*

用"A 比起 B 来 ~/比起 B 来，A ~"改写下面的句子。Rewrite the sentences with the pattern.

1. 我觉得中文不容易学，但法语更难学。

   →＿＿＿＿＿＿＿＿＿＿＿＿＿＿＿＿＿＿＿＿＿。

2. 美国的物价比欧洲的低。

   →＿＿＿＿＿＿＿＿＿＿＿＿＿＿＿＿＿＿＿＿＿。

汉语常用格式330例

解释 *Explanation*

表示只涉及某一范围的情况就已经很突出了，暗含整体就更突出了。不过说话人只强调涉及的情况。

Used to indicate that one part is prominent enough to indicate the whole must be more prominent. But the speaker only stresses what he or she mentions.

例句 *Examples*

1. 我妈每天可忙了。别的不说，就做这四口人的饭，也够她累的。
   Mom is busy enough every day. Besides her other tasks, cooking meals for four is tiring enough for her.
2. 他可是个大款。别的不说，就高档小轿车，至少有三辆。
   He is really a fat cat. He has at least three premium cars, besides other properties.
3. 离开了家以后，别的不说，就说这吃，已经够我伤脑筋的了。
   After leaving home, meals, above all other things, are a headache for me.
4. 政府也很不容易。别的不说，就说修路，得花多少人力财力。
   It is not easy for the government. Besides all other considerations, it spends so much human power and financial resources to construct the roads.

对话 *Dialogues*

1. A: 你每月花多少钱？
   How much do you spend each month?
   B: 别的不说，就说喝酒，也得上千块。
   I spend up to a thousand yuan on drinking, besides everything else.

2. A: 来一趟真不容易呀！
   It's so difficult to come here.
   B: 可不，别的不说，路上就得花一整天时间。
   True. It takes at least one day on the way, let alone all the other headaches.

练习 *Exercises*

用"别的不说，就（说）~"完成句子。Complete the sentences with the pattern.

1. A: 你们平时作业多吗？
   B: 多。_____。

2. A: 准备结婚，筹备婚礼可不容易啊。
   B: 是啊，_____。

汉语常用格式330例

别看 ~ ，其实 ~

解释 *Explanation*

表示实际情况和根据表面现象按常理推出的结论相反。后一分句也可用"但，却，可"等表示转折的词语。

Used to indicate that the actual situation is contrary to what one would think according to common sense. 其实 can be replaced by 但，却，可 or other words indicating a turn or transition.

例句 *Examples*

1. 别看他瘦，其实吃得不少。

   Thin as he looks, he eats a lot.

2. 别看那儿交通不方便，但游客挺多。

   Although the transport is not convenient, that place attracts many visitors.

3. 别看老王住得远，可每天总是第一个到办公室。

   Although Lao Wang lives far away, he is the first in the office every day.

4. 别看他是个小学生，却发现了教科书上的错误。

   Although he's a pupil, he discovered mistakes in the textbook.

对话 *Dialogues*

1. A: 我真羡慕你，精力老是那么充沛。

   I envy how energetic you always are.

   B: 别看我平时工作很紧张，但休息时我充分享受人生。

   I work very hard, but I fully enjoy my leisure time.

2. A: 这么个不起眼的地方足球队居然赢了，真没想到。

   I never expected such a local soccer team to win!

   B: 别看他们队名气不大，其实很有实力。

   Their team isn't famous, but it is very powerful.

练习 *Exercises*

用"别看 ~ ，其实 ~"完成句子。Complete the sentences with the pattern.

1. A: 他个子不高，参加篮球队行吗？

   B: ＿＿＿＿＿＿＿＿＿＿＿＿＿＿＿ 。

2. A: 天气这么冷，你怎么还盖这么薄的被子？

   B: ＿＿＿＿＿＿＿＿＿＿＿＿＿＿＿。

解释 *Explanation*

表示两事物相差不多，"多少"前一般用形容词。

Used to indicate that there is not much difference between the two. An adjective is usually used before 多少.

例句 *Examples*

1. 现在他的经济情况不比你好多少。

   Now his financial condition is not better than yours.

2. 堵车的话，开车不比走路快多少。

   If there is a traffic jam, driving is not faster than walking.

3. 中国南方很多农村的消费水平不比一般城市低多少。

   Consumption in many villages in southern China is not lower than in ordinary cities.

4. 我看就买这个吧，是名牌，价格也不比一般的贵多少。

   Buy this. It's a famous brand, and not really any more expensive than ordinary brands.

对话 *Dialogues*

1. A：我决定转到法语专业，德语太难学了。

   I decide to change my major to French. German is too difficult for me.

   B：我想学法语不比学德语容易多少吧?

   I don't think French is easier than German.

2. A：她真漂亮，身材也好。

   She's so beautiful, with such a good figure.

   B：你也不比她差多少啊。

   You are not less beautiful.

练习 *Exercises*

用"A 不比 B ~ 多少"完成句子。Complete the sentences with the pattern.

1. A：你们学文科的比我们学理科的轻松多了吧?

   B：其实我们学文的也挺辛苦的，_____。

2. A：我想买进口的厨具，质量好。

   B：进口的比国产的贵多了，而且现在国产的质量_____。

不~不~

解释 *Explanation*

两个"不"分别用在意思相反的单音节形容词或方位词前，多表示恰到好处；有时也表示一种不满意的中间状态。用在意思相反的单音节动词（或词素）前，多表示"如果不……就不……"的意思。用在意思相同或相近的单音节词（或词素）前，表示强调否定。

Used with two monosyllabic adjectives or location words with opposite meanings to indicate something is "just right", or sometimes used to indicate a dissatisfying intermediate state. It is also used with antonymic monosyllabic verbs or morphemes to indicate "if not … will not …," or used with two monosyllabic synonyms as an emphatic form of "not".

例句 *Examples*

1. 这条裤子的颜色不深不浅正合适。
   The color of these trousers is neither too dark nor too light. It's just right.
2. 有些年纪大的人看不惯这种不男不女的打扮。
   Some old people can't stand such a sexless style of dress.
3. 那咱们可说好了，7点钟学校门口见，不见不散。
   So, let's meet at 7:00 o'clock at the school gate. Be there or be square.
4. 他不是个好父亲，只知道忙自己的工作，对孩子的事从来都不闻不问。
   He's not a good father. He's always busy with work, and shows no interest in his child.

对话 *Dialogues*

1. A: 你见过小张的女朋友吗？
   Have you seen Xiao Zhang's girlfriend?
   B: 见过，不高不矮，不胖不瘦，很招人喜欢。
   Yes. Neither tall nor short, neither fat nor thin – she's just right.

2. A: 葡萄得洗干净了再吃。
   Wash the grapes clean before eating.
   B: 没关系。俗话说"不干不净，吃了没病"嘛。
   It doesn't matter. As the saying goes, "No cleanness, no disease".

练习 *Exercises*

选词填空。Choose the right phrases to fill in the blanks.

不软不硬	不上不下	不破不立	不言不语

1. 我妈做的饼_____，真好吃。

2. 大家都在热烈地讨论，只有他一个人_____地坐在那儿。

20

解释 *Explanation*

表示没有出现说话人预料的情况，而是发生了跟说话人预料相反或是与一般情理、常规不同的情况。"不但"也可换成"不仅"。

Used to indicate what happened is abnormal, or is contrary to the speaker's expectation. 不但 can be replaced by 不仅.

例句 *Examples*

1. 下了雨之后，不但没凉快点儿，反而更闷热了。
   After the rain, it's stuffier, rather than cooler.

2. 我一直想等房价跌了再买房，可是这些年房价不但没跌，反而飞涨。
   I planned to buy a flat when prices went down, but instead of decreasing, the prices skyrocketed in recent years.

3. 困难不但没吓倒他们，反而坚定了他们的信心。
   They were not daunted by difficulties, instead they became more confident.

4. 这几年一直说要精简机构，可是政府工作人员不仅没减少，反而增加了。你说这是怎么回事？
   Recently, the government has repeated its plan to downsize government bodies. However, the number of public officials has increased. What's your take on this situation?

对话 *Dialogues*

1. A: 听到这样不公平的指责，他一定很生气吧。
   He must be very angry when receiving such unjustified criticism.

   B: 他不但没生气，反而干得更欢了。
   Not only does he not get angry, it makes him work harder.

2. A: 她得了癌症，她的男朋友和她分手了吧？
   She's got cancer. Did her boyfriend break up with her?

   B: 不仅没分手，反而更加体贴她了。
   Instead of breaking up with her, he's more considerate toward her.

练习 *Exercises*

用"不但～，反而～"完成句子。Complete the sentences with the pattern.

1. A: 吃了药以后，你的胃疼是不是好些了？
   B: 哪儿啊，＿＿＿＿＿＿＿＿＿＿＿＿。

2. A: 你提了意见以后，你的邻居是不是比以前安静些了？
   B: 别提了，自从我提了意见，＿＿＿＿＿＿＿＿＿＿＿＿。

汉语常用格式330例

21

不但~，还/而且~

解释 *Explanation*

有更进一层的意思。

Used to indicate a furthering meaning, like "not only . . . but also".

例句 *Examples*

1. 我不但会开车，还会修车呢。你没想到吧？

   Not only can I drive a car, but also repair it. Do you realize that?

2. 他不但收藏名画，还收藏了不少民间剪纸。

   Not only does he collect famous paintings, but also some folk paper-cuts.

3. 王老师不但精通英语，而且精通法语。

   Mr. Wang is not only proficient in English, but also in French.

4. 他对我非常热情，不但请我吃了饭，而且还开车送我回家。

   He was very warm toward me. He treated me a meal and also drove me home.

对话 *Dialogues*

1. A：听说小李对父母不怎么样。

   I heard Xiao Li does not treat his parents well.

   B：没错，不但不孝顺，还经常无理取闹。

   True. Instead of being a dutiful son, he often makes trouble out of nothing.

2. A：你想找一个什么样的女朋友？

   What kind of girlfriend do you want?

   B：我梦中的她不但要聪明、漂亮，而且还得温柔、能挣钱。

   My dream girl should be smart and beautiful. She should also be sweet and have the ability to earn a lot of money.

练习 *Exercises*

用"不但~，还/而且~"完成句子。Complete the sentences with the pattern.

1. A：你为什么不喜欢住在大城市？

   B：住在大城市＿＿＿＿＿＿＿＿＿＿。

2. A：听说你的工作压力比过去更大了？

   B：是啊，我＿＿＿＿＿＿＿＿＿＿。

不但～，连～也/都～

解释 *Explanation*

意思上更进一层，并通过突出的甚至极端的事例表示强调。

Used to indicate "but also" or "moreover" and emphasize it by a prominent or even an extreme example.

例句 *Examples*

1. 今天我忙得不但忘了吃饭，连水都没喝一口。

   I was so busy today that I forgot to eat. I didn't even drink any water.

2. 他最近特勤快，今天不但洗了衣服，连晚饭都做好了。

   He's been hardworking these days. Today he washed clothes, and even cooked dinner.

3. 那座山不但我爬不上去，连登山运动员上去也很难。

   I can't climb that mountain. Even a mountaineer could barely do it.

4. 这个问题太难回答了，不但我不会，可能连老师也回答不出来。

   This problem is so hard that I cannot work it out. Perhaps even the teacher cannot work it out either.

对话 *Dialogues*

1. A: 最近小王没来看你吗?

   Has Xiao Wang visited you recently?

   B: 他不但没来看我，连个电话都没给我打过。

   No. Not even a call from him.

2. A: 大卫的汉语水平真高。

   David has a very good command of Chinese.

   B: 是啊。他不但说得非常流利，连文章也写得很漂亮。

   Yes, he speaks Chinese fluently, and can also write good Chinese articles.

练习 *Exercises*

用"不但～，连～也/都～"完成句子。Complete the sentences with the pattern.

1. 本来打算存钱买房子的，可是近两年工资没怎么增加，物价倒一个劲儿地涨，现在手里这点儿钱_____。

2. 他把所有的积蓄都投进了股市，没想到正赶上股市大跌，结果_____。

解释 *Explanation*

和形容词连用，表示相比之下，差别不大。

Used with an adjective to indicate a similar level when a comparison is made.

例句 *Examples*

1. 我看下周的天气，凉快也凉快不到哪儿去。

   I don't think it will be any cooler next week.

2. 别担心，今年的高考题比往年难也难不到哪儿去。

   Don't worry. This year's university entrance exam won't be more difficult than the previous ones.

3. 你别总觉得自己比别人胖多了，其实也胖不到哪儿去。

   Don't think you are much fatter than others. Actually, you are not any fatter.

4. 在外面吃比自己做省事多了，再说一般餐馆也贵不到哪儿去，还是出去吃吧。

   It's more convenient to eat out than cooking at home. Besides, it's not more expensive to dine at ordinary restaurants. Let's eat out.

对话 *Dialogues*

1. A：这饭店厨师做的菜，比你妈做的好吃吧？

   Do dishes cooked by chefs in this hotel taste better than those cooked by your mother?

   B：我觉得也好吃不到哪儿去。

   I don't think they're any better.

2. A：咱们去那家新开的超市吧。

   Let's go to the new supermarket.

   B：算了，那里的东西也便宜不到哪儿去，还得跑那么远。

   Forget it. Things aren't any cheaper there, and it's further away.

练习 *Exercises*

用"～不到哪儿去"改写句子。Rewrite the sentences with the pattern.

1. 别开车了，现在正堵车呢，开车去也不会太快。

   →_____。

2. 哈哈，你说他不聪明，我看你也不比他聪明多少。

   →_____。

汉语常用格式330例

解释 *Explanation*

表示所涉及的情况或条件是否不同都不会改变结果。"不管"后面常有并列的词语或任指的疑问代词。

Used to indicate the same result despite different circumstances. 不管 is often used before parallel words or interrogative pronouns of general denotation.

例句 *Examples*

1. 不管男女老少，都喜欢参加这种欢庆活动。

   All people, men and women, old and young, like to take part in such celebrations.

2. 一进入中年，不管是谁，都有时光飞逝的感觉。

   Everyone feels that time flies fast once heading into one's middle age.

3. 在互联网时代，不管你有多少经验，都会感觉力不从心。

   In the age of the Internet, no matter how much experience you have you still feel insufficient.

4. 不管那个国家多么强大，也需要国际社会的支持。

   No matter how powerful that country is, it needs the international community's support.

对话 *Dialogues*

1. A: 他是世界金融专家，怎么也赔了呢？

   He is an expert in world finance. Why did he lose too?

   B: 不管什么人，都无法十分准确地预测股票市场。

   It doesn't matter who he is. Nobody can accurately predict the stock market.

2. A: 会有这样的事？真不敢相信。

   Really? I can hardly believe that.

   B: 不管你信不信，这都是事实。

   Believe it or not, it's true.

练习 *Exercises*

用"不管 ~，都/也 ~"改写下列句子。Rewrite the sentences with the pattern.

1. 明天不下雨，我去；明天下雨，我也去。→ _____。

2. 这个东西不贵，我会买；这个东西贵，我还是会买。

   → _____。

不管怎么说，~

解释 *Explanation*

强调不管是在什么情况下都应该承认这个事实。与"无论如何"意思相近。

Used to emphasize that we should admit the fact under any conditions. The meaning is similar to 无论如何.

例句 *Examples*

1. 不管怎么说，他创造了最成功的投资实体。

   After all, he still developed the most successful investment entity.

2. 很多人批评他，但不管怎么说，他在国际上拿了大奖。

   Many people criticized him. But after all, he still won an international prize.

3. 不管怎么说，一个人总得有点儿同情心。

   Anyway, a person should have a bit of compassion.

4. 不管怎么说，烟还是戒掉的好，酒也要适量地喝。

   Anyhow, you'd better give up smoking, and drink moderately.

对话 *Dialogues*

1. A：有人怀疑他从事慈善事业的目的。

   Some people suspect his motivation for engaging in charity.

   B：不管怎么说，搞慈善事业总是好的。

   After all, it's good to engage in charity.

2. A：我真不想和这种人来往。

   I really don't want to have contact with this kind of person.

   B：不管怎么说，他还是你的同学。

   However, he's still your classmate.

练习 *Exercises*

用"不管怎么说，~"完成句子。Complete the sentences with the pattern.

1. A：这门课太没意思了，真不想学了。

   B：_____，这是必修课呀，_____。

2. A：这孩子太不懂事了，有时候气得我真想不管他了。

   B：_____，哪能不管呢？

解释 *Explanation*

表示在任何情况下，某人的态度或决定都不改变。多用于口语。

Used mostly in oral Chinese to indicate the same attitude or decision despite different circumstances.

例句 *Examples*

1. 不管股票行情怎么样，他都稳如泰山。

   Regardless of the stock market situation, he remains calm.

2. 不管父母态度怎么样，他还是乐于冒险。

   Regardless of his parents' attitude, he is happy to take risks.

3. 不管那里的情况怎么样，我一定要去一趟。

   Regardless of the situation, I must go there.

4. 现在不管他对我态度怎么样，我都会像以前一样，谅解他的。

   Regardless of how he treats me, I will forgive him just as I did before.

对话 *Dialogues*

1. A: 有人说为挣钱牺牲休息时间不值得。

   Some people say it's not worth sacrificing your time off for extra money.

   B: 不管别人的看法怎么样，我愿意。

   Regardless of what others think, I'm willing to do so.

2. A: 不少人说这个节目的主持人品行不怎么样。

   Many people gossip about the bad behavior of the host of this program.

   B: 不管传闻怎么样，我认为节目主持得好就行。

   Regardless of what they say, I think it's OK as long as he does a good job.

练习 *Exercises*

用"不管～怎么样，～"完成句子。Complete the sentences with the pattern.

1. A: 天气预报说，明天有四五级大风，你还会去锻炼吗？

   B: _____。

2. A: 妈妈，如果这次考试我考得不好怎么办？

   B: 没关系的，我知道你已经努力了，_____。

解释 *Explanation*

"不惯"前面多用单音节动词，表示对某方面不习惯。肯定式为"动词 + 得惯"。

Often used with a monosyllabic verb before it, 不惯 indicates the subject is unaccustomed to a certain situation. The positive form is "verb + 得惯".

例句 *Examples*

1. 他刚从农村来，过不惯城市生活。

   He just came from the countryside, and has not yet adapted to city life.

2. 有些年轻人生活懒散，真让人看不惯。

   Some young people are so idle that nobody will like them.

3. 南方人到了北方，很多东西都吃不惯。

   Southerners cannot get used to the food in northern China.

4. 我过去学的是繁体字，现在写简体字应该容易，可我就是写不惯。

   I used to learn traditional Chinese characters. Although it should be easy to write simplified ones, I just can't get used to them.

对话 *Dialogues*

1. **A**: 哟，你骑的是小李的新自行车?

   Oh, is that Xiao Li's new bike you are riding?

   B: 是的，可是我骑不惯，车座也不舒服。

   Yes, it is. But I'm not used to it, and the seat is uncomfortable.

2. **A**: 我穿不惯尖头高跟鞋。

   I really can't wear pointed toe high heels.

   B: 我穿得惯。

   I can, I'm used to them.

练习 *Exercises*

用"~不惯"完成句子。Complete the sentences with the pattern.

1. 我是中国人，喜欢喝茶，＿＿＿＿＿＿＿＿＿＿咖啡。

2. 新买的电脑什么都好，就是键盘太软了，我＿＿＿＿＿＿＿＿＿。

（只）不过～罢了

解释 *Explanation*

有"也就是"、"只是"的意思。

Used to indicate "just" or "only".

例句 *Examples*

1. 他那哪是真本事，不过是哄孩子玩儿的把戏罢了。

   That is not his real skill. It's just a trick to amuse children.

2. 他们的煤炭质量很高，不过价格很难接受罢了。

   Their coal is high quality. Only the price is too high.

3. 老百姓对政策还是拥护的，只不过痛恨那些贪官罢了。

   People support the policies, but they hate corrupt officials.

4. 他们的计算机硬件比我们的好，只不过在软件上还稍落后于我们罢了。

   Their computer hardware is better than ours, but their software is slightly behind ours.

对话 *Dialogues*

1. A: 怎么啦，一脸不高兴?

   What's the matter? You look unhappy.

   B: 没什么，只不过不想说话罢了。

   Nothing. I just don't want to talk.

2. A: 他为什么跟你生那么大的气?

   Why did he get so angry with you?

   B: 谁知道! 我不过说了几句公道话罢了。

   Who knows? I just said a few impartial words.

练习 *Exercises*

用"（只）不过～罢了"完成句子。Complete the sentences with the pattern.

1. 别担心，我得的不是什么大病，＿＿＿＿＿＿＿＿＿＿＿＿＿＿＿＿＿＿＿。

2. 我的工作很轻松，＿＿＿＿＿＿＿＿＿＿＿＿＿＿＿＿＿。

不仅（但）不/没～，还～

解释 *Explanation*

表示情况不但不是预料之中的，还向相反的方向更进一步地发展。"不仅"可换成"不但"。

Used to indicate that the situation develops on the contrary to expectation. 不仅 and 不但 can be used interchangeably.

例句 *Examples*

1. 做这种生意不仅不容易赚到钱，搞不好，还会把本钱都搭进去。
   It's not easy to earn money in this business. On the contrary, it's easy to waste all your capital.
2. 印度的软件业，不仅不比我们差，发展速度还比我们快。
   The Indian software industry is not inferior to ours. On the contrary, it is developing faster than ours.
3. 她吃那么多补品，不但没见把身体补好，还新添了胃病。
   She took a lot of different tonics, but did not get better. What's worse, her stomach is now upset.
4. 股票行情不但没好转，股票价格还大幅下跌了。
   The stock market did not change for the better. On the contrary, stock prices dropped sharply.

对话 *Dialogues*

1. A：这孩子太淘气，带他这些天，让你烦了吧？
   That boy is so naughty. Do you get angry when you look after him these days?
   B：看你说的，不仅没烦，还越来越喜欢他了。
   On the contrary, I like him more and more.

2. A：你有什么问题，可以找老王帮忙。
   You can ask Lao Wang for help if you have a problem.
   B：我可了解他，他不但不会帮忙，甚至还会趁机落井下石。
   I know him well. Not only will he not help, but may even take the opportunity to work against you.

练习 *Exercises*

用"不仅（但）不/没～，还～"完成句子。Complete the sentences with the pattern.

1. 我把他心爱的花瓶打碎了，我想他一定会骂我一顿，没想到他_____。

2. 这种减肥药太糟糕了，吃了以后，_____。

解释 *Explanation*

表示某一情况不局限于某个个体或部分群体，而是适合于所有人或事物。

This is used to indicate something is not only applicable to one person or one group, but to all other people or things.

例句 *Examples*

1. 规章制度不仅群众要遵守，任何人都得遵守。

   Rules are not just for ordinary people, they are for all the people.

2. 这一零件不仅这种车可以用，任何牌子的车都能用。

   This part can be used not only in this kind of car, but also in any others.

3. 为了身体健康不仅要少喝白酒，任何酒都不宜多喝。

   For your health you should not just drink less spirits, but also drink less alcohol of any kind.

4. 有了无线网卡，不仅可以在家、在办公室上网，在任何地方都可以上网。

   With the wireless LAN card, you can go online at home, at the office, and also in any other places.

对话 *Dialogues*

1. A: 今天欢迎我来吗？

   Am I welcome today?

   B: 不仅今天欢迎，任何时候来都欢迎。

   Not only today, but at any time.

2. A: 我不相信他会做出这种伤天害理的事。

   I don't believe he did this inhuman thing.

   B: 不仅你不相信，任何人都不会相信。

   Not only you. Nobody believes it.

练习 *Exercises*

用"不仅～，任何～都～"完成句子。Complete the sentences with the pattern.

1. A: 他的要求太高了，我可达不到。

   B: 确实是太高了，＿＿＿＿＿＿＿＿＿＿＿。

2. A: 你是不是很喜欢吃香蕉？

   B: 我喜欢吃水果，＿＿＿＿＿＿＿＿＿＿＿。

～不了多少

解释 *Explanation*

和形容词一起用，用于比较，表示两者相差不大；或和动词一起用，表示数量不多。

Used with an adjective to indicate similarity, or used with a verb to indicate a small quantity.

例句 *Examples*

1. 我看他比过去瘦不了多少。

   In my view he did not get much slimmer than before.

2. 这个平价商店东西的价格和超市也差不了多少。

   The prices at the discount store are almost the same as those at the supermarket.

3. 早饭我一般吃不了多少。喝杯牛奶，吃两片面包。

   I usually don't eat much for breakfast. A glass of milk and two pieces of bread is enough.

4. 我正在编写一本书，不过杂事太多，一天写不了多少。

   I'm compiling a book. But with many other things to do, I can't write much every day.

对话 *Dialogues*

1. A: 小王的外语水平真不错，我很羡慕他。

   Xiao Wang is really good at foreign languages. I'm very envious of him.

   B: 要自信，别谦虚，我看你比他差不了多少。

   Be confident, don't be modest. I don't think you're not as good as him.

2. A: 白糖? 有，要多少?

   Sugar? How much?

   B: 要不了多少，一点儿就够了。

   Not much. A little is enough.

练习 *Exercises*

用 "～不了多少" 完成句子。Complete the sentences with the pattern.

1. 我干这个工作比以前累多了，但是钱却_____。

2. 咳，年纪大了，记性差了，想学点儿外语，可这英语单词一天也_____。

解释 *Explanation*

表示不管在什么情况下，都一定要做某事。"不论"和"不管"意思相同，但后者更口语化。

Used to indicate something must be done under any circumstances. 不论 and 不管 have the same meaning, though the latter is more colloquial.

例句 *Examples*

1. 不论是干什么，你总得找个工作做呀。

   You have to find a job anyway, no matter what it is.

2. 不管他是谁，地位有多高，总得遵纪守法。

   No matter who they are or what they do, everyone must abide by the law.

3. 这些问题，不论多么复杂，总得想办法解决才行。

   We will have to work out these problems, no matter how complicated they are.

4. 这艘失踪的船，不论是沉没了还是被劫持了，总得立即设法寻找。

   Whether this missing boat sank or was hijacked, we must try to find it immediately.

对话 *Dialogues*

1. A: 这电脑一定要急着买吗？

   Do we have to buy a computer immediately?

   B: 是啊。不管新的、旧的，总得有一台呀。

   Yes, we must have one, whether it's new or old.

2. A: 哎呀，晚啦，今天的事又多，来不及吃早饭了。

   Whoops! I'm late. I have so many things today that there is no time for breakfast.

   B: 不论多忙，总得吃点儿东西再走吧。

   No matter how busy you are, you should eat something before going.

练习 *Exercises*

用"不论/不管～，总得～"完成句子。Complete the sentences with the pattern.

1. A: 今天这事真气死我了，什么也吃不下去。

   B: 人是铁，饭是钢，＿＿＿＿＿＿＿＿＿＿＿＿＿＿＿＿。

2. A: 我男朋友要带我去见他的父母，我不想去。

   B: ＿＿＿＿＿＿＿＿＿＿＿＿＿＿＿＿。

～，不免 ～

解释 *Explanation*

表示由于某种原因，免不了会发生某种情况。多用于非理想的状态。

Used mostly to indicate a dissatisfying or upsetting situation that is unavoidable for a certain reason.

例句 *Examples*

1. 马上就要开会了，会场还没布置好，他不免着急起来。

   The meeting will start soon, but the place is still not arranged, so he can't help feeling anxious.

2. 在众人面前受到批评，谁都不免会尴尬的。

   Everyone feels embarrassed when being criticized in public.

3. 恐怖事件接连发生，不免使人感到不安。

   Terrorist incidents keep on occurring, so it's natural for people to feel anxious.

4. 他见人躲躲闪闪的，不免令人生疑。

   He is shifty-eyed when meeting people. Of course people feel suspicious of him.

对话 *Dialogues*

1. A：你看，你女朋友的手在发抖呢！

   Look, your girlfriend's hands are trembling!

   B：这是她第一次登台发表演说，总不免有点儿紧张。

   This is her first speech on stage, so she's a bit nervous.

2. A：他们怎么聊起来没完没了啦？

   Their conversation seems endless!

   B：多年不见的老朋友嘛，不免要多谈几句。

   They are old friends and have not seen each other for many years. Of course they have a lot to talk.

练习 *Exercises*

用"～，不免 ～"完成句子。Complete the sentences with the pattern.

1. 两个人脾气都不好，意见又常不一致，＿＿＿＿＿＿＿＿＿＿＿。

2. 马上要毕业了，看着这生活了多年的校园，心里＿＿＿＿＿＿＿＿＿＿＿。

解释 *Explanation*

用于比较，表示 A 比不上 B。

Used in comparison to show A is not better than B.

例句 *Examples*

1. 我在很多方面都不如你。

   I'm not as good as you in many respects.

2. 他现在的女朋友不如以前那个漂亮。

   His present girlfriend is not as pretty as his ex.

3. 俗话说，求人不如求己。

   As the saying goes, it's better to depend on yourself than to ask for help from others.

4. 他不愿意来就别来，勉强来还不如不来呢。

   If he doesn't want to come, he doesn't need to. It's better not to come at all than to come reluctantly.

对话 *Dialogues*

1. A：自动挡的车和手动挡的车哪种好开？

   Which kind of car is easier to drive, automatic or manual?

   B：手动挡的车当然不如自动挡的好开了。

   A manual car is not as easy to drive as an automatic one, of course.

2. A：给他买什么生日礼物好呢？

   What birthday gift shall I buy for him?

   B：我看买东西不如送他礼品券。

   I think it's better to give him gift coupons.

练习 *Exercises*

用"A 不如 B（～）"完成句子。Complete the sentences with the pattern.

1. A：你开车来的？听说你们城里也下雪了，有我们这里大吗？

   B：_____。

2. A：大夫，我还是吃药吧，我怕打针，太疼了。

   B：可是_____。

不是 ~ ，而是 ~

解释 *Explanation*

表示否定前者，肯定后者。

Used to negate the former and affirm the latter.

例句 *Examples*

1. 我没买那个东西不是因为价钱贵，而是觉得质量差。

   I did not buy it, not because it's expensive, but because I think it's of low quality.

2. 我不是故意不理他，而是根本没听到他叫我。

   I didn't ignore him on purpose. I just didn't hear him.

3. 中国的发展对其他国家不是威胁，而是机遇。

   For other countries, China's development is not a threat, but an opportunity.

4. 我们认为反腐败最重要的不是事后惩罚，而是加强监督和防范。

   We believe that the most important thing for anti-corruption is to strengthen supervision and prevention.

对话 *Dialogues*

1. A: 上课时你怎么从来不主动回答问题?

   Why do you never take the initiative to answer questions in class?

   B: 我不是不想回答，而是不会回答。

   It's not because I don't want to, but because I cannot.

2. A: 第二届研讨会还在洛杉矶开吗?

   Will the second seminar still be held in Los Angeles?

   B: 不是在洛杉矶，而是在中国桂林。

   Not in Los Angeles, but in Guilin, China.

练习 *Exercises*

用"不是 ~ ，而是 ~"完成句子。Complete the sentences with the pattern.

1. A: 刚才和你在一起的那个帅哥是你男朋友吧。

   B: 别开玩笑了，他＿＿＿＿＿＿＿＿＿＿＿＿＿＿＿＿。

2. A: 两点开会，你怎么还不走哇?

   B: 你搞错了吧，＿＿＿＿＿＿＿＿＿＿＿＿＿＿＿＿。

汉语常用格式330例

解释 *Explanation*

表示或者是这样，或者是那样，二者必居其一，没有第三种可能。

Used to indicate "either ... or ..." without a third possibility.

例句 *Examples*

1. 现在买房子可真不容易，不是太贵就是离市区太远。

   It's so difficult now to buy a house. Anything good is either too expensive or too far away from the city center.

2. 现在市场价格大战的结果，不是你死，就是我活。

   The result of the current price war is either you lose or I win.

3. 为了这个课题，她这些天不是泡在图书馆，就是蹲在实验室，夜里才回家。

   In order to complete the research, she stayed in the library or laboratory until night these days.

4. 这个公司破产的原因，我看不是由于管理不善，就是因为违规经营。

   I think the reason behind the bankrupcy of the company is either bad management or illegal dealings.

对话 *Dialogues*

1. A: 假期这几天你干什么了？

   How did you spend your holiday?

   B: 不是吃，就是玩儿，反正没看书。

   I ate and had lots of fun, but I didn't read at all.

2. A: 这串钥匙是谁的？

   Whose keys are these?

   B: 不是爸爸的就是妈妈的。

   If they aren't Dad's, they must be Mom's.

练习 *Exercises*

用"不是~，就是~"完成句子。Complete the sentences with the pattern.

1. 小明的成绩非常好，在班上_____。

2. 我做菜总是拿不准放多少盐，_____。

汉语常用格式330例

~不说 / 不算，~

解释 *Explanation*

表示别的情况姑且不谈，为的是强调所说的内容。后面多用"还"、"也"、"光"和它呼应。

Used to stress the speaker's main point among other things. 还，也 or 光 are often used after the expression for emphasis.

例句 *Examples*

1. 那家大公司要关闭一些店铺不说，同时还要大量裁员。

   The giant company is going to close some stores and also lay off lots of their staff.

2. 这份工作太辛苦了，每天风里来雨里去不说，节假日还常常要加班。

   It is so hard! I work every day, rain or shine. I even often work overtime on holidays.

3. 贷款购房，低收入者不说，就是收入比较高的人也觉得房价贵、利息高。

   Even high-income people are finding housing prices and mortage rates high, not to mention low-income people.

4. 这次去香港旅游我买了好多东西，别的不算，光项链就买了十几条。

   I did a lot of shopping on my trip to Hong Kong, including a dozen necklaces and a whole lot of other stuff.

对话 *Dialogues*

1. A: 你怎么不参加个旅行团出国转转?

   Why don't you travel overseas with a tour group?

   B: 没时间不说，得花好多钱。

   I have no time, besides, it costs a lot of money.

2. A: 咱们就去对面那个小店买吧。

   Let's go to the shop opposite.

   B: 别去那儿，那里的东西价钱贵不说，还不新鲜。

   Don't go there. The goods are expensive, and on top of that they are not fresh.

练习 *Exercises*

用"~不说/不算，~"完成句子。Complete the sentences with the pattern and words in parentheses.

1. 天天在外面吃，→＿＿＿＿＿＿＿＿＿＿＿＿。（花钱多　不卫生）

2. 按揭买房，→＿＿＿＿＿＿＿＿＿＿＿。（利息高　手续复杂）

38

不要说/甭说 ~，就连 ~ 也/都 ~

解释 *Explanation*

通过强调后者的极端情况来说明问题。

Used to make things clear by emphasizing the extreme situation of the latter.

例句 *Examples*

1. 双方和解，不要说我们没想到，就连国际问题专家也未料到。

   The two sides reached compromise. Not only did we not expect it, but experts on international issues also didn't.

2. 中国的古代诗歌，不要说外国留学生，就连中国同学也未必全能看懂。

   Not even Chinese students can understand all the ancient Chinese poems, let alone foreign students.

3. 他的科研成果，甭说在国内，就连外国专家也是公认的。

   His research achievements are not only recognized by Chinese experts, but also by experts of other countries.

4. 这么简单的数学题，甭说大学生了，就连小学生都会做。

   This maths problem is so easy that even primary school students can work it out, let alone a university student.

对话 *Dialogues*

1. A: 你生病的时候他来照顾你了吧?

   Did he come to take care of you when you were sick?

   B: 不要说照顾，就连电话也没打过一个。

   No. He even did not call me.

2. A: 他迷上了游戏机，对学习不管不顾，我要好好劝劝他。

   He's addicted to playing video games, and does not study at all. I must try to persuade him to study more.

   B: 算了吧。甭说你，就连他父母都管不了他。

   Forget it. Even his parents cannot discipline him.

练习 *Exercises*

用"不要说/甭说 ~，就连 ~ 也/都 ~"和括号内的词语完成对话。Complete the sentences with the pattern and words in parentheses.

1. A: 你会不会开车?

   B: 我呀，_____。

   （骑自行车）

2. A: 你去过中国吗?

   B: 当然，_____。

   （非洲）

不~也~

解释 *Explanation*

表示即使没有前面的情况，结果也不受影响。

Used to indicate the result will not change even without what's expressed after 不.

例句 *Examples*

1. 我觉得这样的活动不参加也没什么关系。

   I don't think it matters if I don't take part in that kind of activity.

2. 你不告诉我，我也知道，他一定是你的男朋友。

   Even if you don't tell me, I know he must be your boyfriend.

3. 你不来我也会去看你的。咱们是什么关系呀！

   I will visit you even if you don't come. We are good friends, right?

4. 这里坐公交车很方便，你不买车也行。

   It's convenient to take bus from here. It doesn't matter if you don't buy a car.

对话 *Dialogues*

1. A：让我给你解释一下，好吗？

   Let me explain it to you, OK?

   B：你不解释我也理解。

   I understand that even if you don't explain it.

2. A：这个不幸的消息先别告诉老王，他会承受不住的。

   Don't tell Lao Wang this bad news now. He won't be able to bear it.

   B：不说他早晚也会知道。

   He will know it sooner or later.

练习 *Exercises*

用"不~也~"完成句子。Complete the sentences with the pattern.

1. A：我现在钱有点儿紧，买不了空调了。

   B：其实这里的天气也不算太热，＿＿＿＿＿＿＿＿＿＿。

2. A：你什么时候学的修电脑？

   B：我在电脑公司搞了两三年营销工作，＿＿＿＿＿＿＿＿＿＿。

解释 *Explanation*

表示否定前者，肯定后者。

Used to negate the former and affirm the latter.

例句 *Examples*

1. 考试的目的不在于淘汰学生，而在于督促学生学习。

   The purpose of exams is not to eliminate students, but to encourage them to study harder.

2. 减肥是否能成功，不在于节食，而在于要养成合理的饮食习惯。

   The success of losing weight depends not on dieting, but on good eating habits.

3. 有人认为举行球赛的意义，不在于谁赢谁输，而是为了增进友谊，交流经验。

   Some people think the main aim of ball games is not to win the prize, but to strengthen friendship and exchange experience.

4. 经济全球化发展速度的快慢，不在于某个国家政府的意图，而是一个自然的进程。

   Economic globalization doesn't depend on the intention of a country's government, it's a natural process.

对话 *Dialogues*

1. A：给他买这么个小礼物，真是有点儿不好意思。

   It's a little embarrassing to buy such a small gift for him.

   B：送礼不在于轻重，而是为了表示一点儿心意。

   The value of a gift is not important. It's the regard that counts.

2. A：他们总说要加强对住宅小区的管理。

   They always say they will improve property management of the residential areas.

   B：加强管理不在于怎么说，而在于如何行动。

   What they say is not as important as what they do.

练习 *Exercises*

用"不在于 ~，而是/而在于 ~"完成句子。Complete the sentences with the pattern.

1. 一个人是否有活力，_____。

2. 人生的价值_____。

不怎么 ~

解释 *Explanation*

常用在形容词或动词前，有"不很"、"不太"、"不常"的意思，表示程度不高。

Often used before an adjective or a verb to indicate "not very" or "not often", or to indicate a low degree.

例句 *Examples*

1. 这个苹果看上去又大又红，其实不怎么甜。
   Although the apple looks big and red, it's not very sweet.

2. 有的药品广告做得很多，但效果并不怎么好。
   Some drugs are advertised a lot, but they are not very effective.

3. 他们互相还不怎么了解，就急于合作，肯定不会成功。
   They don't know each other very well, and they are too eager to work together. They definitely will not succeed.

4. 我们原来是很亲密的好朋友，可现在不怎么来往了。
   We used to be very good friends, but now we rarely contact each other.

对话 *Dialogues*

1. A: 这些资料对了解事实真相会有价值。
   In order to get the truth, these materials are valuable for us.
   B: 但有的部分不怎么可靠。
   But some are not very reliable.

2. A: 风这么大，我不想出门了。
   The wind is blowing too strongly. I don't want to go out.
   B: 风虽大，但不怎么冷。
   The wind is strong, but it isn't very cold.

练习 *Exercises*

用"不怎么 ~"完成句子。Complete the sentences with the pattern.

1. A: 你常常运动吗？
   B: 我这人很懒，_____。

2. A: 学习汉语挺难的吧？
   B: 如果找到了适合自己的学习方法，其实也_____。

汉语常用格式330例

解释 *Explanation*

意思是不太好。

Used to show not being good.

例句 *Examples*

1. 因为贪玩儿，他的学习成绩一直不怎么样。

   He doesn't care about anything except having fun. That's why his marks are so bad.

2. 这幅画儿的构思还可以，但色彩不怎么样。

   The idea of this painting is OK, but the color is not so good.

3. 虽然他长得很帅，脑子也很活，但是人品不怎么样。

   Although he's handsome and smart, he's not a decent person.

4. 他们两国关系 21 世纪以前还不错，现在不怎么样了。

   The relationship between the two countries was fairly good before the 21st century, but things have since cooled.

对话 *Dialogues*

1. A：我们这儿河水污染很严重，你们那儿没什么问题吧?

   The rivers in our area are seriously polluted. What about yours?

   B：也不怎么样。

   Not so good either.

2. A：听说老金借了几个朋友的钱都不还。

   I heard Lao Jin borrowed money from his friends and didn't pay them back.

   B：这种人真不怎么样。

   This is not a decent kind of person.

练习 *Exercises*

用"~不怎么样"完成句子。Complete the sentences with the pattern.

1. A：我觉得他的汉字写得很漂亮啊。

   B：可＿＿＿＿＿＿＿＿＿＿＿＿＿＿＿＿＿。

2. A：这套房子你喜欢吗?

   B：＿＿＿＿＿＿＿＿＿＿＿＿＿＿＿＿＿＿。

不只~，就连~都/也~

解释 *Explanation*

"不只"意思同"不但"、"不仅"，与"就连~都/也~"一起用，表示强调。

With the same meaning as 不但 and 不仅，不只 is used with 就连~都/也~ for emphasis.

例句 *Examples*

1. 这问题不只在国内引起了争论，就连国外也很重视。

   This issue not only caused widespread discussion in China, but was also discussed in other countries.

2. 我刚到国外时，不仅没什么朋友，就连个说话的人也没有。

   When I first arrived overseas, I had no friends. There was not even a single person to talk to.

3. 该厂改革以后，不只产量增加了，就连人的精神面貌都变了。

   After the factory was reformed, not only did output increase, but people's attitudes were also improved.

4. 这首歌非常流行，不仅年轻人喜欢，就连七八十岁的老人也爱唱。

   The song is very popular, and not just with young people. Old people in their seventies and eighties also like to sing it.

对话 *Dialogues*

1. A: 这部中文电影你看懂了吗？

   Did you understand this Chinese movie?

   B: 不只内容明白了，就连对话也基本上听懂了。

   Yes, not only the content, but also the dialogue.

2. A: 现在的大学生英语水平真不错。

   University students now have a good command of English.

   B: 不仅大学生，就连一些中学生也能说一口流利的英语。

   Not to mention university students, even some middle school students can speak fluent English.

练习 *Exercises*

用"不只~，就连~都/也~"完成句子。Complete the sentences with the pattern.

1. 今年我们公司裁了很多人，＿＿＿＿＿＿＿＿＿＿＿＿＿＿＿。

2. 她非常能干，＿＿＿＿＿＿＿＿＿＿＿＿＿＿＿。

解释 *Explanation*

表示出现某种情况是不可能的。

Used to indicate impossibility.

例句 *Examples*

1. 你看老朱这副模样，有哪个姑娘会喜欢他才怪。

   Lao Zhu is so ugly. It's impossible for any girl to like him.

2. 他整天这么吊儿郎当的，能考上大学才怪。

   He fools around all day. It'll be a miracle if he can enter a university.

3. 胸无大志的人能成功才怪呢。

   It'll be a miracle if an unambitious person can succeed.

4. 他是高度近视，不戴眼镜能看清楚这些字才怪呢。

   He has high myopia. It's impossible for him to discern these characters without glasses.

对话 *Dialogues*

1. A：我今天一定要把这些杂七杂八的事都处理完。

   I must finish all these chores today.

   B：哪儿这么容易，你今天能处理完才怪呢。

   It's not so easy. It'll be a miracle if you can finish them today.

2. A：我的门钥匙不知放在哪里了。

   I don't know where I put the door key.

   B：你这么粗心大意，不丢东西才怪呢。

   You're so careless that no wonder you lose things.

练习 *Exercises*

用"～才怪（呢）"完成句子。Complete the sentences with the pattern.

1. A：我怎么有这么多蛀牙？

   B：你这么爱吃糖，又不好好刷牙，＿＿＿＿＿＿＿＿＿＿＿＿＿＿＿。

2. A：你能不能看懂中文报纸？

   B：我才学了三个月汉语，＿＿＿＿＿＿＿＿＿＿＿＿＿＿＿。

才 ~ 就 ~

解释 *Explanation*

表示前后两件事情紧接着发生。

Used to indicate that two things happened one after the other.

例句 *Examples*

1. 你怎么才来就要走了？

   You just came. Why go now?

2. 他出国才两个月就用掉了几万美金。

   Within two months living abroad, he had spent tens of thousands of dollars.

3. 他们才搞了一年房地产就退了出来。

   They quit the real estate industry only a year after they started.

4. 这家公司才营业了几个月，就赚了不少钱。

   Although the company has only been in business for a few months, they have already made a lot of money.

对话 *Dialogues*

1. A: 他们才认识三个月就结婚了。

   They got married only three months after meeting each other.

   B: 真是一见钟情啊。

   It really was love at first sight.

2. A: 这是我的女儿，刚从国外回来。

   This is my daughter. She has just returned from overseas.

   B: 哟，才几年不见，就变成亭亭玉立的大姑娘了。

   I haven't seen her for only a few years, she turns out to be a pretty young lady.

练习 *Exercises*

用 "才 ~ 就 ~" 完成句子。Complete the sentences with the pattern.

1. 这里靠近北极，天黑得早，冬天的时候，＿＿＿＿＿＿＿＿＿＿。

2. 因为家里穷，他没有继续上高中，＿＿＿＿＿＿＿＿＿＿。

解释 *Explanation*

表示强调所说的事情或情况，多暗含对比。常含有不同意对方看法的意思。

Used to emphasize what's talked about, implying comparison. It often indicates disagreement.

例句 *Examples*

1. 不少人喜欢吃山西刀削面，可我觉得兰州拉面才好吃呢！

   Many people like Shanxi sliced noodles, but I think Lanzhou hand-pulled noodles are more delicious.

2. 现在买房才不合适呢，有人推断房价下降趋势已不可逆转。

   It's not appropriate to buy apartments now. Some people draw an inference that it is an irreversible trend that the housing price will drop.

3. 这点儿小灾小难算什么，那些在地震中突然失去亲人的家庭，才悲惨呢！

   Such a small disaster is no big deal. Those families who lost relatives in the earthquake are really miserable.

4. 中国古代美人西施才漂亮呢，淡妆浓抹都好看，现在的美女哪比得上啊。

   The ancient Chinese beauty Xi Shi was extremely pretty, whether richly adorned or plainly dressed. No beauty of our times can equal her.

对话 *Dialogues*

1. A：你是不是爱上那新来的博士后了？

   Have you fallen in love with the post-doctorate who newly came?

   B：谁说的？你才爱上他了呢！

   Who told you? It's impossible!

2. A：听说哈尔滨的姑娘长得漂亮。

   I hear that girls in Harbin are beautiful.

   B：苏州、杭州一带的漂亮姑娘才多呢！

   There are prettier girls in Suzhou and Hangzhou.

练习 *Exercises*

用"~才~呢"完成句子。Complete the sentences with the pattern.

1. A：猫是人最好的朋友。

   B：＿＿＿＿＿＿＿＿＿＿。

2. A：这里的风大得吓人。

   B：你没经历过台风吧？＿＿＿＿＿＿＿＿＿＿。

除非 ~，不然/否则 ~

解释 *Explanation*

表示一定要这样，要不然将是另一种结果。

Used to indicate a necessity, without which the result will be different.

例句 *Examples*

1. 除非有各方面的支持，不然我们完不成任务。

   We can't finish our task unless we get support from other departments.

2. 除非抓到凶手，不然我决不罢休。

   I won't give up until the criminal is caught.

3. 除非你采取果断措施来解决这个问题，否则必将酿成大祸。

   This problem will cause a disaster unless you take decisive measures to solve it.

4. 除非打赢这场比赛，否则不能进入决赛。

   You won't get into the finals unless you win this match.

对话 *Dialogues*

1. A: 让我进去看看比赛吧！

   Let me in to watch the game!

   B: 进去？除非你有票，不然，没门儿！

   Let you in? Unless you have a ticket, otherwise, no way!

2. A: 老师，上周借的那本参考书让我给弄丢了。

   Mister, I lost the reference book that I borrowed last week.

   B: 除非交纳一百元罚款，否则停止借书。

   You will not be allowed to borrow books again, unless you pay a fine of 100 yuan.

练习 *Exercises*

用"除非 ~，不然/否则 ~"完成句子。Complete the sentences with the pattern.

1. A: 妈妈，我能不能看会儿电视？

   B: _____。

2. A: 北京的交通真成问题，到处都堵车。

   B: 是啊，_____。

48

解释 *Explanation*

表示一定要这样，才会有某种结果。多为积极方面的结果。

Used to indicate something happens under certain conditions, mostly positive.

例句 *Examples*

1. 除非双方都让步，才能达成和解。

   The compromise will only be reached when both sides give some ground.

2. 除非太阳从西边出来，他这样的人才能发大财。

   People like him will get rich only when the sun rises in the west.

3. 除非你改变学习方法，多听多说，才有可能学好汉语。

   You will learn Chinese well only when you change your methods, and practice speaking and listening more.

4. 除非你少吃麦当劳、肯德基，才能变苗条。

   You won't lose weight unless you eat less McDonald's and KFC.

对话 *Dialogues*

1. A：咱们一起去参加他的生日晚会吧。

   Let's go to his birthday party together.

   B：除非你答应我一定不喝醉，我才去。

   I will not go unless you promise me you won't get drunk.

2. A：你有什么心事，跟我说说吧。

   Tell me what's on your mind.

   B：除非你答应替我保密，我才跟你说。

   I won't unless you promise to keep it a secret for me.

练习 *Exercises*

用"除非 ~，才 ~"改写下列句子。Rewrite the sentences with the pattern.

1. 如果不出现奇迹，这个病人就活不过明天。

   →_____。

2. 我刚工作，现在不贷款就不可能买房子。

   →_____。

除了 ~（以外），都 ~

解释 *Explanation*

表示提出的部分不包括在内。

Used to indicate what's mentioned is excluded.

例句 *Examples*

1. 除了刮风、下雨，他每天都去锻炼。

   He exercises every day, unless it's windy or rainy.

2. 在中国，除了香菜，我什么蔬菜都吃。

   In China, I eat all vegetables except for coriander.

3. 除了两极以外，世界各地他几乎都跑遍了。

   He has been everywhere in the world except for the two poles.

4. 眼下是旅游旺季，除了这儿以外，别处都住满了。

   It's the tourist season now. Everywhere is full except for here.

对话 *Dialogues*

1. A: 今天你干什么了？

   What did you do today?

   B: 除了睡觉，什么都没干。

   Nothing, except for sleep.

2. A: 大家的英语水平都有了很大的提高。

   They have all improved their English.

   B: 是的。除了我以外，大家都有所提高。

   Yes. All have improved except for me.

练习 *Exercises*

用"除了 ~（以外），都 ~"改写下列句子。Rewrite the sentences with the pattern.

1. 我这一生只爱她一个人。→_____。

2. 只有我能帮你这个忙。→_____。

解释 *Explanation*

表示只有这两种情况存在，没有别的，带有强调的语气。

Used as an emphatic form to indicate "either … or …".

例句 *Examples*

1. 这几天除了刮风就是下雨，天气糟透了。

   It has been either windy or rainy lately. The weather is really bad.

2. 这书架上的书，除了文学的，就是语言的。

   The books on this shelf are either about literature or language.

3. 出事地点周围，除了消防员就是武警。

   There are either firemen or armed policemen at the scene of the accident.

4. 我每天除了忙工作，就是忙家务，一点儿休闲时间也没有。

   I'm busy with either work or housework every day. I have no leisure time.

对话 *Dialogues*

1. A: 她整天待在家里干什么呀?

   What does she do at home all day?

   B: 她呀，没别的事，除了看小说，就是聊天。

   Nothing in particular. She either reads novels or chats.

2. A: 你们学校的食堂怎么样?

   What do you think of the food of your school dining hall?

   B: 没什么好吃的，除了白菜就是豆腐。

   It's nothing special. If it's not Chinese cabbage, it's beancurd.

练习 *Exercises*

用"除了 ~，就是 ~"改写下列句子。Rewrite the sentences with the pattern.

1. 他很懒，每天只吃饭、睡觉、玩儿牌，什么事也不干。

   →_____。

2. 商店里卖的胶卷只有柯达和富士两种。

   →_____。

汉语常用格式330例

除了 ~（以外），也/还 ~

解释 *Explanation*

表示不仅是前面所说的包括在内，后者也包括在内。

Used to indicate "besides", "apart from" or "in addition to".

例句 *Examples*

1. 这次中学同学聚会，除了小王不能去，我也去不了。

   Not only Xiao Wang, I can't attend the middle school mates' party either.

2. 除了学好各门功课，他还积极参加各种活动。

   He works hard on all subjects in addition to playing an active role in various activities.

3. 现在，除了南极气温升高以外，北极也有变暖的趋势。

   Now apart from the South Pole, the North Pole is getting warmer too.

4. 来参加婚礼的除了双方的亲朋好友，还有双方单位的领导。

   Along with friends and relatives, leaders from the couple's companies also attended the wedding.

对话 *Dialogues*

1. A：你喜欢什么球类运动?

   What kind of ball games do you like?

   B：除了高尔夫，我还喜欢保龄球。

   Besides golf, I also like bowling.

2. A：上次你去中国，都到了哪些城市?

   Which cities did you visit during your last trip to China?

   B：除了北京、上海，还去了西安和广州。

   In addition to Beijing and Shanghai, I also went to Xi'an and Guangzhou.

练习 *Exercises*

用"除了~（以外），也/还~"完成句子。Complete the sentences with the pattern.

1. A：周末你一般干什么?

   B：＿＿＿＿＿＿＿＿＿＿＿＿＿＿＿＿＿。

2. A：听说他汉语说得呱呱叫，根本听不出是个外国人。

   B：对，他很有语言天赋，＿＿＿＿＿＿＿＿＿＿＿＿＿。

解释 *Explanation*

本义指离开原来所在的地方，到别的地方去。引申为考虑或处理问题时以某一方面为着眼点。

Used to indicate "going from some place to another place", and in extension it indicates the basis on which to consider or handle a problem.

例句 *Examples*

1. 参加野营的学生们已经整理好行装，准备从学校出发。
   Students going camping have packed up and are ready to start from school.
2. 访问团定于明日上午 9 时从北京出发。
   The delegation is leaving Beijing at 9：00 am tomorrow.
3. 搞经济建设不能急于求成，要从实际情况出发。
   We can't be hasty in developing the economy. We must proceed according to the actual situation.
4. 找什么工作，要从自己的实际水平出发。
   The job you look for must be suited to your practical ability.

对话 *Dialogues*

1. A: 能告诉我这次的旅行计划吗?
      Can you tell me your plan for this trip?
   B: 21 号从北京出发经南京到上海。
      I will leave Beijing on the 21ˢᵗ, and go to Shanghai via Nanjing.

2. A: 有些人反对这项改革。
      Some people oppose this reform.
   B: 我看他们是从个人利益出发的。
      I think they are against it only out of consideration of their personal interests.

练习 *Exercises*

用"从～出发"完成句子。Complete the sentences with the pattern.

1. A: 这次冬季长跑活动的线路是什么?
   B: ＿＿＿＿＿＿＿＿＿＿＿。

2. A: 你为什么放弃优厚待遇，又去读书呢?
   B: 我是＿＿＿＿＿＿＿＿＿＿。只有读书，才能有更大的发展。

从 ~ 角度说

解释 *Explanation*

表示从某个方面来看问题。

Used to indicate to judge or speak from a certain perspective.

例句 *Examples*

1. 从营养的角度说，蔬菜生吃比较好。

   In terms of nutrition, it's better to eat uncooked vegetables.

2. 从技术角度说，制造这种产品有一定的难度。

   Technically, it's a bit difficult to manufacture such kind of products.

3. 从实用的角度说，这款轿车更合适。

   This car is more appropriate for practical purpose.

4. 从中医的角度说，这叫气虚，需要补。

   In traditional Chinese medicine, this is called "deficiency of vital energy" which demands nourishment.

对话 *Dialogues*

1. A: 我觉得张艺谋导演的这部电影比前几部成功。

   I think this movie, directed by Zhang Yimou, is more successful than his previous ones.

   B: 那要看从哪个角度说。

   It depends on from which angle you judge it.

2. A: 你说我为什么会做这样的一个梦？

   Could you please tell me why I had such a dream?

   B: 从心理学的角度说，这个梦说明你缺乏安全感。

   Psychologically, this dream shows you have no sense of security.

练习 *Exercises*

完成下列句子。Complete the following sentences.

1. 从安全的角度说，＿＿＿＿＿＿＿＿＿＿＿＿＿＿＿＿＿＿。

2. 从经济学的角度说，＿＿＿＿＿＿＿＿＿＿＿＿＿＿＿＿。

解释 *Explanation*

表示根据某一方面，或从某种角度来观察。

Used to indicate "from some aspect or angle".

例句 *Examples*

1. 从目前情况看，还不至于发生世界规模的战争。

   Judging from the current situation, I don't think it's serious enough to cause a world war.

2. 从各方面来看，医疗制度急需改革。

   All the evidence indicates that the medical care system needs immediate reform.

3. 这几个方案各有利弊，但从总体上说，这个方案优于其他方案。

   The plans all have their pluses and minuses, but overall this plan is better than the others.

4. 从配置来说，这台电脑比那台高多了。

   In terms of configuration, this computer is better than that one.

对话 *Dialogues*

1. A: 这个年轻人怎么样？

   What do you think of this young man?

   B: 从工作态度来说，这小伙子还是很不错的。

   Judging from his attitude to work, he is quite satisfying.

2. A: 这次考试情况如何？

   What are the results of the exam?

   B: 从成绩来看，优、良者居多。

   The marks show most students got "excellent" or "good".

练习 *Exercises*

用"从 ~（来）看/说"和所给的词语完成对话。Complete the sentences with the pattern and words in parentheses.

1. A: 你觉得这两款车哪款比较好？

   B: 很难说，_____。（驾驶性能　舒适程度）

2. A: 我们月底以前能完成任务吗？

   B: _____，没有问题。（目前情况）

从哪儿~起（呢）

解释 *Explanation*

表示不知道应该从何开始。后面有"呢"时含有自问的语气。

Used to indicate that someone does not know where to start. When followed by 呢, it has a tone of self-interrogation.

例句 *Examples*

1. 我有很多感想，可是从哪儿说起呢？

   I have many reflections, but where shall I start?

2. 这么多的展厅，我们从哪儿看起呢？

   There are so many exhibition halls. Which one shall we go to first?

3. 内容这么丰富多彩，从哪儿写起？

   There is so much to describe. Where shall I start to write?

4. 你认为孩子的教育应该从哪儿抓起？

   In your opinion, from which aspect shall we start to improve children's education?

对话 *Dialogues*

1. A: 给我们讲讲这次旅行的见闻吧。

      Tell us what you saw and heard during this trip.

   B: 这次去了这么多地方，从哪儿讲起呢？

      I've been to so many places. Where shall I start?

2. A: 你来介绍一下情况吧。

      Will you please tell us the situation?

   B: 从哪儿介绍起呢？好吧，我想到哪儿就说到哪儿吧。

      Where shall I start? OK, I will speak out what comes into my mind.

练习 *Exercises*

用"从哪儿~起（呢）"完成句子。Complete the sentences with the pattern.

1. 要我们谈谈恋爱经过？_____？

2. 没有教练指导，真不知道_____。

解释 *Explanation*

表示从某个时间或地方开始。"自"多用于书面语。

Used to indicate "from a date or place". 自 is mostly used in written Chinese.

例句 *Examples*

1. 经理说从下月起给大家涨工资。

   The manager said all of us would get a pay rise from next month.

2. 很多人都不知道月亮是从东边升起的。

   Many people don't know the moon rises from the east.

3. 本条例自公布之日起实行。

   The regulation comes into force upon promulgation.

4. 《中华人民共和国物权法》自 2007 年 10 月 1 日起正式施行。

   The Property Law of the People's Republic of China came into effect as of October 1st, 2007.

对话 *Dialogues*

1. A：咱们得好好锻炼啦，不然真的要长啤酒肚了。

   Unless we want to get beer bellies, we should exercise.

   B：好，咱们从明天起就开始锻炼。

   OK, let's start from tomorrow.

2. A：听说中国个税起征点要调整？

   I heard that China would adjust personal income tax exemption threshold. Is it true?

   B：没错，自 2008 年 3 月 1 日起个税起征点提高到 2000 元。

   Yes. It will rise to 2,000 yuan from March 1st, 2008.

练习 *Exercises*

用"从/自~起"完成句子。Complete the sentences with the pattern.

1. A：你什么时候才能下决心戒烟呢？

   B：_____。

2. A：中国改革开放的新时期从哪年算起？

   B：_____。

从/自~以来

解释 *Explanation*

表示从过去某一时期起直到说话时为止。

Used to indicate the period from a certain time in the past to the present.

例句 *Examples*

1. 从新技术展览会开幕以来，参观者达数十万人。

   Since this new technology exhibition was opened, the number of visitors has reached several hundred thousand.

2. 从认识那个女孩儿以来，他变了不少，也学会了珍惜时间。

   Since he met that girl, he has changed a lot and learned to value time.

3. 自古以来，男大当婚，女大当嫁。

   Throughout history, men and women marry at the right age.

4. 自今年一月以来，人民币升值逾六百个基点。

   Since January this year, Renminbi has risen in value by over 600 percentage points against the US dollar.

对话 *Dialogues*

1. A: 王部长很注意听取各方面的意见。

   Minister Wang attaches a great deal of importance to gathering opinions from a wide range of sources.

   B: 从他当部长以来，大家的情绪高多了。

   Since he was promoted to the ministerial post, public sentiment has improved.

2. A: 湖南几十年没下过这么大的雪了。

   It has been several decades since Hunan saw such heavy snow.

   B: 是啊，自上世纪五十年代以来没下过这样的冰雨、暴雪。

   Yes. There hasn't been so much hail and snow since the 1950s.

练习 *Exercises*

用"从/自~以来"和所给的词语造句。Make sentences with the pattern and words in parentheses.

1. _____。（大学毕业）

2. _____。（自然灾害）

解释 *Explanation*

表示从某种情况发生以后。"打"用于口语，"自"用于书面语，"从"都可以。

Used to indicate after or since something happened. 打 is often used orally, while 自 is used in written Chinese. 从 can be used in both oral and written Chinese.

例句 *Examples*

1. 经理助理刘小姐打结婚以后就不工作了。

   Since she got married, Manager Assistant Ms. Liu has not worked.

2. 打王部长听取汇报以后，他决心加快机构改革。

   After Minister Wang heard the report, he decided to accelerate the institutional re-structuring.

3. 从大学毕业以后，我就再也没听到过他的消息了。

   Since graduating from university, I have heard no news of him.

4. 自他去西部考察以后，就决定加强生态环境建设。

   After he came back from his inspection tour to the western regions, he decided to make a bigger effort to improve ecological environment.

对话 *Dialogues*

1. A: 我们还是十年前在美国见的面吧?

   Was it ten years ago when we met in the United States?

   B: 可不，从那以后，咱们就没见过。

   Exactly, but since then we haven't seen each other.

2. A: 现在这个医院由谁负责?

   Who's in charge of the hospital now?

   B: 自院长出国以后，无人负责。

   No one took charge after the president went abroad.

练习 *Exercises*

用"打/从/自～以后"完成句子。Complete the sentences with the pattern.

1. A: 你最后一次看见他是什么时候?

   B: 是去年年底，＿＿＿＿＿＿＿＿＿＿＿＿＿。

2. A: 你是什么时候开始对中国文学感兴趣的?

   B: 我高中的时候读了《三国演义》，＿＿＿＿＿＿＿＿＿＿＿＿。

大～大～

解释 *Explanation*

表示规模大、程度深。两个"大"后用意思相近或相关的单音节名词、形容词或动词。

Used respectively before a monosyllabic noun, adjective or verb of similar or relevant meanings, to indicate scale or magnitude.

例句 *Examples*

1. 不少农村妇女逢年过节都喜欢穿大红大绿的衣服。

   Quite a few rural women like to wear bright red or green clothes on festival days.

2. 年轻人花钱总是大手大脚的，还没到月底呢，工资就花光了。

   Young people always overspend. Some even use up their salary before the end of the month.

3. 政府反对公务员大吃大喝，然而收效甚微。

   The government prohibits public officials from extravagant dining, but to little effect.

4. 他的一生大起大落，既过过十分贫穷的日子，也享受过少有的荣华富贵。

   He experienced great ups and downs in his life, including periods of wealth and prestige as well as periods of destitution.

对话 *Dialogues*

1. A: 你为什么要搬家?

   Why are you moving?

   B: 隔壁邻居老是大吵大闹的，受不了。

   My neighbor is always too loud, and I can't take it anymore.

2. A: 哎，体重又增加了。

   Oh, I've put on more weight.

   B: 每天大鱼大肉的，能不胖吗?

   You eat too much meat every day. Of course you put on weight.

练习 *Exercises*

选词填空。Choose the right phrases to fill in the blanks.

> 大是大非　　大富大贵　　大红大紫　　大摇大摆

1. 这不是小问题，而是_____的原则性问题，我们绝不能让步。

2. 她再也不是过去那个不起眼的小丫头了，她现在是_____的明星。

60

解释 *Explanation*

"大"和"的"中间一般是表示某些季节、节假日、时令的词语，强调在某种特定的情况下应该或不应该怎样。

Words indicating seasons, holidays, festivals or times between 大 and 的 usually show what should or should not be done under certain circumstances.

例句 *Examples*

1. 大清早的，是谁叫门呢？

   It's early in the morning. Who's knocking at the door?

2. 大雪天的，外面滑，别出去了。

   It's snowing, and the ground is slippery. Don't go out.

3. 大过年的，别说让人不愉快的事。

   It's the Spring Festival. Don't talk about unhappy things.

4. 大周末的，老待在家里多没意思。

   It's the weekend! It's boring to stay at home all day.

对话 *Dialogues*

1. A: 我想出去逛逛。

   I want to take a walk.

   B: 大中午的，太阳这么毒，去哪儿逛呀。

   It's noon and the sun is burning. Where will you go?

2. A: 我今晚要穿这条超短裙去参加晚会。

   I will wear this miniskirt to the party tonight.

   B: 大冬天的，你穿裙子不怕冷吗？

   It's winter. Isn't it too cold wearing a skirt?

练习 *Exercises*

用"大 ~ 的，~"和所给词语完成句子。Complete the sentences with the pattern and words in parentheses.

1. A: 我要吃蛋糕，你现在去给我买。

   B: ＿＿＿＿＿＿＿＿＿＿＿＿＿＿＿＿，明天再买好不好？（半夜）

2. A: 我怕鬼。

   B: ＿＿＿＿＿＿＿＿＿＿＿＿＿＿＿＿，你别自己吓自己了。（白天）

解释 *Explanation*

"大"、"特"用在两个相同的单音节动词前,表示规模大、程度深。带夸张语气。

Each used before the same monosyllabic verb to indicate an exaggerated scale or magnitude.

例句 *Examples*

1. 会上他大谈特谈改革,会下却是另一回事。

   At the meeting he talked a lot about reform, but afterwards acted in a different way.

2. 在会上老板大讲特讲如何开发海洋资源问题。

   At the meeting, the boss gave a long-winded talk on how to develop marine resources.

3. 她听到法院的判决后,大骂特骂,说太不公平了。

   When she heard the court's judgment she cursed terribly, and claimed it was unfair.

4. 香港真是购物天堂,很多人到了那里都大买特买。

   Hong Kong really is a shopping paradise. People go there to buy to their hearts' content.

对话 *Dialogues*

1. A:这次连放七天假,你有什么打算?

   It's a seven-day holiday. What are your plans?

   B:我要大睡特睡,这些日子太辛苦了。

   I want to sleep to my heart's content. These days have been hectic.

2. A:这个剧本怎么样?

   What do you think of this script?

   B:情节不合理,语言也别扭,需要大改特改。

   The plot is unreasonable and the language is strange; a lot needs to be revised.

练习 *Exercises*

选词填空。Choose the right phrases to fill in the blanks.

大错特错　　大吃特吃　　大批特批　　大改特改

1. 你以为他沉默不语就是同意了,那就＿＿＿＿＿＿＿＿＿了。说明你根本不了解他。

2. 今天的晚饭这样丰盛,大家心情又好,于是就＿＿＿＿＿＿＿＿＿了一顿。

解释 *Explanation*

表示到特指的或某个适当的时候。

Used to indicate a special or proper time.

例句 *Examples*

1. 别担心，该给你的钱到时候自然会给你的。

   Don't worry. When the time comes, your money will be given to you.

2. 首先必须筹足资金，要不到时候经费不足怎么办？

   First we have to make sure we have enough money. Otherwise, what shall we do if we're short of funds by then?

3. 他们长期组织文艺演出，到时候一定会有很好的舞台效果。

   They have been engaged in organizing performances for a long time. Therefore, you will see good stage effects.

4. 这个星期天我要上台演出，这次我要早点儿做好准备，免得到时候着急。

   I have a performance this Sunday. This time I'm going to get prepared earlier, so I won't get so anxious.

对话 *Dialogues*

1. A: 后天就出国了，我还什么都没准备呢！

   I will go abroad the day after tomorrow, but I still haven't started preparing anything!

   B: 别急，到时候我都会帮你准备好的。

   Don't worry. I will help you get ready by then.

2. A: 那边的情况，我一点儿也不了解。

   I don't know anything about the situation there.

   B: 到时候我会告诉你的。

   I will tell you by that time.

练习 *Exercises*

用"到时候 ~"完成句子。Complete the sentences with the pattern.

1. 奥运会是世界性的体育盛事，＿＿＿＿＿＿＿＿＿＿＿＿＿。

2. 我们下个月举行婚礼，＿＿＿＿＿＿＿＿＿＿＿＿＿。

倒(是) ~

解释 *Explanation*

表示跟意料或一般情理相反。有时表示相反的意思较明显，有时表示相反的意思较轻微。

Used to indicate that something is contrary to what is expected or thought. Sometimes the contrast is sharp and sometimes not.

例句 *Examples*

1. 你不喜欢这本书？我倒觉得这位作者写得挺好的。

   Don't you like this book? But I think the author did a good job.

2. 原想省点儿事才这么处理的，没想到倒更费事了。

   Instead of saving trouble, I made it more troublesome by handling it this way.

3. 你看你，该说的没说，不该说的倒是说个没完。

   You don't tell us what should be told. Instead, you talk endlessly about what should not be told.

4. 你觉得她很高傲吗？我倒是没这个感觉。

   You think she is arrogant, don't you? I don't think so.

对话 *Dialogues*

1. A: 我不爱吃柚子，又酸又苦的。

   I don't like grapefruit. It's sour and bitter.

   B: 我倒是挺爱吃的。

   I like it.

2. A: 远足回来大家都累了，躺下就不想动了。

   After the hike, everyone is so tired and reluctant to move after lying down.

   B: 我倒是来了精神。

   But I'm more energetic.

练习 *Exercises*

用"倒(是) ~"完成句子。Complete the sentences with the pattern.

1. A: 为了让钱不贬值，应该把闲钱投资。

   B: _____。

2. A: 一般十二三岁的孩子逆反心理严重。

   B: 我的女儿_____。

解释 *Explanation*

用来界定所叙说的某种情况的时间范围。

Used to set a limit to the time of a situation mentioned.

例句 *Examples*

1. 到目前为止，他们是北京最有实力的电子商务公司。

   So far, their company is the strongest e-commerce company in Beijing.

2. 到昨天为止，有400人报名参加这个语言学研讨会。

   By yesterday, 400 people had signed up for the linguistics seminar.

3. 他是退而不休，他说他要一直干到完全丧失工作能力为止。

   He has retired but he doesn't rest. He said that he would work until the day he can't work any longer.

对话 *Dialogues*

1. A: 听说有两个中国人骑自行车环游了世界。

   I heard two Chinese traveled around the world by bike.

   B: 是啊，到现在为止，中国只有他们两个人以骑车方式宣传了健康之路。

   Yes. Up till now, they are the only two Chinese people promoting a healthy way of living by traveling by bike.

2. A: 台湾有多少人参观过西安的兵马俑？

   How many Taiwanese have visited the Terracotta Warriors in Xi'an?

   B: 听说到2002年为止，就已经超过五十万人次了。

   It is said that by 2002, the number had exceeded 500,000.

练习 *Exercises*

用"到～为止"完成句子。Complete the sentences with the pattern.

1. A: 今年你炒股赚了不少钱吧？

   B: 嗯，_____。

2. A: 你上大学的时候一直是你父母给你付学费吗？

   B: _____，我三年级的时候开始打工。

汉语常用格式330例

65

解释 *Explanation*

表示程度很高。

Used to indicate a high degree or intensity.

例句 *Examples*

1. 高级商场的商品，质量虽好，但价格贵得不得了。

   The products in high-grade shopping malls are of good quality, but are extremely expensive.

2. 展览厅挤得水泄不通，人多得不得了。

   The exhibition hall is overcrowded. There are far too many people.

3. 几场足球赛都赢了，大家高兴得不行。

   We won all the football matches. Everyone is ecstatic.

4. 错过了那次机会，我后悔得不行。

   I can't regret more to have missed that opportunity.

对话 *Dialogues*

1. A：你怎么一回家就躺下了？

   Why did you go to bed as soon as you got home?

   B：我一夜没睡，困得不行啦。

   I didn't sleep last night, and even now I can hardly keep my eyes open.

2. A：老李知道今天会上的情况吗？

   Does Lao Li know what happened at today's meeting?

   B：知道了，他气得不得了。

   Yes, he's furious.

练习 *Exercises*

用"～得不得了/得不行"完成句子。Complete the sentences with the pattern.

1. 屋子里开了暖气，温度太高，＿＿＿＿＿＿＿＿＿＿＿。

2. 她看到我新买的玩具，＿＿＿＿＿＿＿＿＿＿，所以我就送给她了。

汉语常用格式330例

解释 *Explanation*

表示假设关系，可以和"如果"、"要是"搭配使用。

Used to indicate an assumption. It can be used with 如果 or 要是.

例句 *Examples*

1. 钱都投在股票上的话，太危险了。

   It's very dangerous to invest all your money in the stock market.

2. 如果各方面条件都允许的话，应该去周游世界。

   If circumstances permit, you should travel around the world.

3. 一个公司长期资金周转困难的话，只好宣布倒闭。

   If a company has long-term difficulties with capital turnover, it has to announce bankruptcy.

4. 要是你不介意的话，我想给大家读一下你的这篇文章。

   If you don't mind, I want to read your article to everybody.

对话 *Dialogues*

1. **A:** 你是 MBA，怎么不开个公司？

   You have an MBA. Why don't you start your own company?

   B: 赔钱的话，怎么办？

   What will I do if it loses money?

2. **A:** 你这个周末怎么过？

   How will you spend the weekend?

   B: 有兴致的话，去长城玩儿。

   I may go to the Great Wall if I am in the mood.

练习 *Exercises*

用"~ 的话，~"完成句子。Complete the sentences with the pattern.

1. _____，一定能取得好成绩。

2. _____，对谁都没有好处。

A 的 A，B 的 B

解释 *Explanation*

两个"的"字前后，各用相同的动词或形容词，表示有的这样，有的那样。

Used with the same verb or adjective before and after each 的 to indicate that some are (doing) this and some are (doing) that.

例句 *Examples*

1. 大家推的推，拉的拉，行李很快运走了。

   With some pushing and some pulling, they quickly carried away the luggage.

2. 他们家高朋满座，说的说，笑的笑。

   There are many guests in their home, talking and laughing.

3. 看到那些孩子，吵的吵，闹的闹，我的头都大了。

   These children are so noisy that they are giving me a headache.

4. 现在是秋高气爽的季节，山上的树红的红，绿的绿，黄的黄，真好看。

   It's now pleasant autumn weather. Trees on the mountains turn red, yellow or stay green. It's beautiful.

对话 *Dialogues*

1. A：这苹果是论堆卖的，便宜。

   The apples sell in a pile. They are cheap.

   B：怪不得大的大，小的小呢。

   No wonder some are big and some are small.

2. A：每天早上，街心公园可热闹啦！

   The corner park is buzzing with activities every morning.

   B：可不，跳舞的跳舞，练剑的练剑，唱歌的唱歌，遛鸟的遛鸟。

   Yes. Some people dance, some practice swordplay, some sing, and others take a walk with their birds.

练习 *Exercises*

用"A 的 A，B 的 B"完成句子。Complete the sentences with the pattern.

1. 办公室里大家都在忙着，_____。

2. 大家都喝醉了，_____。

解释 *Explanation*

分别用在两个意义相同或相近的动词或数量词前，表示"这里~那里~"和"到处~，乱~"的意思。

Used before two verbs or quantifiers with the same or similar meanings to indicate being disorganized or being scattered everywhere.

例句 *Examples*

1. 为了投诉，我东一趟西一趟，好不容易才找到负责人。

   To lodge my complaint, I went there again and again, and finally found the person in charge.

2. 有什么话请直截了当地说，别东拉西扯的。

   Just say what you want to say; don't beat about the bush.

3. 他年轻的时候不务正业，整天东游西荡。

   When he was young he didn't have a proper job, and just wasted his time away.

4. 这篇论文是东拼西凑的，甚至有些观点是相互矛盾的。

   This thesis is a "cut and paste" job. Some of the arguments are even contradictory.

对话 *Dialogues*

1. A: 这些人东倒西歪的，怎么啦？

   These people are staggering. What's the matter?

   B: 八成是喝醉了。

   They must be drunk.

2. A: 这孩子钢琴学了还没两个月，又不学了，改学二胡了。

   The child quit piano after less than two months, and started to learn erhu.

   B: 他就是这样，东一榔头西一棒槌，什么也学不好。

   His method of study is very disorganized, so ultimately he learns nothing.

练习 *Exercises*

选词填空。Choose the right phrases to fill in the blanks.

东躲西藏　　东奔西走　　东跑西颠　　东一句西一句

1. 他欠了别人的钱还不起，只好＿＿＿＿＿＿＿＿＿＿。

2. 他整天＿＿＿＿＿＿＿＿＿＿的，也不知在忙些什么。

汉语常用格式330例

动不动就 ~

解释 *Explanation*

表示常常发生某种情况，后面跟动词性词语，带有不满的口气。

Used before a verbal phrase to indicate that something happens frequently, embodying discontent.

例句 *Examples*

1. 物价动不动就涨，这日子还怎么过！

   The prices grow now and then. It's almost impossible to make a living!

2. 有些名人的生活小事动不动就闹得满城风雨。

   Some celebrities frequently create a great sensation over trifles.

3. 小姚也太意气用事了，动不动就撂挑子不干了。

   Xiao Yao is too emotional and frequently throws up his work.

4. 那里的老百姓有游行的自由，动不动就上街示威游行。

   People there have the freedom to demonstrate, and they often hold demonstrations on streets.

对话 *Dialogues*

1. A：你好像不太喜欢跟施太太聊天儿？

   It seems you don't like to chat with Mrs. Shi, do you?

   B：嗯，她总是动不动就抱怨，看社会的消极面太多。

   Yes. She is always ready to complain because she tends to see the seamy side of society.

2. A：你女朋友真是个多愁善感的人，像林黛玉似的。

   Your girlfriend is really sentimental, just like Lin Daiyu.

   B：可不是吗？动不动就伤心流泪，我老得哄着她。

   It's true. She's apt to cry and I always have to please her.

练习 *Exercises*

用"动不动就 ~"完成句子。Complete the sentences with the pattern.

1. 这孩子身体太弱了，＿＿＿＿＿＿＿＿＿＿＿＿＿＿。

2. 职员们都不喜欢这个老板，他＿＿＿＿＿＿＿＿＿＿＿＿＿。

解释 *Explanation*

表示"已经~了"的意思。

Used to indicate "already".

例句 *Examples*

1. 都四月了，怎么还这么冷！

   It's already April, but still so cold!

2. 都夜里一点了，孩子还在学习呢。

   It is one am, but the child is still studying.

3. 都十二月了，一场雪还没下过呢。

   It's already December, but has not snowed yet.

4. 利息都这么低了，可以说是负利息，还存什么钱。

   Bank interest is low; compared with the inflation rate, it is even negative. There is no point in saving money in a bank.

对话 *Dialogues*

1. A: 这位老先生身体真够棒的！

   This old man is in very good health.

   B: 可不是吗？都八十多岁了，还跳舞呢。

   Yes, that's true. He's over 80, but can still dance.

2. A: 饭都凉了，还不快吃！

   The food is getting cold. You should eat first!

   B: 你没看见我忙着呢吗？

   Can't you see I'm busy?

练习 *Exercises*

用"都~了，~"完成句子。Complete the sentences with the pattern.

1. 那位著名的画家_____，还画了不少画儿呢。

2. 这些鱼肉罐头_____，千万别吃了。

都这时候了，~

解释 *Explanation*

表示时间已经很晚，或到了比较紧急的时候。后句常用"还"与它呼应。也说"都什么时候了。"

Used before a sentence often with 还 to indicate it's already late or urgent. Sometimes the pattern becomes 都什么时候了.

例句 *Examples*

1. 都这时候了，还玩儿牌呢！

   You're still playing cards at this hour?

2. 都这时候了，你还有心思开玩笑！

   You're still inclined to joke at a time like this?

3. 都什么时候了，她还不回家，真急人！

   It's so late and she hasn't come back. It worries me!

4. 都什么时候了，你怎么还不准备动身哪？

   It's late. Why aren't you ready to go?

对话 *Dialogues*

1. A：你说都这时候了，小孙他们还会来吗？

   It's already late. Do you think Xiao Sun and others will come?

   B：我想他们不会来了。

   I don't think they will come.

2. A：咱们去逛逛商店吧。

   Let's go shopping.

   B：都什么时候了，商店早关门了。

   It's late, and shops are closed.

练习 *Exercises*

用"都这时候了，~"完成句子。Complete the sentences with the pattern.

1. A：哎呀，那份重要的文件没带，我得回去拿。

   B：_____。

2. A：我还有很多事情没做完呢。

   B：_____。

72

解释 *Explanation*

表示从某人、某事的角度来看问题。强调跟可谈到的情况或看法有关的人或物。

Used to indicate that what it is like for someone or something. It stresses the people and conditions connected with the things mentioned.

例句 *Examples*

1. 对企业来说，流动资金是很重要的。

   For business enterprises, capital flow is very important.

2. 对某些人来说，唠叨也是他们的生活乐趣。

   For some people, pointless chatter is one of life's interests.

3. 对运动员来说，积累比赛经验十分重要。

   For athletes, gaining competition experience is very important.

4. 对生产商来说，最关心的是市场动态。

   For manufacturers, market trends are critical.

对话 *Dialogues*

1. A: 张大爷，春节好！恭喜发财呀！

   Grandpa Zhang, happy Spring Festival! Best wishes for a prosperous New Year!

   B: 谢谢。不过，对我们老年人来说，健康更重要，是不是？

   Thank you. But for old people health is more important, isn't it?

2. A: 我想那个人，贼头贼脑的，很可能是盗窃嫌疑犯。

   That man is shifty. I think he is probably the theft suspect.

   B: 可是，对法官判案来说，要有真凭实据。

   But the judge needs concrete evidence to convict him.

练习 *Exercises*

用"对 ~ 来说，~"完成句子。Complete the sentences with the pattern.

1. A: 我觉得在网上用 MSN 聊天儿真有意思。

   B: _____。

2. A: 我得回去戴手套，今天好冷啊！

   B: 是吗？我是东北人，_____。

对了，~

解释 *Explanation*

表示忽然想起某事或转换话题提醒对方注意。

Used as a reminder to indicate that the speaker suddenly remembers something or changes the subject.

例句 *Examples*

1. 睡觉吧。对了，你上闹钟了吗？

   Let's go to bed. Wait! Did you set the alarm clock?

2. 现在准备动身吧！对了，小王还没到呢。

   Let's get ready to leave now. Oh wait! Xiao Wang has not come yet.

3. 春节就要到了。对了，火车票还没订吧？

   The Spring Festival is coming. But hey, you haven't booked your train ticket, have you?

4. 今天的会就开到这儿。对了，晚上经理请大家吃全聚德烤鸭。

   The meeting will finish now. Oh, yes, the manager will treat us to Beijing Duck at Quanjude this evening.

对话 *Dialogues*

1. A: 小李现在精神状态怎么样？

   Is Xiao Li in good spirits?

   B: 挺好的。对了，你怎么突然提起他了？

   Very good. But hey, why did you suddenly mention him?

2. A: 今天几号？

   What's the date?

   B: 15 号。对了，该发工资了。

   The 15th. Oh, it's payday.

练习 *Exercises*

用"对了，~"写两句话。**Make two sentences with the pattern.**

1. _____。

2. _____。

解释 *Explanation*

中间用形容词或动词，表示肯定，但数量不多或程度不高。

Used with an adjective or a verb in the middle to indicate a small quantity or degree.

例句 *Examples*

1. 朋友聚会，大家高兴，你多少也喝点儿吧？

   It's a happy gathering of friends. Drink a little, will you?

2. 她是我的好朋友，向我借钱，我虽不富裕，多少也得借她点儿。

   She's a good friend of mine. When she asked to borrow money, I lent some to her, even though I don't have a lot myself.

3. 经过上次比赛的失败，现在他多少成熟了一点儿。

   After failing in the previous match, he is now a little more mature.

4. 中国西部某些地方的老百姓现在仍然贫困，但比早些年多少好了一点儿。

   People in some places of western China are still poor now, but a little better off than in the past.

对话 *Dialogues*

1. A：那里的干部作风怎么样？

   What style of work do the cadres have there?

   B：和过去比，多少民主了点儿。

   A bit more democratic than in the past.

2. A：我真的不想吃，别勉强我吧。

   I really don't want to eat. Don't force me.

   B：为了身体，多少吃一点儿，好吗？

   For the sake of your health, try to eat some, OK?

练习 *Exercises*

用"多少 ~（一）点儿"完成句子。Complete the sentences with the pattern.

1. A：现在你身体怎么样了？

   B：休息了一个月，＿＿＿＿＿＿＿＿＿＿＿＿＿＿。

2. A：你的英语口语有很大提高吧？

   B：我天天练习听说，＿＿＿＿＿＿＿＿＿＿＿＿＿＿。

多少有点儿 ~

解释 *Explanation*

表示虽然程度不高，但某种性质、状态或变化是存在的。后面可以用名词、形容词、动词。

Used before a noun, an adjective or a verb to indicate "more or less", "somewhat" or "to some extent", showing the existence of certain nature, state or change, though not in high degree.

例句 *Examples*

1. 现在他们老板的态度多少有点儿改变。

   Now their boss has changed his attitude to some extent.

2. 他们这么快就结婚了，大家多少有点儿意外。

   It was somewhat unexpected that they got married so quickly.

3. 尽管她比较有钱，但是丢了这么多钱，多少有点儿不痛快。

   Although she is rich, she still felt somewhat unhappy to lose so much money.

4. 孩子还小，突然到了一个完全陌生的环境，多少有点儿害怕。

   The child is still young, and will definitely be somewhat scared to be suddenly placed in a strange environment.

对话 *Dialogues*

1. A：现在那里乡镇居民生活怎么样？

   Now what's life like in that town?

   B：多少有点儿改善吧。

   It's improved a bit.

2. A：他这么大年纪，能干得了这么重的活吗？

   He is so old. Is he able to do this kind of hard work?

   B：我看多少有点儿吃力。

   I think it's somewhat difficult for him.

练习 *Exercises*

用"多少有点儿 ~"完成句子。Complete the sentences with the pattern.

1. 他以前做过这方面的工作，＿＿＿＿＿＿＿＿＿＿。

2. 这个运动员骨折刚好，上场比赛＿＿＿＿＿＿＿＿＿＿。

解释 *Explanation*

表示不管情况或事态处于哪一种程度，都不会影响后面的结论。前面可以和"不管"配合。

Used sometimes after 不管... to indicate the same result at whatever a degree or to whatever an extent.

例句 *Examples*

1. 对吝啬的人来说，多么有钱也不舍得花。

   A stingy person is unwilling to spend money, no matter how wealthy he or she is.

2. 不管遇到多么大的困难，我们都会克服的。

   No matter how big the difficulty is, we will overcome it.

3. 他真了不起，不管遇到多复杂的情况，都能应付。

   He's amazing. He can handle even the most complicated situation.

4. 她男朋友对她百依百顺，只要她喜欢，多贵的东西都给她买。

   Her boyfriend does everything she says and buys her everything she likes, no matter how expensive it is.

对话 *Dialogues*

1. A: 我已经是中年人了，才开始学英语，感到很吃力。

   I'm already a middle-aged man. It's difficult for me to start learning English now.

   B: 不管多吃力也要坚持，否则会影响未来的发展。

   You must persist no matter how difficult it is. Otherwise, it will affect your future development.

2. A: 统计这些数字太麻烦了。

   It's too much trouble counting up these figures.

   B: 多麻烦你也得干哪，那是你的本职工作。

   No matter how difficult it is, you have to do it. It's your work.

练习 *Exercises*

用"多（么）~也/都 ~"完成句子。Complete the sentences with the pattern.

1. A: 明天要下大雨，咱们别去了吧。

   B: 我都期待了这么久了，_____。

2. A: 他这么有钱，你怎么还不愿意跟他交往？

   B: 对我来说，感情和人品最重要，他_____。

凡（是）~，都 ~

解释 *Explanation*

表示在某个范围内的人或事物都包括进去，毫无例外。

Used to indicate all people or things in a certain scope without exception.

例句 *Examples*

1. 凡是邓丽君的歌，我都收藏了。

   I collect any song by Teresa Teng.

2. 凡是帮助过我的人，我都会感恩，永远不会忘记。

   I feel grateful to and will never forget anyone who has helped me.

3. 宪法规定凡年满18岁的公民，都有选举权和被选举权。

   The Constitution states that every citizen over 18 has the right to vote and to stand for election.

4. 凡贪污腐败的，不管职务高低，都应严惩。在法律面前人人平等嘛。

   All those who abuse their power should be punished seriously regardless of their position, because all men are equal before the law.

对话 *Dialogues*

1. A：贵公司招聘工作人员，外地的也可以申请吗？

   Can non-local people apply to your company?

   B：凡有高等学历的，无论本地外埠，都欢迎。

   We welcome anyone with a diploma of higher education, whether they are local or not.

2. A：凡买这家公司股票的，都赔得很惨。

   Anyone who bought this company's shares suffered great loss.

   B：没办法，只好认倒霉了。

   There is nothing they can do. They just have to accept it.

练习 *Exercises*

用"凡（是）~，都 ~"完成句子。Complete the sentences with the pattern.

1. 他太溺爱孩子了，_____。

2. 中国实行九年制义务教育，_____。

解释 *Explanation*

强调在任何情况下都不改变态度或影响结果，有时也强调是某种情况或原因，有"既然"的意思。

Used to indicate the same attitude or result despite different circumstances, and sometimes to emphasize a certain condition or cause as a similar expression to 既然.

例句 *Examples*

1. 你要喝就喝吧，反正我不喝。

   If you want to drink then drink, but I won't anyway.

2. 反正没事儿，多聊一会儿吧。

   Since we have nothing to do, let's chat a little longer.

3. 反正事情已经这样了，无法挽回，你多想也毫无用处。

   Since it has already happened, it can't be helped. It's no use thinking about it any-more.

4. 不管她是否还要和我继续交往，我都无所谓，反正也没谈婚论嫁。

   I don't care whether she will be with me or not, because we haven't decided to marry.

对话 *Dialogues*

1. A: 这个消息可靠吗？

   Is this news reliable?

   B: 信不信由你，反正我信。

   Whether you believe it or not is up to you. I believe it anyway.

2. A: 这个案子牵扯的人很多，你说能破吗？

   This case involves many people. Do you think it can be solved?

   B: 反正要查个水落石出。

   They will certainly get to the bottom of the case.

练习 *Exercises*

用"反正 ~"和所给的词语完成句子。Complete the sentences with the pattern and words in parentheses.

1. 你再劝我也没有用，＿＿＿＿＿＿＿＿＿＿＿＿。（改变主意）

2. 今天我们聊个通宵也没关系，＿＿＿＿＿＿＿＿＿＿＿。（周末睡懒觉）

汉语常用格式330例

解释 *Explanation*

表示提醒、劝告或警告听话人，对其动作、行为的某一方面提出要求。

Used to remind, persuade or warn the listener in regard to one of his actions or behaviors.

例句 *Examples*

1. 动作还要放慢一点儿、柔韧一点儿，打太极拳不能太快太硬。

   Be slower and more flexible. You cannot move fast and stiff when practicing Taiji Boxing.

2. 你呀，就是太老实，吃了个大亏，下次放机灵点儿。

   You suffered big losses as you are too honest. Next time, be smarter.

3. 先生，请你放尊重点儿，把手拿开。

   Behave yourself, sir. Remove your hand.

4. 劝你放明白点儿，你要是敬酒不吃吃罚酒，可别怪我对你不客气。

   You should understand the situation. If you turn down my request, I will exert more pressure; don't blame me then.

对话 *Dialogues*

1. A：这事不是我干的，你们抓错人了吧。

   I did not do this. You must have the wrong man.

   B：人证物证俱在，放老实点儿！坦白从宽，抗拒从严。

   Eyewitnesses and material evidence are both available. Be honest! We are lenient to those who confess their crimes and severe to those who do not.

2. A：相亲的时候应该注意些什么？

   What shall I pay attention to at a blind date?

   B：我看你呀，只要放大方点儿就行了。

   I think it's OK as long as you are natural and poised.

练习 *Exercises*

用"放~点儿"完成句子。Complete the sentences with the pattern.

1. 儿子，今天你爸爸心情不好，你可要_____，别惹他生气。

2. 脚步_____，她累了一天啦，刚睡着。

解释 *Explanation*

表示应该做的没做，反而做了不该做的；或放弃了好条件，做了不容易做的。

Used to describe a situation where something that needs to be done remains undone, and something unnecessary is done instead; or to give up a good and easy situation and instead choose to do something difficult.

例句 *Examples*

1. 放着好好的日子不过，整天吵架，真没意思。

It's no good quarreling and fighting all day. You should lead a better life.

2. 你放着工作不干，书不看，老去玩儿牌、喝酒，太不像话了。

You often play cards or drink when you have work to do or books to read. What a shame.

3. 这里各项设施都很齐备，咱们要是放着这么好的条件不利用，太可惜了。

This place has complete facilities. It's a pity if we don't make use of such good conditions.

4. 她可真跟一般人不一样，放着大机关的工作不做，跑到农村来吃苦。

She's quite different from ordinary people. She gave up a good job in the government to come and work under harsh conditions in the country.

对话 *Dialogues*

1. A: 我要出去一下。

   I'm going out.

   B: 这都几点了？放着觉不睡，去哪儿呀？

   Isn't it late? Where are you going when it's time for bed?

2. A: 我还是穿这身儿旧衣服吧，舒服。

   I will wear the old clothes. They are so comfortable.

   B: 放着新衣服不穿，买它干吗呀？

   You don't wear your new clothes. Why did you buy them?

练习 *Exercises*

用"放着～不～"和所给的词语完成句子。Complete the sentences with the pattern and words in parentheses.

1. 她是个闲不住的人，退休了，＿＿＿＿＿＿＿＿＿＿，还去做义工。（清闲的日子）

2. 为了省过路费，司机＿＿＿＿＿＿＿＿＿，绕小路，多花了两个小时。（高速公路）

非(得) ~ 不可/不行

解释 *Explanation*

表示一定要这样，必须这样，或一定会这样。

Used to indicate something has to be done or is certain to happen.

例句 *Examples*

1. 这几个贪官贪污的钱都到哪儿去了，非查清不可。

   We must find out where the money embezzled by the corrupt officials goes.

2. 这个问题关系到国计民生，我们非下大力气解决不可。

   This problem has a direct bearing on the nation's economy and people's livelihood, so we must work hard to solve it.

3. 发生这种情况非同小可，非得你亲自去一趟不行。

   It is indeed no trivial matter. You must go there in person.

4. 幸亏你拉了我一把，不然我非被车撞上不可。

   Fortunately you pulled me away; otherwise I would surely have been hit by the car.

对话 *Dialogues*

1. A: 我看这种事你最好别插手。省得惹麻烦。

   I think it's better if you don't take part in it. It sounds like too much trouble.

   B: 不行，我非管不可。

   No, I must take part in it.

2. A: 这么贵的玩具你也舍得给孩子买?

   You didn't hesitate to buy such an expensive toy for the kid?

   B: 没办法，她又哭又闹，非要买不行。

   I had no choice. She cried and wailed. I had to buy it.

练习 *Exercises*

用"非(得) ~ 不可/不行"完成句子。Complete the sentences with the pattern.

1. 不管你怎么说，我还是爱她，＿＿＿＿＿＿＿＿＿＿＿＿。

2. 这个读书报告明天要交给老师，今天＿＿＿＿＿＿＿＿＿＿＿。

解释 *Explanation*

表示根据情况应该怎样做的，就怎样做；或应该怎么处理的，就怎么处理。

Used to indicate to do what should be done according to the condition.

例句 *Examples*

1. 把房间整理一下，该收的收，该洗的洗。

   Tidy the room. Sort out what needs to be sorted out and wash what needs to be washed.

2. 你也别太节省了，该吃的吃，该喝的喝。别难为自己。

   Don't be too thrifty. Eat and drink as much as you like. Don't be so hard on yourself.

3. 根据法律，该判刑的判刑，该释放的释放。

   According to the law, sentence whoever should be sentenced and release whoever should be released.

4. 我们得赏罚分明，该批评的批评，该奖励的奖励。

   We have to be fair and strict in giving out rewards and punishments. Criticize whoever should be criticized and reward whoever deserves reward.

对话 *Dialogues*

1. A: 行李整理好了，还剩下这么多东西，怎么办？

   The luggage has been packed. What shall we do with all these leftover things?

   B: 该扔的扔，该送人的送人。

   Throw out what needs to be thrown out, and send what needs to be sent.

2. A: 你既然了解到一些情况，为什么不说呢？

   Since you know something about the situation, why don't you tell me?

   B: 该说的时候说，不该说的时候不说，我不能没搞清楚事实就瞎说。

   I will tell you when the time is right. I shouldn't say anything before I'm clear about the truth.

练习 *Exercises*

用"该 A 的 A，该 B 的 B"和所给的词语完成句子。Complete the sentences with the pattern and words in parentheses.

1. 她是个勤快的家庭主妇，每天在家里＿＿＿＿＿＿＿＿＿＿＿＿＿＿＿＿＿，屋子收拾得可干净了。(洗 擦)

2. 今年咱们要添些新衣服了，这些旧的＿＿＿＿＿＿＿＿＿＿。(扔 捐)

该 ~ 就 ~

解释 *Explanation*

表示不必顾虑太多，应该怎样就怎样。

Used to indicate to do what should be done without giving much thought to it.

例句 *Examples*

1. 病了就请假吧，该休息就得休息。

   When you're sick, take time off. Rest when you need to.

2. 不合格的产品，该销毁就销毁，绝对不能流入市场。

   Regarding sub-standard products, if they should be destroyed, then destroy them. Don't allow them into the market.

3. 别舍不得花钱，根据需要，该买就买。

   Don't always save money. If there are things you should buy, then buy them.

4. 效益不好的企业，该宣布破产的就宣布破产。

   Enterprises with poor returns should announce bankruptcy at the appropriate time.

对话 *Dialogues*

1. A: 企业合并之后，债务怎么办？

   What will happen to the outstanding debts after the entenprises have merged?

   B: 该谁还就谁还。

   Whoever is supposed to pay them should pay.

2. A: 上级来了解情况时，我们该怎么说？

   What shall we say when the authorities come to collect information?

   B: 该怎么说就怎么说。

   Say what you should say.

练习 *Exercises*

用"该~就~"和所给的词语完成句子。Complete the sentences with the pattern and words in parentheses.

1. 对孩子不能太娇惯，＿＿＿＿＿＿＿＿＿＿＿＿＿＿＿＿＿。（批评）

2. 对于别人过分的要求，＿＿＿＿＿＿＿＿＿＿＿＿＿＿，别不好意思。（拒绝）

汉语常用格式330例

解释 *Explanation*

"该"后用代词或名词，表示轮到或应该是；用动词则表示理应出现某种情况，或表示是到做某件事的时候了。

Used with a pronoun or noun to indicate to be one's turn or "should be"; or used with a verb to indicate something is supposed to happen or it's time to do something.

例句 *Examples*

1. 下面该唐副总裁发言了，请准备。

   Next the floor goes to Vice President Tang. Please get ready.

2. 下次出国考察，该软件中心的工程师去了。

   Next time, Software Center engineers will go for the study tour overseas.

3. 都十二点了，该休息了，有什么事明天再说吧。

   It's 12 o'clock and you should rest. If you still have things to do, look after them tomorrow.

4. 孩子都十好几岁了，该懂点儿礼貌了。

   The child is over ten years old, and should be more polite.

对话 *Dialogues*

1. A：今天该谁值班了？

   Who will be on duty today?

   B：该我了。

   I will.

2. A：周处长该回来了，请稍等一会儿吧。

   Director Zhou should come back soon. Please wait for a while.

   B：好，谢谢！

   OK. Thanks.

练习 *Exercises*

用"该～了"完成句子。Complete the sentences with the pattern.

1. 你们都请过客了，这次＿＿＿＿＿＿＿＿＿＿＿＿＿＿。

2. 已经三十多了，＿＿＿＿＿＿＿＿＿＿＿＿＿，再不生就太晚了。

刚 ~ 就 ~

解释 *Explanation*

表示两件事紧接着发生。

Used to indicate that one thing happens immediately after another.

例句 *Examples*

1. 这老吴刚戒了烟没两天就又抽上了。

   No sooner had Lao Wu quitted smoking than he began to smoke again two days later.

2. 真巧，我刚出家门就碰到邻居谢医生了。

   What a coincidence! I met my neighbor Doctor Xie the moment I walked out.

3. 筋疲力尽的梁总刚到家，电话就又追来了。

   The exhausted Manager Liang had hardly arrived home when he got another call.

4. 这款摄像机刚上市就赶上市场价格大战，只好降价。

   Right after the launch of this video camera, a price war broke out. And the producer had to reduce the price.

对话 *Dialogues*

1. A: 奇怪，他俩刚度完蜜月回来就吵着要离婚。

   It's odd that they quarreled and wanted to divorce the moment they came back from honeymoon.

   B: 以前可是爱得死去活来的恋人哪。

   They used to be deep in love with each other.

2. A: 你怎么了？刚跑了几步就上气不接下气的了。

   What's wrong with you? You have hardly run a few steps when you are out of breath.

   B: 咳，我好久没跑步了，身体虚了。

   Well, I'm weaker because I haven't run for a long time.

练习 *Exercises*

用"刚~就~"完成句子。Complete the sentences with the pattern.

1. A: 你是什么时候接到她的电话的？

   B: _____ 。

2. A: 他是什么时候来的？

   B: _____ 。

汉语常用格式330例

解释 *Explanation*

前面用动词，表示某个动作连续不断。

Used after a verb to indicate the action is continuous.

例句 *Examples*

1. 我们该出发了，可雨还下个不停。

   We should leave, but the rain hasn't stopped.

2. 除夕夜里12点，鞭炮声响个不停。

   Around 12 o'clock on Chinese New Year's Eve, the sound of firecrackers doesn't stop.

3. 妈妈走了，孩子一直哭个不停，真可怜。

   The mother left and the baby didn't stop crying. Poor baby.

4. 这位著名的钢琴演奏家刚上场，观众的掌声就响个不停。

   As soon as the famous pianist went on stage, the audience would not stop applauding.

对话 *Dialogues*

1. **A:** 你看他们俩，一直说个不停。

   Look, those two haven't stopped talking.

   B: 多年不见了嘛！

   It's because they have not seen each other for so many years!

2. **A:** 我只是感冒，没什么，甭担心。

   I just have a cold. Nothing serious. Don't worry.

   B: 可你一直咳个不停，还是去看看大夫吧。

   But you keep coughing. Go see a doctor.

练习 *Exercises*

用"~个不停"完成句子。Complete the sentences with the pattern.

1. 他太幽默了，逗得大家_____。

2. 我每天下班回家，又要照顾孩子又要干家务，真是_____。

各 ~ 各的 ~

解释 *Explanation*

表示各自做各自的事，或各自有不同的特点、态度、做法等。

Used to indicate "each does his own business", or "each has his own characteristics, attitude or method".

例句 *Examples*

1. 在谈判桌上，双方各说各的观点。

   At the table, each side states their own points of view.

2. 据说这次拳击比赛，各有各的绝招，胜负难分。

   It's said that in this bout both boxers have their strengths, so it's hard to know who will win.

3. 公司即将倒闭，对今后的出路员工们各有各的打算。

   The company will close down. Regarding the future, each employee has his or her own plan.

4. 这个班的班风很好，遵守纪律。考试时大家各做各的题，没有人作弊。

   The students in this class have a good attitude and are disciplined. During the exam, they all worked on their own papers. No one cheated.

对话 *Dialogues*

1. **A：**这两本字典哪本好？

   Out of these two dictionaries, which one is better?

   B：各有各的特点。

   Each has its own attributes.

2. **A：**昨天散会以后，大家去喝酒了吧？

   Did you have a drink after the meeting yesterday?

   B：没有，会后就各回各的家了。

   No. After the meeting, everyone went home.

练习 *Exercises*

用"各 ~ 各的 ~"完成句子。Complete the sentences with the pattern.

1. AA 制就是大家一起吃完饭后＿＿＿＿＿＿＿＿＿＿＿＿＿。

2. 我喜欢看连续剧，丈夫喜欢看球赛，所以我们家有两台电视，＿＿＿＿＿＿＿＿＿。

解释 *Explanation*

"个够" 多用在单音节动词后边，表示做某事做到尽兴。

Used after a monosyllabic verb to indicate to do something to one's heart's content.

例句 *Examples*

1. 这个消息太让人激动了，走，咱们去喝个够！

   That's such an exciting news! Let's go and drink our fill.

2. 今天我没有别的安排，咱们去咖啡厅聊个够！

   I don't have other arrangements today. Let's go to a café and chat to our hearts' content!

3. 今天周末，咱们去唱卡拉 OK 吧，我们要唱个够。

   Today's the weekend. Let's go to karaoke and sing until we can sing no more.

4. 啊，这美丽的大草原，我要看个够。

   Wow, I want to appreciate the beautiful grassland as much as I like.

对话 *Dialogues*

1. A: 明天又是周末了，去国家大剧院看演出吧。

   Tomorrow is the weekend. Let's go to the National Centre for the Performing Arts to watch a performance.

   B: 这些天累死我了，对什么都毫无兴趣，只想在家睡个够。

   I've been so tired these past few days. I'm not interested in doing anything except going home and sleeping to my heart's content.

2. A: 今天是新年夜，各商场营业时间延长两小时。

   Today is New Year's Eve. All shopping malls will open two hours longer.

   B: 那真太好了，咱们不着急，慢慢逛个够。

   Great! We don't need to hurry. We can shop as leisurely as we like.

练习 *Exercises*

用 " ~ 个够 " 写两个复合句。Make two compound sentences with the pattern.

1. _____。

2. _____。

解释 *Explanation*

表示不满意，有责备或命令的口气。

Used to express dissatisfaction, with a tone of reproach or order.

例句 *Examples*

1. 你少给我 找点儿麻烦好不好！

   Don't cause so much trouble for me, OK?

2. 那是你的座位吗？给我 起来！

   Is that your seat? Stand up!

3. 你给我 闭嘴！怎么能这样不尊重别人。

   You shut up! How can you be so disrespectful toward others?

4. 叫他给我 走，我永远不想再见到他。

   Tell him to go. I don't want to see him again.

对话 *Dialogues*

1. A: 爸爸，我想去踢球。

   Dad, I want to play football.

   B: 不行！你老老实实地给我 做作业去！

   No way! Go do your homework!

2. A: 别生气了，咱们去喝咖啡吧。

   Don't be angry. Let's get some coffee.

   B: 少啰嗦，给我 走开。

   Stop talking. Leave me alone!

练习 *Exercises*

用"（你）给我 ~ "完成句子。Complete the sentences with the pattern.

1. 小偷偷了王先生的手机，王先生在后面一边追一边喊"_____！"

2. 小明期末考试有两三门不及格，爸爸生气地对他说："_____！"

解释 *Explanation*

表示很相近，相差很少。

Used to indicate similarity or a little difference.

例句 *Examples*

1. 她没什么变化，还跟当学生时差不多。

   She has not changed much. She looks almost the same as when she was a student.

2. 几年来他从不与人交往，跟生活在另一个世界差不多。

   For several years he had no contact with any people. It seems he was living in another world.

3. 现在的经济形势，和上次金融危机开始时差不多。

   The current economic situation is similar to that at the start of the previous financial crisis.

4. 减了半天肥也没什么效果，我的体重还是跟减肥前差不多。

   This method of losing weight isn't very effective. My weight is still almost the same as before.

对话 *Dialogues*

1. A: 我希望有更多属于自己的时间。

   I want to have more time for myself.

   B: 我跟你的想法差不多。

   I have a similar thought.

2. A: 我觉得他勤奋、勇敢，还有点儿傲气。

   I think he is diligent, brave and a bit proud.

   B: 这和一个成功运动员的特征差不多。

   These are similar attributes to a successful athlete.

练习 *Exercises*

用 "~ 跟/和 ~ 差不多" 和所给的词语完成对话。Complete the sentences with the pattern and words in parentheses.

1. A: 好久没见了，你看我老多了吧？

   B: _____。(上次)

2. A: 你新搬的房子有多大？

   B: _____，但是离单位近多了。(以前的)

~跟/和～过不去

解释 *Explanation*

表示与某人为难。

Used to indicate to make things difficult for somebody.

例句 *Examples*

1. 对人对事不冷静，实际上是跟自己过不去。

   To lose one's nerve when dealing with something or someone is actually being hard with oneself.

2. 不要老跟别人过不去，宽容待人是美德。

   Don't embarrass others. It is a virtue to be tolerant.

3. 这份报告老板又让我重写，我觉得他有点儿和我过不去。

   My boss asked me to rewrite the report again. I think he is making things a little difficult for me.

4. 你为什么总是和我过不去？我说什么你都反对！

   Why do you always embarrass me? You disagree with everything I say!

对话 *Dialogues*

1. A: 他气死我了，我哪能吃得下饭？

   He made me so angry! How am I supposed to eat?

   B: 别跟自己过不去嘛！

   Don't be hard on yourself.

2. A: 省吃俭用存下的钱都丢了，以后的日子可怎么过啊！

   I lost the money that I had saved by living so frugally. How am I going to live?

   B: 别急，老天爷不会和你过不去的。

   Don't worry. The heavens won't be hard on you.

练习 *Exercises*

用 "～ 跟/和～过不去" 完成句子。Complete the sentences with the pattern.

1. A: 你为什么要辞职啊？

   B: _____。

2. A: 会上小王怎么那么顶撞小李？一点儿都不顾影响。

   B: 是啊，_____。

解释 *Explanation*

表示说话人认为某人、事、情况、状态等达到了某种很高的程度。多用于口语。

Used to indicate that the speaker thinks people, things, conditions or states have reached a high level of certain conditions. It is often used colloquially.

例句 *Examples*

1. 现在的孩子们是够累的，除了正常上课，周末还要上各种补习班。

   Nowadays children are always exhausted. As well as normal school, they have weekend lessons.

2. 他的记忆力真够好的，很多材料过目不忘。

   He has an excellent memory. He can remember a large amount of material after reading just once.

3. 这个人真够啰嗦的，怪不得大家都烦他。

   This guy loves the sound of his own voice. That's why people find him annoying.

4. 别发牢骚了，你现在够幸福的了，知足吧。

   Don't complain. You are really happy right now, so you should be content.

对话 *Dialogues*

1. A: 她和交往了三年的男朋友分手后，哭了两天。

   After breaking up with her boyfriend of three years, she cried for two whole days.

   B: 怪不得我这几天见她老是闷闷不乐的，真够让她伤心的。

   No wonder I find her so miserable recently. She is really upset.

2. A: 咱们去请吴先生帮个忙吧。

   Let's ask Mr. Wu for help.

   B: 他已经够忙的了，别再去给他添麻烦了。

   He is quite busy. Don't bother him again.

练习 *Exercises*

用"够～的（了）"完成句子。Complete the sentences with the pattern.

1. 怎么，考了 95 分你还不满意？ _____。

2. 哇！你的妹妹真_____。

汉语常用格式330例

解释 *Explanation*

表示程度比较高，和"挺～的"意思相近。"怪"后用形容词或表示心理状态的动词，多用于口语。

Used with an adjective or a verb depicting certain mood to indicate a rather high degree. The expression is similar to 挺～的 in meaning and is often used colloquially.

例句 *Examples*

1. 女儿去深山探险，我怪担心的。

   My daughter went to explore in a high mountain, so I'm quite worried right now.

2. 听说老朋友受伤了，他心里怪难受的。

   When he heard that his old friend had been injured, he felt quite sorry.

3. 这孩子从小就失去了母爱，怪可怜的。

   The child lost his mother when he was very young. Poor child!

4. 你看这个地方怪有诗意的，我们照张相吧。

   Look, this is quite a scenic place. Let's take a picture.

对话 *Dialogues*

1. A: 妈，我出去一会儿。

   Mom, I'm going to go out for a while.

   B: 刚下过雨，路上怪滑的，小心点儿。

   It just rained, and the road is quite slippery. Be careful.

2. A: 这两个孩子是双胞胎，很像吧?

   These babies are twins. Don't they look alike?

   B: 嗯，怪好玩儿的。

   Yes. It's quite interesting.

练习 *Exercises*

用"怪～的"完成句子。Complete the sentences with the pattern.

1. 晚上一个人走这条没有路灯的小路，_____。

2. 一边工作一边读博士，_____。

汉语常用格式330例

解释 *Explanation*

"管"在这里同"把",只用于口语,用来称说人或事物。

Used only in oral Chinese to call somebody or something as a certain name. Here 管 has the same meaning as 把.

例句 *Examples*

1. 他说话非常快,大家都管他叫"机关枪"。

   He speaks very fast. Everybody calls him "machine gun".

2. 中国人管娇生惯养的孩子叫"小皇帝"。

   Chinese people call any pampered child "little emperor".

3. 我们管飞扬着黄沙的天气叫"沙尘暴"。

   We call the weather with floating sand a "sandstorm".

4. 因为她长得胖,大家都开玩笑地管她叫"肥肥"。

   Since she is plump, people jokingly call her 肥肥 (Feifei), as 肥 means fat.

对话 *Dialogues*

1. A: 你知道古代人管眼睛叫什么吗?

   Do you know what ancient people called an eye?

   B: 这还不知道? 叫"目"。

   That's easy. They called it 目.

2. A: 你堂弟管你妈叫什么?

   How does your cousin address your mother?

   B: 婶子。

   Auntie.

练习 *Exercises*

用"管 ~ 叫 ~"改写句子。Rewrite the sentences with the pattern.

1. 妈妈的兄弟我叫"舅舅"。→_____。

2. 白薯西方人叫"甜土豆"。→_____。

汉语常用格式330例

光/单～就～

解释 *Explanation*

有"仅仅/只～就～"的意思，表示在所指的范围里数量已经很多或时间已经很长了。"就"后常有表示数量或时间的词语。

Used often with words signifying quantity or time after 就 to indicate that the quantity is quite large or the time is very long in the specified range.

例句 *Examples*

1. 这个老板光公开的财产就有好几亿人民币。

   This boss is very rich. The wealth he made public alone accounts for a few hundred million yuan.

2. 中国十几亿人口，一年光吃饭就得多少粮食啊。

   China has a population of over 1 billion, and to feed them alone accounts for a lot of grain.

3. 在中国的外国留学生很多，光韩国的就有六万多人。

   In China, there are many foreign students. The number of Korean students alone exceeds 60,000.

4. 这一年物价涨得很厉害，单猪肉就涨了一倍多。

   Prices have soared this year. Pork price alone has more than doubled.

对话 *Dialogues*

1. A: 你们的会怎么开得那么长啊?

   Why did your meeting take so long?

   B: 光邓院长就讲了两个小时。

   President Deng alone spoke for two hours.

2. A: 去那里旅行得用多少钱?

   How much did it cost to travel there?

   B: 不少，单机票就得950美元，还不含税。

   Quite a lot. Airfare alone cost me $950, excluding tax.

练习 *Exercises*

用"光/单～就～"完成句子。Complete the sentences with the pattern.

1. 今天各门课的老师都布置了书面作业，我做了三个多小时才做完，_____。

2. 她有各种各样的首饰，_____。

解释 *Explanation*

两个"归"的前后各用相同的词语，表示不同的人或事界线分明，相互之间不发生关联。

Used respectively between identical words to indicate a clear boundary and no contact or connection between different people or things.

例句 *Examples*

1. 有些人说归说，做归做，只说不做。

   Some people never practice what they preach.

2. 友谊归友谊，爱情归爱情，不能混为一谈。

   Friendship is one matter and love is another; do not confuse them.

3. 朋友归朋友，钱归钱，借你的钱我一定要还。俗话说，亲兄弟，明算账嘛。

   Friendship is one matter and money is another. I must return the money I borrowed from you. As the saying goes, "Money matters should be accounted for even among brothers."

4. 从今以后我们桥归桥，路归路，不再来往。

   From now on, we will go different ways and never see each other again.

对话 *Dialogues*

1. **A**：你挺欣赏她的，为什么这次把她批评得这么狠？

   You appreciate her very much. Why do you criticize her so harshly?

   B：欣赏归欣赏，批评归批评。

   Appreciation is one thing, and criticism is another.

2. **A**：你们的房费一起结算吗？

   Do you share the hotel expenses?

   B：不，他的归他的，我的归我的。

   No, we pay separately.

练习 *Exercises*

用"A 归 A，B 归 B"完成句子。Complete the sentences with the pattern.

1. 她把衣橱收拾得整整齐齐，_____，找起来很方便。

2. 你最好不要让你的家人在你的公司工作，_____，把亲情和工作混在一起，会很麻烦。

解释 *Explanation*

用反问形式来表示程度已经够高的了，常含有反驳的语气。

Used in a rhetorical question to indicate that the degree is high enough. It often has a tone of retort.

例句 *Examples*

1. 我一个小时就赶过来了，这还不快啊？

   I came here in only one hour. Isn't it quick enough?

2. 这菜还不丰盛啊？鸡、鸭、鱼、肉都有了。

   Isn't it a sumptuous meal? There are chicken, duck, fish and meat.

3. 这苹果还不甜啊？我没吃过比这更甜的了。

   Isn't the apple sweet enough? I have never had apples sweeter than it.

4. 一个抗震帐篷要几千块，甚至一万多块，这还不贵呀？

   A tent to shelter earthquake victims costs several thousand yuan or even over 10,000 yuan. It's so expensive!

对话 *Dialogues*

1. **A:** 你的屋子怎么弄得这么乱七八糟的？

   Why is your room in such a mess?

   B: 这还不够整齐啊？别对男生宿舍要求太高了。

   Isn't it tidy enough? Don't expect too much for a boy's dormitory.

2. **A:** 我不想跟他交往，我选男朋友首先要个儿高的。

   I don't want to date him. My boyfriend should be tall first of all.

   B: 什么？他一米七五，这还不够高哇？

   What? He is 1.75 meters. Not tall enough?

练习 *Exercises*

用"这还不 ~ 啊"完成句子。Complete the sentences with the pattern.

1. **A:** 这篇作文还不算太差吧？

   B: _____。

2. **A:** 我起得也不晚哪。

   B: _____。

解释 *Explanation*

表示"只是"的意思。含有说话人认为某种情况并不特别、并不复杂，有可想而知的意思。多用于答话。

Used mostly in a reply with the meaning of "just" or "only". Its tone shows that everything is as usual, and that there is nothing special or complicated occurring.

例句 *Examples*

1. 说来说去你还不就是嫌人家长得丑吗？

   What it comes down to is that you dislike him only because he's ugly.

2. 他这么小能有什么心事？还不就是想考个第一名。

   He's just a child. Why would he be worried? He just wants to come top in the exam.

3. 我一个人过节能怎么过啊，还不就是在家看看电视。

   What else could I do during the festival? I just watched TV at home.

4. 你以为他真想学习什么知识呀？还不就是为了混个文凭。

   Do you really think he wants to learn something? He only wants to get a diploma.

对话 *Dialogues*

1. A: 这次去中国的旅行线路怎么样？

   What is the route of the trip to China?

   B: 还不就是北京、西安、南京、上海、广州这几个大城市。

   Just several big cities: Beijing, Xi'an, Nanjing, Shanghai and Guangzhou.

2. A: 昨天参加聚会的有哪些人？

   Who took part in the gathering yesterday?

   B: 还不就是老冯、小朴、大崔、金姐他们几个。

   Only Lao Feng, Xiao Piao, Da Cui and Sister Jin.

练习 *Exercises*

用"还不就是 ~"完成句子。Complete the sentences with the pattern.

1. A: 每次回老家你都干什么？

   B: _____。

2. A: 听说你现在会点不少中国菜了？

   B: _____这几个最普通的。

还～哪

解释 *Explanation*

答话中使用，表示不同意对方的看法，多用于反问，有时带责备、讽刺的意味。

Used to indicate disagreement in a reply, mostly in rhetorical questions and sometimes with a tone of reproach and irony.

对话 *Dialogues*

1. A: 干吗这么早就叫我？人家还困着呢！

   Why do you get me up so early? I am still sleepy!

   B: 还早哪？你看看都几点了？

   So early? Look, what time is it?

2. A: 你的西班牙语考得不错嘛！

   You got a quite good mark in the Spanish exam!

   B: 还不错哪？刚及格。

   Quite good? I just passed.

3. A: 美国的东西真贵。

   The prices are really high in the United States.

   B: 还贵哪？比欧洲便宜多了。

   High? They are much lower than those in Europe.

4. A: 今天的菜挺好吃的。

   Today's dishes are very tasty.

   B: 还好吃哪？咸死人了！

   Very tasty? They are too salty!

练习 *Exercises*

用"还～哪"完成句子。Complete the sentences with the pattern.

1. A: 他干的这种活儿真轻松。

   B: ＿＿＿＿＿＿＿＿＿＿＿＿＿？你干干试试。

2. A: 这间屋子挺大的呀。

   B: ＿＿＿＿＿＿＿＿＿？只有 12 平方米，两个人住挤得要命。

解释 *Explanation*

表示某种现象或动作还没结束，或尚未发生。略带强调。与"没 ~"相比，隐含有某种现象或动作会发生、会完成的意思。

Used for slight emphasis to indicate that some phenomenon or action has not ended or taken place. Compared with 没 ~, it implies that certain phenomenon or action will take place or be completed.

例句 *Examples*

1. 雨下了半天了，还没停呢。

   It has been raining for half a day, but hasn't stopped yet.

2. 这次社会调查报告，我还没写完呢。

   I have not finished the social survey report.

3. 这本小说他看了一个月了，还没看完呢。

   He has been reading the novel for a whole month, but hasn't finished yet.

4. 他们俩谈恋爱已经有五年了，还没结婚呢。

   They have been in love for five years, but haven't got married yet.

对话 *Dialogues*

1. A: 就这么点儿活儿，你们怎么还没干完呢？

   It is not a lot of work. Why haven't you finished yet?

   B: 快了，快了，就完了。

   Very soon. We will finish it in a moment.

2. A: 这么晚了，你们怎么还不睡？

   It's so late. Why don't you get to bed?

   B: 我们俩还没聊够呢。

   We have not chatted enough yet.

练习 *Exercises*

用"还没 ~ 呢"完成句子。Complete the sentences with the pattern.

1. 她可真能逛街，都逛了一天了，＿＿＿＿＿＿＿＿＿＿＿。

2. 孩子都爱玩儿游戏，你瞧我这儿子，玩儿了一晚上了，＿＿＿＿＿＿＿＿＿＿。

还 ~ 呢（1）

汉语常用格式330例

解释 *Explanation*

表示强调仍继续属于某种情况或处于某种状态。中间用形容词或动词性词语。

Used to emphasize a remaining condition or state. An adjective or a verb phrase is placed in between the words.

例句 *Examples*

1. 你别急着上班，刚大病了一场，身体还虚着呢。

   Don't rush back to work. You have just recovered from a severe illness, and are still very weak.

2. 孩子还小呢，对她的培养教育你不能操之过急。

   Your child is still young. Take your time raising and educating her.

3. 哎呀，都两天了，你的衣服怎么还泡着呢？

   Oh no, two days have passed, why are your clothes still soaking wet?

4. 这个杯子的保温性真好，我两个小时以前泡的茶还热着呢。

   This cup has such good insulation that the tea I made two hours ago is still warm.

对话 *Dialogues*

1. A: 你女儿上大学了吧？

   Has your daughter gone to university?

   B: 哪儿啊，她还在读高中呢。

   Not yet. She is still in high school.

2. A: 这个牙膏可以扔了吧？

   Should we just throw this toothpaste out?

   B: 别扔啊，还能用几次呢。

   Don't. It can be used several more times.

练习 *Exercises*

用"还 ~ 呢"完成句子。Complete the sentences with the pattern.

1. A: 咱们快走吧。

   B: 你别催我，时间_____。

2. A: 小赵，下课后咱们打球去。

   B: 不去了，昨天打得时间太长了。今天胳膊_____。

解释 *Explanation*

表示说话人认为某人的所作所为或水平与其身份不相称；或表示不同意别人的某个说法，认为离事实相差甚远。

Used to indicate that the speaker thinks that the actions and behavior of somebody is not in keeping with his/her rank, or that they disagree with other's opinions because they find them untruthful.

例句 *Examples*

1. 还金融学院的教授呢，就这水平！

   How can a professor at the Finance College be so dismal?

2. 还美国留学回来的呢，英语就说成这样？

   How come he/she speaks such bad English even after studying in the US?

3. 还哥哥呢，你就这样对待弟弟呀。

   You are the elder sibling. How can you treat your younger brother like this?

4. 还中文系毕业的呢，连篇调查报告都写不好。

   A Chinese major can not even write a report well.

对话 *Dialogues*

1. A: 你呀，车子、房子都有了，算是富翁了。

   You have your own car and house and are rich now.

   B: 还富翁呢，"负翁"还差不多。

   Rich? I am actually a rich debtor.

2. A: 她是博士毕业吧?

   Is she a PhD graduate?

   B: 还博士呢，连本科都没读完。

   A PhD graduate? She didn't even finish college.

练习 *Exercises*

用"还 ~ 呢"完成句子。Complete the sentences with the pattern.

1. A: 人家可是名校毕业的博士。

   B: _____，素质这么差。

2. A: 你去过欧洲吧?

   B: _____，我连北京城都没出过。

还是 ~ 好

解释 *Explanation*

表示经过比较，做出选择。

Used to indicate making a choice after comparison.

例句 *Examples*

1. 吃多了发胖，还是少吃点儿好。

   You will get fat if you eat too much. You'd better eat less.

2. 我考虑来考虑去，觉得还是亲自去一趟好。

   After thinking it over, I decided that I'd better go there by myself.

3. 这个问题先不下结论，还是再深入调查调查好。

   Don't jump to conclusions. You'd better make deeper investigation first.

4. 孩子们的事情，父母还是让他们自己决定好。

   It's better for parents to let children decide for themselves.

对话 *Dialogues*

1. A: 你喜欢这里的冬天还是夏天?

   Do you like summer or winter better here?

   B: 还是春天好。

   I like spring better.

2. A: 陈总，明天的大会请您讲话。

   Manager Chen, please make a speech at tomorrow's meeting.

   B: 我看，我还是不发言好。

   Well, I'd better not.

练习 *Exercises*

用"还是 ~ 好"完成句子。Complete the sentences with the pattern.

1. A: 下个星期才考试呢，不着急准备。

   B: 我觉得_____。

2. A: 你看今天天儿挺好的，不用带伞了吧。

   B: 现在是雨季，随时可能会下雨，_____。

解释 *Explanation*

表示创造某种条件，以利于达到某种目的。

Used to indicate that a certain condition is created for a purpose.

例句 *Examples*

1. 我们赶快把活儿干完，好早点儿回家。

The sooner we finish the work, the earlier we can go home.

2. 请给我你的手机号码，好随时联系。

Please give me your cell phone number, so I can contact you anytime.

3. 我想住在当地人家里，好练习口语。

I want to live with a local family, so as to practice my spoken language.

4. 新产品理所当然要多作广告，好扩大影响啊。

Of course we will advertise more to promote new products so they will be better known.

对话 *Dialogues*

1. A: 夏天的阳光太厉害了。

   Summer sunlight is scorching.

   B: 多搽点儿防晒霜吧，好保护皮肤。

   Put more sun lotion on to protect your skin.

2. A: 明天是去游览长城吗？

   Are we going to the Great Wall tomorrow?

   B: 是啊，早餐多吃点儿，好爬山。

   Yes. Eat more breakfast for climbing the Wall.

练习 *Exercises*

用"~，好~"完成句子。Complete the sentences with the pattern.

1. 今天太累了，我要泡个热水澡，_____。

2. 生病了，就该按时吃药，_____。

好 ~ 啊

解释 *Explanation*

"好"后用形容词，表示程度深，和"多么"意思相同，带感叹语气。"啊"发生音变时可写做"呀"、"哪"或"哇"。

Used with an adjective to indicate scale or magnitude in an exclamatory tone. It means the same as 多么. 啊 can be written phonetically as 呀, 哪 or 哇.

例句 *Examples*

1. 上海外滩的建筑群好漂亮啊！
   The buildings in the Bund of Shanghai are so beautiful!
2. 她的头发好黑好亮啊，像黑锦缎似的。
   Her hair is amazingly black and beautiful. It is like black brocade.
3. 我从电视上看到地震灾区的景象好惨哪！
   I saw the earthquake-striken areas on TV. What a tragic scene!
4. 我当时迷迷糊糊地听到有人跟我说话，声音好熟悉呀。
   At the time I was dazed, I heard a voice talking to me. It was an extremely familiar voice.

对话 *Dialogues*

1. A: 这是我的朋友小黄，刚从国外回来。
   This is my friend Xiao Huang. He just came back from overseas.
   B: 哟，小伙子好酷哇。
   Oh, what a cool young man!

2. A: 你看那孩子哭得好可怜哪。
   Look, that child is crying. Poor little thing!
   B: 是迷路了吧。
   He is probably lost.

练习 *Exercises*

用"好 ~ 啊"完成句子。Complete the sentences with the pattern.

1. A: 这是我女儿的照片。她今年五岁了。
   B: _____。

2. A: 尝尝我刚买的绿茶，是今年的杭州龙井。
   B: _____。

解释 *Explanation*

"好不"和部分双音节形容词一起用表示肯定的意思，如"好不热闹"与"好热闹"意思相同，表示程度更高。

Used with some disyllabic adjective to indicate affirmation. For example, 好不热闹 means the same as 好热闹 but implies a higher degree.

例句 *Examples*

1. 大热天，吹来一股风，好不凉爽。

   With breezes in such a hot day, it feels so cool!

2. 老朋友在一起开怀畅饮，好不痛快！

   When old friends get together for a drink, it's really pleasant!

3. 听说朋友坐的那艘船失事了，他好不着急。

   When he heard that his friend was on the ship that was wrecked, he was so worried.

4. 节日的街头，人山人海，好不热闹！

   At festival time, the streets are really crowded. It's bustling!

对话 *Dialogues*

1. A：这部连续剧打动了很多人。

   This TV series touched many people.

   B：是的，情节跌宕起伏，特别是女主人公的不幸遭遇，令人好不心酸！

   Yes, really. The plot is quite complex, and the heroine in particular endures some terrible experiences. It really makes people's hearts ache.

2. A：这件事办得太不顺利了。

   The thing is not going well.

   B：真是的，跑来跑去，好不麻烦！

   Yes, it's proving to be a real headache. I have to run around for it.

练习 *Exercises*

用"好不 ~"改写句子。Rewrite the sentences with the pattern.

1. 他的变化太大了，真令人吃惊。→＿＿＿＿＿＿＿＿＿＿＿＿＿＿＿＿＿＿。

2. 究竟该怎么选择呢？让我很烦恼。→＿＿＿＿＿＿＿＿＿＿＿＿＿＿＿＿＿＿。

汉语常用格式330例

107

~好了

解释 *Explanation*

表示按照所提出的建议去做可以解决问题。

Used to indicate that the problem can be solved if following the suggestion offered.

例句 *Examples*

1. 你觉得无聊? 那看电视好了。

   Are you bored? Then watch TV.

2. 想买些鱼、虾等半成品? 去超市好了。

   If you want to buy semi-processed fish or shrimp, go to the supermarket.

3. 雨下得太大，不能出去，在家玩儿好了。

   It is raining heavily. You can't go out, so play at home.

4. 如果去你家不方便的话，就到我家来聚会好了。

   If it's not convenient to gather at your place, you can come to mine.

对话 *Dialogues*

1. A: 要不要我陪你去商场?

   Should I go with you to the shopping mall?

   B: 你在家休息吧，我一个人去好了。

   No. You have a rest at home. I will go by myself.

2. A: 真抱歉，今天没时间买菜。

   I'm really sorry. I didn't have time to buy groceries.

   B: 没关系，吃方便面好了。

   It doesn't matter. Let's have instant noodles.

练习 *Exercises*

用"~好了"完成句子。Complete the sentences with the pattern.

1. A: 我有点儿不舒服。

   B: _____，剩下的工作我来做。

2. A: 这里的路我不太熟悉。

   B: _____，我开车，很方便。

解释 *Explanation*

"好容易才"和"好不容易才"意思相同，都表示费了很大力气才做到。

Both of these two expressions indicate to manage with great difficulty.

例句 *Examples*

1. 我好容易才买到明天的足球票。

It was with great difficulty that I finally managed to buy tickets for tomorrow's football match.

2. 他好容易才找到这份工作，能不积极干吗？

He managed to find this job only with great difficulty. Of course he works hard.

3. 他假期住在乡下，我好不容易才找到他的家。

He lived in the countryside during the vacation. I managed to find his home only with great difficulty.

4. 我好不容易才打听到朱先生的消息，原来他去了新加坡。

It was with great difficulty that I managed to find out what happened to Mr. Zhu. It turned out he had gone to Singapore.

对话 *Dialogues*

1. A：那本法国小说买到了吗？

   Did you buy that French novel?

   B：上哪儿去买呀？我好容易才借到一本。

   Where can I buy it? It was only with great difficulty that I finally managed to borrow one.

2. A：对不起，那份材料我落在出租车上了。

   Sorry, I left the material in a taxi.

   B：哎呀，那是我好不容易才弄到的。

   What? That was very difficult to find.

练习 *Exercises*

用"好（不）容易才 ~"完成句子。Complete the sentences with the pattern.

1. 减肥实在是太难了，我又是节食又是锻炼，＿＿＿＿＿＿＿＿＿＿＿＿。

2. 这本书是繁体字的，读起来好费劲，＿＿＿＿＿＿＿＿＿＿＿＿。

解释 *Explanation*

表示已具备某种有利条件和情况，否则就会出现不如意的情况。

Used to indicate that there is some favorable condition or situation, otherwise something unsatisfactory may occur.

例句 *Examples*

1. 好在今天阳光好，要不然这些衣服根本干不了。

   Fortunately it's sunny today, otherwise these clothes wouldn't dry up.

2. 好在我多买了些鱼呀肉的，要不然哪儿够吃的呀。

   Luckily I bought much fish and meat, otherwise there won't be enough food to eat.

3. 好在现在上网很方便，要不然一个人在异国他乡太寂寞、无聊了。

   Fortunately it's convenient to get online now, otherwise I would be too lonely and bored being alone in a foreign country.

4. 好在这合同漏洞发现得及时，要不然我们的经济损失就大了。

   Fortunately we found out the loophole in the contract in time, otherwise we would suffer great economic losses.

对话 *Dialogues*

1. A: 你今天起晚了，上课没迟到吗？

   You got up late today. Were you late for class?

   B: 好在路上没堵车，要不然肯定迟到。

   Luckily there was no traffic jam, otherwise I would have been late.

2. A: 你这个马大哈，出门没关火，那多危险啊！

   You scatterbrain! You didn't turn off the oven before going out. How dangerous!

   B: 是啊！好在妈妈回家早，要不然我就闯大祸了。

   I'm sorry. Luckily Mom came home early, otherwise I would have brought a big disaster.

练习 *Exercises*

用"好在 ~ , 要不然 ~"完成句子。Complete the sentences with the pattern.

1. A: 经理让我告诉你，出差日期延后两天。

   B: 好在我还没买机票，＿＿＿＿＿＿＿＿＿＿＿＿＿＿＿。

2. A: 天这么阴，我看马上要下大雨了！

   B: 好在我带了伞，＿＿＿＿＿＿＿＿＿＿＿＿＿＿＿。

A 和 B 比起来，～／和 B 比起来，A

解释 *Explanation*

表示用 A 和 B 进行比较，A 的情况如何。

Used to indicate how A is in comparison to B.

例句 *Examples*

1. 和昨天比起来，今天冷多了。

   Today is much colder than yesterday.

2. 上海话和苏州话比起来要硬一些。

   Shanghai dialect is rougher than Suzhou dialect.

3. 哥哥长得很高，但和弟弟比起来还矮五公分。

   The elder brother is very tall, but five centimeters shorter than his younger brother.

4. 和十年前比起来，中国人的生活水平真是大大提高了。

   Compared with ten years ago, the living standard of Chinese people has greatly improved.

对话 *Dialogues*

1. A: 你的汉语水平真不错。

   Your Chinese is quite good.

   B: 哪儿呀，和你比起来差多了。

   Not at all. I'm not half as good as you.

2. A: 这位歌星嗓音不错，挺甜的。

   This pop star has a good voice, very sweet.

   B: 我觉得她和邓丽君比起来还差得远呢。

   I don't think she comes close anywhere to Teresa Teng.

练习 *Exercises*

用"A 和 B 比起来，～／和 B 比起来，A～"改写句子。Rewrite the sentences with the pattern.

1. 他比同龄人成熟。→＿＿＿＿＿＿＿＿＿＿＿＿＿＿＿＿。

2. 美国的物价比欧洲的便宜。→＿＿＿＿＿＿＿＿＿＿＿＿＿。

何必 ~ 呢

解释 *Explanation*

表示没有必要这样做，常用于劝说对方。

Used often in persuasion to indicate that there is no need for something.

例句 *Examples*

1. 天都这么晚了，末班车也没了，何必非要走呢。

   It's so late and the last bus has gone. Why insist on leaving?

2. 人家都已经道歉了，你何必再计较呢。

   He has apologized. There is no need to argue with him.

3. 你冷静些，何必为了图一时痛快而酿成大错呢。

   Calm down. There is no need to vent your anger at the expense of committing big mistakes.

4. 人生就是有得有失，有苦有甜，你又何必想不开呢。

   Life has gains and losses, roses and thorns. Why do you take it to heart?

对话 *Dialogues*

1. A: 不行，你快告诉我，这到底是怎么回事?

   Do tell me, what's the matter?

   B: 人有时候还是糊涂点儿好，何必什么事情都要一清二楚呢。

   It's better to be ignorant sometimes. There is no need to know everything clearly.

2. A: 我得换个手机，这个已经过时了。

   I must change my cell phone. This one is obsolete.

   B: 这手机还能用，何必赶时髦呢。

   This phone still works. Why should you follow the fashion?

练习 *Exercises*

用"何必 ~ 呢"完成句子。Complete the sentences with the pattern.

1. A: 这件事没办好，都是我的错。

   B: 你已经尽力了，_____。

2. A: 虽然我们已经分手了，可我还是忘不了她。

   B: 既然这样放不下，当初_____。

解释 *Explanation*

用反问语气表示更进一层。有"更不用说"的意思。

Used to indicate "much less" or "let alone" in a tone of retort.

例句 *Examples*

1. 虎毒还不食子呢，何况是人！

   Even a hungry tiger does not eat its own cubs, let alone man!

2. 村镇的师资也缺乏，何况偏僻的山区。

   Teachers are inadequate in villages and towns, let alone in remote mountain areas.

3. 她住的地方很难找，何况你还是个外国人，就别去了。

   The place she lives is hard to find, even if you weren't a foreigner. Don't go.

4. 这段山路一般人爬起来都很吃力，何况是一个腿有毛病的老人。

   This mountain path is difficult for ordinary people, let alone an old man with a bad leg.

对话 *Dialogues*

1. A：学外语真不容易。

   It is really difficult to learn a foreign language.

   B：学母语也要花时间哪，何况学外语。

   It takes time to learn your native language, let alone a foreign one.

2. A：她在那里人生地疏的，我有点儿担心。

   I am a bit worried about her, because she's a total stranger there.

   B：都这么大了，何况还有她姑姑在呢。

   She has already grown up. Furthermore, her aunt is there.

练习 *Exercises*

用"~，何况 ~"完成句子。Complete the sentences with the pattern.

1. 这么简单的问题，小学生都会回答，＿＿＿＿＿＿＿＿＿＿。

2. 这么重的活儿男人干也费力，＿＿＿＿＿＿＿＿＿＿。

A 和 B 相比

解释 *Explanation*

表示互相比较。书面语常用"与/同～相比"。

Used to indicate comparison. In written Chinese, 与/同～相比 is often used.

例句 *Examples*

1. 和发达国家相比，中国的生产力还很低下。

   Compared with developed countries, China still has quite low productivity.

2. 电子产品的价格，和几年前相比，差别很大。

   The prices of electronic products are quite different from several years ago.

3. 现在冬天的平均气温和几十年前相比，高了不少。

   The average winter temperature now is much higher than that of several decades ago.

4. 北京今年3月份二手房交易量与去年相比，有下跌趋势。

   In Beijing, sales of second hand housing in March turned out to be lower than those of last year.

对话 *Dialogues*

1. A：你们国家的人权状况还不理想。

   Human rights situation in your country are not ideal.

   B：和过去相比，已经民主多了。

   It is much better than in the past.

2. A：中国国民的文化素质和以前相比，有很大提高。

   The educational level of Chinese people has improved greatly.

   B：重视文化教育了嘛。

   This is because the government attaches importance to culture and education.

练习 *Exercises*

用"A 和 B 相比"完成句子。Complete the sentences with the pattern.

1. A：现在中国年轻人的求职观念有什么改变？

   B：＿＿＿＿＿＿＿＿＿＿＿＿＿＿＿＿＿＿＿。

2. A：你的新工作单位怎么样？

   B：＿＿＿＿＿＿＿＿＿＿＿＿＿＿＿＿＿＿＿。

解释 *Explanation*

表示两种事物相像。书面语常用"与/同 ~ 相似"。

Used to indicate similarity. In written Chinese, 与/同 ~ 相似 is often used.

例句 *Examples*

1. 这辆轿车和董事长的奔驰车外貌相似。

   This car looks like our president's Mercedez Benz.

2. 现在亚洲的经济形势和几年前相似吗?

   Is the current economic situation in Asia similar to that of several years ago?

3. 听说现在那里的情况和中国文革时期很相似。

   I heard that the situation there is similar to China's Cultural Revolution.

4. 科学家发现鳄鱼祖先的鼻子结构与狗相似。

   Scientists discovered that the nose structure of crocodile's ancestors is similar to that of dogs.

对话 *Dialogues*

1. A: 有人说现在的晚礼服和 19 世纪的相似。

   Some people say modern evening dresses resemble those of the 19th century.

   B: 是吗? 我没注意过。

   Really? I have never noticed that.

2. A: 大卫和小蒋的性格、举止都有些相似。

   David and Xiao Jiang are similar in personality and behavior.

   B: 怪不得他们是形影不离的朋友呢。

   That's why they are such good friends, and are always together.

练习 *Exercises*

用"A 和 B 相似"写两个句子。Make two sentences with the pattern.

1. _____。

2. _____。

忽 ~忽 ~

解释 *Explanation*

表示不稳定，一会儿这样，一会儿那样。也可用"忽而~忽而~"。两个"忽"后限用词义相反的单音节词。"忽而"后不限。

Used with monosyllabic antonyms to indicate an unstable state. 忽而~忽而~ can also be used with words not as monosyllabic.

例句 *Examples*

1. 山区的气候，忽晴忽雨，变化无常。
   The weather is changeable in mountain areas. It changes quickly from sunny to rainy.
2. 近来他的血压不太稳定，忽高忽低的。
   Recently his blood pressure has not been too stable. It has been swinging from high to low.
3. 我的电脑显示屏好像出了问题，忽明忽暗的。
   Something is wrong with my computer screen. One minute it's bright and the next it's dim.
4. 最近中国的股市忽上忽下，让不少股民心神不定。
   Recently the Chinese stock market has been fluctuating, upsetting stock-holders.

对话 *Dialogues*

1. A: 小李的脾气真让人猜不透。
   It is really hard to figure out Xiao Li's temperament.
   B: 是啊，忽而高兴，忽而生气。
   Yes, he is happy one minute and angry the next.

2. A: 这篇文章思路很乱。
   This article is very disorganized.
   B: 就是，忽东忽西的，没个中心。
   I agree. It has no theme, sometimes talking about this and sometimes about that.

练习 *Exercises*

选词填空。Choose the right phrases to fill in the blanks.

> 忽多忽少   忽快忽慢   忽左忽右   忽隐忽现

1. 前面的车大概是故意要挡我的路，＿＿＿＿＿＿＿＿＿＿，我没法超过去。

2. 一日三餐最好定量，不要＿＿＿＿＿＿＿＿＿＿。

解释 *Explanation*

表示先承认对方所说的有道理、是事实，然后再提出自己补充的看法。

Used to indicate that the speaker acknowledges that what the other person said is reasonable or realistic, and then puts forth his own opinion.

例句 *Examples*

1. 朋友之间应多来往、多了解，话是这么说，可是大家都忙，哪有时间哪。
   It's true that we should have more contact for better understanding. But we are all busy and don't have much time to do so.
2. 条条道路通罗马，话是这么说，可是有的路走起来太艰辛了。
   It is said that every road leads to Rome. But some road is so hard to walk on.
3. 一分钱一分货，话是这么说，可是有时多花钱也不一定能买到好货。
   It's right that you get what you pay for. But sometimes you don't necessarily get quality goods by paying more.
4. 日子一个人也能过，话是这么说，可是那还是挺孤单的。
   It's fair to say that one can live all by oneself. However, one will feel lonely.

对话 *Dialogues*

1. A: 夫妻本是同林鸟，大难临头各自飞。
   Husband and wife are like birds in the same forest. When disaster approaches, they fly their own ways.
   B: 话是这么说，可是患难夫妻也不少。
   It's said so. But there are quite a few couples who could go through thick and thin together.

2. A: 强震已经过去，不会有更大的破坏了。
   The strong earthquake has stopped, and there won't be bigger damage.
   B: 话是这么说，可是有时候余震也挺厉害的。
   It is said so. But sometimes aftershocks are really severe and can cause damage too.

练习 *Exercises*

用"话是这么说，可是 ~"完成句子。Complete the sentences with the pattern.

1. A: 对学生来说，没有比学习更重要的了。
   B: 话是这么说，_____。

2. A: 孩子大了，应该注意培养他的独立生活能力。
   B: 话是这么说，_____。

话又说回来

汉语常用格式330例

解释 *Explanation*

表示退一步想，或从另一个角度来看问题。常和"可是、不过"一起用。

Used often with 可是 or 不过 to indicate a second thought or another angle for thinking.

例句 *Examples*

1. 今天我起得太晚了，可是，话又说回来，早了我也起不来。

   I got up too late today. But on the other hand, I can't get up early.

2. 我应该跟他一起去上海，可是话又说回来，哪有时间呢！

   I should go to Shanghai with him. But on second thought, I realize there's no time.

3. 丈夫有很多地方让她不满意，可话又说回来，这世上哪有十全十美的人呢。

   She isn't satisfied with her husband for many reasons. But then again, nobody in the world is perfect.

4. 我对他做的这个项目不太满意，不过话又说回来，这个项目确实很难做，换成我，可能还不如他呢。

   I am not quite satisfied with the project he worked on. But on second thought, the project is very difficult, and perhaps I would not have done as well as him.

对话 *Dialogues*

1. A: 附近超市的东西太贵。

   Things at the nearby supermarket are too expensive.

   B: 那你到远处的大超市去买呀。

   Then go shopping in the large supermarket that's farther out.

   A: 不过，话又说回来，附近有这个超市还是挺方便的。

   Whatever, it is convenient to have a supermarket nearby.

2. A: 天天做饭挺麻烦的。

   It is so tiring to cook every day.

   B: 那就去饭馆吃呗。

   Then let's eat out.

   A: 可是，话又说回来，自己做比较省钱。

   On second thought, cooking at home can save a lot money.

练习 *Exercises*

用"话又说回来"完成句子。Complete the sentences with the pattern.

1. 养个孩子真累人哪，可＿＿＿＿＿＿＿＿＿＿＿＿＿＿＿＿＿＿＿＿＿。

2. 这份工作是不理想，不过，＿＿＿＿＿＿＿＿＿＿＿＿＿＿＿＿＿＿＿。

解释 *Explanation*

表示要么这样，要么那样。

Used to indicate "either ... or ..."

例句 *Examples*

1. 或者打针，或者吃药，都可以。

   Either having an injection or taking pills is OK.

2. 或者明天，或者后天，我得去一趟上海。

   I must go to Shanghai either tomorrow or the day after tomorrow.

3. 你或者同意，或者反对，总得表示个态度。

   You can either agree or disagree, but you must express an opinion.

4. 这个会，或者你去，或者他去，你们两个谁都行。

   You or he will attend this meeting. Either is OK.

对话 *Dialogues*

1. A: 我去买水果，你看要帮你带点儿什么？

   I am going to buy some fruit. What can I buy for you?

   B: 或者苹果，或者香蕉，随便。

   Either apples or bananas are OK.

2. A: 中午去哪儿吃饭？

   Where shall we have lunch?

   B: 或者中餐馆，或者西餐厅，随你挑。

   Either a Chinese or Western restaurant; you make the decision.

练习 *Exercises*

用"或者~或者~"完成句子。Complete the sentences with the pattern.

1. A: 这个总结报告上边要求什么时候交？

   B: _____。

2. A: 暑假你打算去哪儿？

   B: _____。

汉语常用格式330例

即使 ~ 也 ~

解释 *Explanation*

表示假设一个让步的条件，在这个条件下结果也不受影响。

Used to indicate the same result under the concession.

例句 *Examples*

1. 明天即使没汽车，走路我也要去。

   Even if there is no bus tomorrow, I will walk there.

2. 这次即使考上的希望很小，我也要去试试。

   Even if there is little hope of passing the test, I will still try.

3. 即使你对工作没兴趣，也得去上班，年轻人不能总啃老吧。

   Even though you have no interest in your work, you still have to work. Young people can't always depend on their parents.

4. 要想提高听力就得多听，即使听不懂也要硬着头皮听。

   If you want to improve your listening comprehension, you have to listen more, even if you don't understand.

对话 *Dialogues*

1. A: 这是一家非常好的公司，机会难得，赶快申请吧。

   It is an extremely good company, this is a rare opportunity. Apply for it now.

   B: 谢谢，不过即使待遇非常优厚，我也不想去，因为专业不对口。

   Thank you. But although the pay is good, I don't think I'll apply. It does not suit my major.

2. A: 参加爬山活动，你的身体行吗？

   Are you well enough to go climbing?

   B: 行，即使爬到山顶也没问题。

   Yes. Even climbing to the top is no problem.

练习 *Exercises*

用"即使 ~ 也 ~"完成句子。Complete the sentences with the pattern.

1. A: 那个重要文件我已经设了密码，你放心吧。

   B: 现在电脑高手很多，很多时候_____，不要大意。

2. A: 那个顾客，老是大喊大叫的，我真不想理她。

   B: 顾客就是上帝，_____。

既然 ~（那么）就 ~

解释 *Explanation*

表示先提出一个前提，然后根据这个前提做出推论，说明因果关系。也可用"也"或"还"与"既然"搭配。

Used to indicate a cause-and-effect relationship. 也 or 还 can also be used with 既然.

例句 *Examples*

1. 既然想去，那你就去吧。

   Since you want to go, just go.

2. 既然你已经考虑成熟了，就大胆地去做吧。

   Now that you've thought it over, do it bravely.

3. 你既然来了，还不多坐一会儿？

   Since you are already here, why don't you stay a little longer?

4. 既然你一定要这样做，那我也不多说什么了。

   Since you insist on doing like that, I'm not going to say anything.

对话 *Dialogues*

1. A: 你既然想去留学，那么就得好好学习外语。

   Since you want to go overseas to study, you should work hard to learn a foreign language.

   B: 就是。

   Certainly.

2. A: 这套衣服，你既然那么喜欢，还犹豫什么？买吧！

   Since you like the suit so much, why hesitate? Just buy it!

   B: 你说得倒轻松，我哪有那么多钱哪！

   That's easy for you to say. Where can I get so much money?

练习 *Exercises*

用"既然 ~（那么）就 ~"完成句子。Complete the sentences with the pattern.

1. A: 我挺喜欢那个女孩儿的。

   B: _____。

2. A: 这是我第一次在网上聊天，感觉挺好的。

   B: _____。

既 ~ 又/也 ~

解释 *Explanation*

表示两方面同时具备。

Used to indicate "both... and..." or "as well as".

例句 *Examples*

1. 她既不胖，又不瘦，体形真棒。

   She is neither fat nor thin. She has a good figure.

2. 孩子考上了名牌大学，要去外地就读，当妈妈的既高兴又有些舍不得。

   The child has been accepted into a famous university. Although Mom is happy, she is also a little unwilling to be separated from her child.

3. 他们的公寓小区，既有健身房，也有游泳池。

   Their apartment complex has both a gym and a swimming pool.

4. 沈先生既有学历、资历，也有能力，所以老板很器重他。

   Mr. Shen has a good educational background and qualification, as well as capability, and therefore the boss has a very high opinion of him.

对话 *Dialogues*

1. A: 这座建筑既有传统特色，又有现代气息。

   This building combines both traditional and modern features.

   B: 可以看出，设计师很高明。

   We can see that the designer is quite brilliant.

2. A: 昨天的联欢会开得怎么样？

   How was the party yesterday?

   B: 很好，既生动又活泼。

   Very good. It was lively and entertaining.

练习 *Exercises*

用"既~又/也~"改写句子。Rewrite the sentences with the pattern.

1. 旅游可以欣赏风景。旅游可以增加见闻。

   → _____。

2. 游泳可以健身。游泳可以减肥。

   → _____。

解释 *Explanation*

表示在某种事物或情况发生之后，出现了另一种事物或情况。

Used to indicate that another thing or situation occurs following something or some situation.

例句 *Examples*

1. 继去年突破一千万之后，今年高考人数将再创新高。

   The number of students taking part in the college entrance exam hit a new high this year, after it exceeded 10 million last year.

2. 澳大利亚成为继英美之后世界第三大留学中心。

   Australia has become the third destination for overseas study in the world, second only to the United Kingdom and the United States.

3. 继肯德基之后，麦当劳也将进驻这家大型购物广场。

   Following KFC, McDonald's will also enter this large shopping square.

4. 这家网站继去年推出简约风格的搜索首页之后，又一次做出修正。

   This website made another revision, following its launch of simple search homepage last year.

对话 *Dialogues*

1. A：听说您又出版了一本书？

   I heard you published another book. Is it true?

   B：是的，这是继去年那本畅销书之后的第二本小说。

   Yes. It's my second novel, following the bestseller last year.

2. A：中国现在也是石油消费大国。

   China is also a big petroleum consumer now.

   B：对，中国是继美国之后，世界第二大石油消费国。

   It's true. It's the second biggest petroleum consumer after the United States.

练习 *Exercises*

用"继~之后，~"写两个句子。Make two sentences with the pattern.

1. _____。

2. _____。

假如 ~，就 ~

解释 *Explanation*

表示假设出现某种情况，就会做出某种选择或引起某种结果。"就"也可换成"那"。

Used to indicate that a certain assumption will lead to a certain choice or result. 就 can be replaced by 那.

例句 *Examples*

1. 假如没有太阳，世界上就没有生命。

   If the sun didn't exist, there would be no life in the world.

2. 假如我能选择，我就选择轻松的活法。

   If I could choose, I would choose an easier lifestyle.

3. 假如人真有下辈子，那我来世一定要嫁给你。

   If the next life really existed, I would definitely marry you then.

4. 假如有一天生活欺骗了你，那你也不要对生活失去信心。

   Even if life cheats you one day, you should not lose confidence in it.

对话 *Dialogues*

1. A: 假如你年轻二十岁，那你会干什么？

   If you were 20 years younger, what would you do?

   B: 或许会当舞蹈家。

   Perhaps I would be a dancer.

2. A: 假如我有很多钱的话，我就会去环游世界。

   If I had lots of money, I would travel around the world.

   B: 我也是。

   Yes, so would I.

练习 *Exercises*

用"假如 ~，就 ~"写两个句子。Make two sentences with the pattern.

1. _____。

2. _____。

解释 *Explanation*

"叫"有"被"的意思，常表示某人、某事物遭遇不如意的情况。多用于口语。

Used as a passive voice, often to indicate an unexpected bad consequence. It is often used informally.

例句 *Examples*

1. 这么大的树，叫风给刮倒了。

   Such a big tree was blown down by the wind.

2. 我心爱的小狗叫人给抓走了，能不伤心吗？

   Somebody snatched my beloved puppy. Of course I am sad.

3. 付钱时我发现钱包叫小偷给偷走了，让我真尴尬。

   When I went to pay, I was embarrassed to find that my wallet had been stolen.

4. 这么重要的文件叫他给落在出租车上了，能不挨批吗？

   He left such an important file in a taxi. No wonder he was blamed.

对话 *Dialogues*

1. A: 你去瑞士旅行时买的那块儿金表呢？

   Where is that gold watch you bought on the trip to Switzerland?

   B: 唉，叫我的女儿给弄丢了。

   Well, my daughter lost it.

2. A: 今天的晚会太让人扫兴了。

   This evening's party was really disappointing.

   B: 是啊，全叫那帮酒鬼给搅和了。

   Yes. Those drunken people ruined it.

练习 *Exercises*

用"叫 ~ 给 ~"完成句子。Complete the sentences with the pattern.

1. A: 我的那双高筒靴子呢？

   B: 太旧了，打扫卫生时_____。

2. A: 你这次考得不好，你妈妈说你了吗？

   B: 那还用说，_____。

解释 *Explanation*

表示虽然承认存在某种情况，但是不因此改变"可是"后提及的事情。"可是"也可换成"但是"、"然而"。

Used to indicate that despite of a certain fact led by 尽管，the fact does not change something led by 可是，which can be replaced by 但是 or 然而.

例句 *Examples*

1. 尽管这些天我忙得焦头烂额，可是过得非常充实。
   Although I am extremely busy these days, I feel my life is very rewarding.
2. 尽管他没有明说，可是我能猜到发生了什么事。
   Although he did not say it openly, I can guess what had happened.
3. 尽管对手实力很强，但是我们一定要想办法打败他。
   We must find a way to defeat him in spite of his power.
4. 尽管大家都投票给他，然而各人的想法并不一样。
   Although everybody voted for him, their opinions are not exactly the same.

对话 *Dialogues*

1. A: 这次展销会，展位租金很贵。
   To rent a booth at this exhibition is very expensive.
   B: 尽管贵，但是还要争取参展。
   Even though the rent is expensive, we should still try to participate.

2. A: 你想考北大、清华？没那么容易。
   You want to get into Peking University or Tsinghua University? It's not that easy.
   B: 尽管难考，可是我还是想试试。
   Although it's difficult, I still want to have a try.

练习 *Exercises*

用"尽管 ~，可是 ~"完成句子。Complete the sentences with the pattern.

1. A: 明天有四五级大风，你还去滑雪吗？
   B: ＿＿＿＿＿＿＿＿＿＿＿＿＿＿＿＿。

2. A: 你这么忙，还能来参加校友聚会吗？
   B: ＿＿＿＿＿＿＿＿＿＿＿＿＿＿＿＿。

汉语常用格式330例

解释 *Explanation*

表示两件事紧接着发生，也表示前后两件事有因果关系。

Used to indicate two things taking place one after another, or a cause-and-effect relationship.

例句 *Examples*

1. 到了国外，就知道该学的东西太多了。

   As soon as I went overseas, I knew I had a lot to learn.

2. 她身体不好，就在家多待了一天，不必指责。

   She didn't feel well, so she stayed at home an extra day. Don't blame her.

3. 一知道情况不好，她便坐立不安起来。

   As soon as she knew the situation was bad, she couldn't sit still.

4. 我敲了一下门，没人应，我便垂头丧气地往回走了。

   I knocked at the door, but no one answered. So I walked back, crestfallen.

对话 *Dialogues*

1. A: 小杨在家吗？

   Is Xiao Yang at home?

   B: 刚回来就又出去了。

   As soon as he came back, he went out again.

2. A: 你怎么这么快回来了？

   How did you get back so fast?

   B: 我送她上了车便回来了。

   As soon as she was on the train, I came back.

练习 *Exercises*

用 "~就/便~" 完成句子。Complete the sentences with the pattern.

1. 今天的菜太好吃了，我＿＿＿＿＿＿＿＿＿＿，结果吃得太饱了。

2. 看他那一副不想说话的样子，我＿＿＿＿＿＿＿＿＿。

~就~吧

解释 *Explanation*

"就" 放在两个相同成分之间，表示还可以接受或对不利情况抱无所谓的态度。

就 is used between two identical words or expressions to express tolerance or indifference to an adverse situation.

例句 *Examples*

1. 远就远点儿吧，反正有车。

   It't true that it's a bit far. Anyway, there is a bus going there.

2. 他不来就不来吧，你别勉强他。

   If he does not come, let it be. Don't push him.

3. 这式样老气就老气吧，我都这把年纪了。

   It's fine if the dress is old-fashioned. I am at this age anyway.

4. 今年高考落榜就落榜了吧，早点儿工作也好。

   You can't change the fact that you failed the college entrance exam, so don't worry about it. It is also good to take up a job earlier.

对话 *Dialogues*

1. A: 那房子是朝北的。

   The house faces north.

   B: 朝北的就朝北的吧，反正住不了几天。

   So be it. Anyway, we are only staying for a few days.

2. A: 这些盘子好看是好看，但都是塑料的，还买吗？

   These dishes look good, but they are plastic. Do you still want to buy them?

   B: 塑料的就塑料的吧，瓷的也贵。

   So be it. Porcelain dishes are more expensive.

练习 *Exercises*

用 "~就~吧" 完成句子。Complete the sentences with the pattern.

1. A: 我不爱喝牛奶嘛！干嘛非要我喝？

   B: 好，好，_____，真拿你没办法。

2. A: 哎呀！真糟糕！今天有大雨，可我的伞丢了！

   B: _____，我再给你买一把。

解释 *Explanation*

表示能否成功或成为现实的决定性因素是什么。

Used to indicate a decisive factor for a success or the reality.

例句 *Examples*

1. 能否买到真古董，就看你识别的眼力了。

   Buying genuine antiques depends on your ability to judge real from fake.

2. 明天能不能去春游，就看下不下雨了。

   Whether we can go on a spring excursion or not tomorrow depends on if it will rain.

3. 能否达成停火协议，就看双方是否有诚意。

   Whether the truce can be reached depends on if the two sides sincerely try to work together.

4. 他是我们队里最优秀的，能不能拿下冠军就看他的了。

   He is the best on our team. Whether we can be the champions or not depends on him.

对话 *Dialogues*

1. A: 你们和培信公司的合作有戏吗？

   Will your cooperation with Peixin Company succeed?

   B: 成不成就看今天的谈判了。

   That depends on whether today's negotiations are successful.

2. A: 听说他应聘到一家外资企业当市场经理了，不知能不能干长。

   I heard that he joined a foreign enterprise as a market manager. I wonder whether he will work there for long.

   B: 那就看他的工作业绩怎么样了。

   It depends on his performance.

练习 *Exercises*

用"～就看～"完成句子。Complete the sentences with the pattern.

1. A: 现在大学生好找工作吗？

   B: _____。

2. A: 这条食品街有这么多餐馆，咱们去哪一家好呢？

   B: _____。

解释 *Explanation*

表示从某方面讲，或根据某种情况来看问题。多用于书面语。

Used to indicate to judge from a certain perspective. It is often used in written form.

例句 *Examples*

1. 就我的经验来说，这样做没问题。

   In my experience, there is no problem doing it like this.

2. 他哥哥，就技术来说，绝对是一流的。

   His brother is absolutely first-class in terms of skill.

3. 就病人目前的情况来看，手术不是十分理想。

   The operation was not as good as expected judging from the patient's current condition.

4. 这本书我还没看完，但就读过的章节来看，还是很不错的。

   I have not finished the book. However, judging from the chapters I've read, it's quite good.

对话 *Dialogues*

1. A: 这里的咖啡怎么样?

   How's the coffee here?

   B: 就浓度来说，还差点儿。

   It is not so good as far as consistency is concerned.

2. A: 你这篇科普文章翻译得真棒，比我强多了。

   You did a very good job in translating this science popularization article. You are much better than me.

   B: 可就专业知识来说，我远不如你。

   But I am not half as good as you in terms of professional knowledge.

练习 *Exercises*

用"就 ~ 来说/来看"完成句子。Complete the sentences with the pattern.

1. A: 索尼的相机和富士的相机哪个牌子的好?

   B: _____。

2. A: 这个电视剧拍得怎么样?

   B: _____。

解释 *Explanation*

强调肯定，确定范围。

Used for emphasis or affirmation to indicate the range.

例句 *Examples*

1. 你要找林主任？左边第三位就是。

   You are looking for Director Lin? He is the third from the left.

2. 韩国人最喜欢的中国酒就是"二锅头"和"五粮液"。

   The Chinese liquors that Korean people like best are Erguotou and Wuliangye.

3. 立交桥南边那座高楼就是中国大饭店。

   The tall building to the south of the flyover is the China Grand Hotel.

4. 你知道他说的那个人就是我，还明知故问。

   You know he referred to me, but you asked as if you didn't know.

对话 *Dialogues*

1. A: 地铁站在哪儿？

   Where is the subway station?

   B: 到前面路口，一拐弯就是。

   Turn at the next corner, and you will see it.

2. A: 这个班上最调皮的学生是谁？

   Who is the naughtiest student in the class?

   B: 就是我儿子，不过他是绝顶聪明的。

   My son. But he is extraordinarily clever.

练习 *Exercises*

用"~就是（~）"完成句子。Complete the sentences with the pattern.

1. A: 请问，哪位是高小姐？

   B: _____。

2. A: 这里有这么多种啤酒，哪种是他要我们买的？

   B: _____。

~就是了

解释 *Explanation*

用在句子末尾。表示"只不过~"或"只要~就行了",不必过于在意。

Used at the end of a sentence to affirm a certain condition that does not deserve too much attention.

例句 *Examples*

1. 谁都会犯错误的,以后改正就是了。

   Everyone makes mistakes. It is OK as long as you correct them.

2. 他哪里会真想当老师! 说说就是了。

   He does not really want to be a teacher! He was just saying.

3. 我怎么可能开公司当大老板? 开个玩笑就是了。

   How could I start a company and become a boss? I'm just kidding.

4. 别再为这事难受了,以后接受教训,当心点儿就是了。

   Don't feel bad about this anymore. It will be OK as long as you learn your lesson, and be careful in the future.

对话 *Dialogues*

1. A: 你倡议举办的这个晚会真不错。

   The party that you organized was really good.

   B: 算不上是晚会,大家聚在一起热闹热闹就是了。

   It wasn't really a party. It was just some people getting together and having fun.

2. A: 我很欣赏这个小摆设,造型真可爱。

   I like this ornament a lot. Its design is really cute.

   B: 你喜欢的话,拿去就是了。

   You can take it if you like.

练习 *Exercises*

用"~就是了"改写第一个句子,完成第二个句子。Rewrite the first sentence and complete the second with the pattern.

1. 她哪里是爱他,只不过喜欢他的钱罢了。

   →_____。

2. 我的小皇帝,你别哭了,想要什么,我_____。

解释 *Explanation*

前半句表示肯定，后半句表示在某一方面有点儿不足。

Used to indicate an affirmation in the first half and a deficiency or shortcoming in the latter half of a sentence.

例句 *Examples*

1. 这位主持人很有风度，就是矮了点儿。

   This host is well-mannered, but a little short.

2. 那座公寓环境不错，就是远了点儿。

   That apartment has a good environment, but is a bit far.

3. 这个牌子的轿车很受欢迎，就是贵了点儿。

   This brand of car is very popular, but a bit expensive.

4. 现在的孩子都挺聪明的，就是娇气了点儿。

   Children nowadays are smart, but a bit spoiled.

对话 *Dialogues*

1. **A:** 你看这件衣服怎么样？

   What do you think of the clothes?

   B: 样子、花色都好，就是颜色暗了点儿。

   The design and patterns are quite good, but the color is a bit dark.

2. **A:** 这部电影拍得不错。

   This movie is quite good.

   B: 对，就是武打镜头多了点儿。

   Yes, but it has too many kung fu scenes.

练习 *Exercises*

用"～，就是～了点儿"完成句子。Complete the sentences with the pattern.

1. 你这篇文章写得挺好的，＿＿＿＿＿＿＿＿＿＿＿。

2. 他这个人挺热心的，＿＿＿＿＿＿＿＿＿＿＿。

就是/就算 ~也~

解释 *Explanation*

表示假设的让步，有"即使"的意思。

Used to indicate a concession, meaning "even (if)".

例句 *Examples*

1. 这孩子智力过人，就是高等数学题也会做。

   The child is very intelligent. He can even work out higher math problems.

2. 他有充足的论据，就是专家要驳倒他也不容易。

   He has adequate proof. Not even experts can easily refute him.

3. 他武功可不一般，就算你们再加几个人也不是他的对手。

   He is very good at kung fu. Even if you had other people helping, you can't defeat him.

4. 她的手真巧，就算工艺美术家也不一定能赶上她。

   She is highly skilled. Not even craftsmen have better skills than her.

对话 *Dialogues*

1. A: 这帐篷很结实。

   The tent is very strong.

   B: 这下好啦，就是下暴雨也不怕了。

   Good. Even if it rains heavily, we don't need to be afraid.

2. A: 鲁迅的杂文你都能看懂了吧?

   Can you understand all of Lu Xun's essays?

   B: 别拿我开心了，就算我再学两年也不见得能行啊。

   Are you kidding me? Even if I study for two more years, I probably won't be able to understand them.

练习 *Exercises*

用"就是/就算 ~也~"完成句子。Complete the sentences with the pattern.

1. 当年这首流行歌曲，＿＿＿＿＿＿＿＿＿＿＿＿＿＿＿。

2. 法律面前人人平等，＿＿＿＿＿＿＿＿＿＿＿＿＿＿＿。

解释 *Explanation*

表示拿某人、某事做例子。

Used to take somebody or something as an example.

例句 *Examples*

1. 我们俩有很多地方不一致，就说吃饭吧，一个爱吃米饭，一个爱吃面食。

   We two have many differences. Take food as an example, one likes rice while the other likes wheaten food.

2. 谁说北方男人不干家务活？就说我们家吧，家务活多半儿是我干的。

   Who tell you men from the north don't do housework? Take my family as an example. I do most of the household chores.

3. 这几天事事不顺，就说今天吧，刚出门就崴了脚。

   Things haven't been going very well for me lately. Take today as an example, I sprained my ankle not long after I walked out home.

4. 我对这家旅行社的服务不满意，就说旅游车吧，又破又脏。

   I'm not satisfied with the services of this travel agency. Take the coach as an example, it's old and dirty.

对话 *Dialogues*

1. A: 你怎么那么爱吃水果?

   Why are you so fond of fruits?

   B: 营养丰富嘛，就说苹果吧，可以预防好多病呢。

   Fruits are nutritious. Take apple as an example, it can prevent many diseases.

2. A: 你觉得她哪点儿好看？让你这么着迷。

   Which part of her do you think is beautiful? What fascinates you?

   B: 哪儿都好看，就说头发吧，又黑又亮。

   Her every part is beautiful. Take her hair as an example, it's black and shiny.

练习 *Exercises*

用"就说 ~ 吧， ~"完成句子。Complete the sentences with the pattern.

1. 我们班的同学都挺不错的，_____ 。

2. 他是个特别节省的人，_____。

解释 *Explanation*

表示要求不高，只要有某种起码的条件，或达到某个小目的就可以了。

Used to indicate a basic condition or a minor goal, which is not a high standard.

例句 *Examples*

1. 你们有什么事找服务员就行。

   If you need help, please look for a service person.

2. 这篇文章您过一下目，签个名就行。

   Please go over the article, and then sign your name.

3. 我对衣服的样式无所谓，能穿就行。

   I don't mind the design of the clothes, as long as I can wear them.

4. 她没什么大病，只是疲劳过度，多休息休息就行。

   She is not seriously ill, just too tired. She will recover with more rest.

对话 *Dialogues*

1. A: 今天我们好好聊聊，中午饭就做得简单点儿。

   Let us have a good chat today. Make the lunch simple.

   B: 对，吃方便面就行。

   OK. Let's just have instant noodles.

2. A: 这个文件下午去送可以吗?

   Is it OK if I send this file this afternoon?

   B: 没问题。明天送到就行。

   No problem, as long as it will arrive by tomorrow.

练习 *Exercises*

用"~就行"完成句子。Complete the sentences with the pattern.

1. 吃完不用洗碗，_____。

2. 他干的这个行业，特别自由，不用去单位，_____。

解释 *Explanation*

表示强调某种人或事物的特点、关键所在。

Used to emphasize the attributes of somebody or something.

例句 *Examples*

1. 她的这身儿打扮，俏就俏在帽子上。

   She looks so beautiful, just because of her hat.

2. 这套衣服贵就贵在面料上。

   The suit is expensive because of the material.

3. 他这人可气就可气在有钱不还，所以有人骂他是无赖。

   He is irritating, because he doesn't return money even if he has it. So some people say he is a man without any virtue.

4. 这个商店好就好在品种齐全，特别受白领们的欢迎。

   This shop is good because it has a wide variety of products. It is especially popular among white-collar workers.

对话 *Dialogues*

1. A: 昨天的足球赛我们输了。

   We lost yesterday's football match.

   B: 你们输就输在整体配合差。

   You lost because you lacked teamwork.

2. A: 这明明是骗局，为什么还有这么多人上当受骗?

   It's obviously a swindle. Why are so many people falling for it?

   B: 问题出就出在不少人有贪财、占小便宜的心理。

   The problem is that a lot of people have a money-loving mentality, and are always looking for small advantages.

练习 *Exercises*

用"A 就 A 在～（上）"完成句子。Complete the sentences with the pattern.

1. A: 你说她哪儿漂亮?

   B: _____。

2. A: 为什么中国足球队三十年来老输给韩国呢?

   B: _____。

就这样（～），～还～呢

解释 *Explanation*

意思是虽然十分尽力，或已具备一定的条件，但还达不到客观的或他人的要求。

Used to indicate that although efforts have been made or certain conditions have been met, it is still far from the objective or others' requirements.

例句 *Examples*

1. 他就这样起早贪黑地干，老板还不满意呢。

   He works hard from dawn to night, but his boss is still not satisfied.

2. 我每月的工资，就这样省吃俭用，还不够花呢。

   I live very frugally on my salary, but I still don't have enough to spend.

3. 我一天只吃一顿饭，就这样，体重还减不下来呢。

   I only eat one meal a day. Even so, I do not lose any weight.

4. 开夜车对她来说已经是家常便饭，可就这样她父母还逼她抓紧呢。

   It's normal for her to work late into the night. Even so, her parents still force her to work harder.

对话 *Dialogues*

1. A: 你不用花那么多时间给孩子辅导。

   You don't need to spend so much time tutoring your child.

   B: 就这样他的成绩还上不去呢。

   Even so, his marks don't improve.

2. A: 你真算得上是个贤妻良母啊。

   You are really a good wife and a loving mother.

   B: 就这样我老公还不满意呢。

   Even so, my husband is not satisfied.

练习 *Exercises*

用"就这样（～），～还～呢"完成句子。Complete the sentences with the pattern.

1. A: 你怎么穿得这么多?

   B: ＿＿＿＿＿＿＿＿＿＿。穿少了还不得冻死我了。

2. A: 你真有耐心，给他讲了一遍又一遍。

   B: 没办法啊，＿＿＿＿＿＿＿＿＿＿。

解释 *Explanation*

强调指出对方或他人某种情感的程度极高，省略了程度补语，意在引人注意。

Used to emphasize a high degree of an emotion and a feeling with the degree complement omitted, aiming to attract attention.

例句 *Examples*

1. 看把他得意的，不就是当个小科长吗？

   He is so complacent. It's nothing more than a small section chief.

2. 你这次得了学习优秀奖，看把你妈妈乐的。

   This time you got an award for good marks. Look, how happy your mother is!

3. 看把他气的，我只是跟他开个玩笑，至于吗？

   Why he is so angry? I'm just kidding him.

4. 孩子真的离不开妈妈，你才走几天，看把孩子想的。

   Children can not leave their mothers. You were away for only several days, and the child has been missing you so much.

对话 *Dialogues*

1. A: 我的鹦鹉被人偷走了！

   My parrot was stolen!

   B: 看把你伤心的，再买一只不就行了。

   Don't be so sad. Buy another one.

2. A: 我的女儿真的骨折了吗？

   Does my daughter really get a fracture?

   B: 看把你吓的，老黄蒙你的。

   Don't freak out. Lao Huang is kidding you.

练习 *Exercises*

用"看把你/他~的"完成句子。Complete the sentences with the pattern.

1. A: 这个暑假我妈妈要带我去欧洲旅游！

   B: _____。

2. A: 你看我穿这件衣服更漂亮了吧？

   B: _____。

解释 *Explanation*

表示一种估计，有"看来"的意思。多用于从外表、外部情况看。

Used to indicate an estimation as judged mostly from the apperance, meaing "it seems …" or "sb. looks …".

例句 *Examples*

1. 她已经三十岁了，看上去也就是二十来岁。

   She is 30 years old, but looks as if in her twenties.

2. 他高高大大的，看上去像个威武的军官。

   He is tall, looking like an awesome officer.

3. 雷声不断，乌云密布，看上去要下雨了。

   Thunder rolls and dark clouds gather. It seems to rain.

4. 这姑娘，皮肤白里透红，看上去很健康。

   With a fair and rosy complexion, the girl looks very healthy.

对话 *Dialogues*

1. A：他们来了多少人？

   How many people are they?

   B：看上去有三十多人，个个都是棒小伙子。

   It seems there are more than 30, and each one of them is strong lad.

2. A：这座仿古建筑物，看上去像是星级宾馆。

   This pseudo-classic building looks like a star-rated hotel.

   B：哪儿呀，这是文化部的办公楼。

   Well, it's the office building of the Ministry of Culture.

练习 *Exercises*

用"看上去 ~"完成句子。Complete the sentences with the pattern.

1. A：你看这件真丝睡衣怎么样？

   B：＿＿＿＿＿＿＿＿＿＿＿＿，穿上应该也很舒服。

2. A：听说林局长出院了，他恢复得怎么样？

   B：他气色红润，＿＿＿＿＿＿＿＿＿＿＿＿。

汉语常用格式330例

解释 *Explanation*

表示从表面看到的现象做出某种推断。

Used to draw some inference from a phenomenon.

例句 *Examples*

1. 今天的晚霞真好，看样子明天是个晴天。

   There is beautiful sunset glow today. It seems tomorrow will be a sunny day.

2. 他沉着脸从经理的办公室出来，看样子是挨批了。

   With a long face, he came out of the manager's office. Apparently, he was criticized.

3. 她对你这么在意，看样子是喜欢上你了。

   She pays so much attention to you. Apparently she likes you.

4. 这几天没人提公司重组的事了，看样子这事要搁浅了。

   These days, nobody talks of the issue of corporate restructuring. It seems to be held up.

对话 *Dialogues*

1. A: 星期天你能来参加同学聚会吗?

   Will you come to our classmates' party on Sunday?

   B: 家里要来客人，看样子去不了。

   I have visitors to my home on Sunday. Apparently, I won't make it.

2. A: 这次海啸，有好几百人失踪呢。

   Several hundred people were missing in this tsunami.

   B: 已经过去一个多月了，看样子他们生还的可能性不大了。

   It has been more than a month since the tsunami. It seems that their chances of survival are very slim.

练习 *Exercises*

用"看样子 ~"完成句子。Complete the sentences with the pattern.

1. A: 你说他今天还会来吗?

   B: 都这么晚了，_____。

2. A: 他多大年纪?

   B: 我也不太清楚，_____。

~，可不就 ~

解释 Explanation

表示由于某种原因，当然会出现某种结果。

Used to indicate that certain cause brings along the result.

例句 Examples

1. 她八点才起床，九点才吃早饭，可不就晚了。

   She got up at eight and had breakfast at nine. No doubt she was late.

2. 整天生闷气，可不就憋出病来了嘛。

   You have fits of the sulks all day long. No doubt you get sick.

3. 外边天寒地冻的，你穿得这么少跑出去，可不就感冒了。

   It's freezing outside and you ran out wearing so little. No doubt you caught a cold.

4. 我看他喝得醉醺醺的，可不就生气了嘛。

   I saw he was drunk and certainly became angry.

对话 Dialogues

1. A：这台机器的噪音怎么越来越大？

   Why is the noise of the machine getting louder and louder?

   B：光用不维修，可不就出毛病了。

   It receives no maintenance and will certainly go wrong.

2. A：这个月我花的钱可超支了不少。

   I overspent much this month.

   B：天天下馆子，可不就费钱。

   You ate out every day. It's certainly too much.

练习 Exercises

用"~，可不就 ~"和所给的词语完成对话。Complete the sentences with the pattern and words in parentheses.

1. A：你说我为什么老长肉？我吃得也不多呀。

   B：_____。（不运动）

2. A：这家商店的运动服怎么都这么贵？

   B：_____。（名牌）

解释 *Explanation*

表示从上文或对方所叙述的情况，可以得出判断性的结论。

Used to indicate a judgmental conclusion drawn from the above text or what the other speaker said.

例句 *Examples*

1. 再冷的天，他都去户外游泳，可见他身体多棒了。

   He goes swimming outdoors even in cold days; it is thus clear that he is very healthy.

2. 每次谈判，老板都把你带着，可见很器重你。

   The boss brings you along to each negotiation; it is thus evident that he has a very high opinion of you.

3. 现在"可口可乐"家喻户晓，可见广告的作用很大。

   Now Coca-Cola is known to every household, showing that advertisement has a huge influence.

4. 离婚后，两人都感到天像塌下来一样，可见离婚对人是有极大伤害的。

   After divorce, they both felt like the heaven fell down; it is thus evident that divorce hurts people deeply.

143

对话 *Dialogues*

1. A: 好多乐器，他都能演奏一段。

   He can play a lot of musical instruments.

   B: 可见他对音乐很内行。

   Obviously he is an expert in music.

2. A: 有什么好吃的，妈妈总要给我留着点儿。

   When there is something delicious, Mom always saves a little for me.

   B: 可见你妈妈特别偏爱你。

   It shows your mother loves you more.

练习 *Exercises*

用"~，可见~"完成句子。Complete the sentences with the pattern.

1. 他什么事都告诉你，＿＿＿＿＿＿＿＿＿＿＿＿＿＿＿＿。

2. 现在学汉语的学生越来越多了，＿＿＿＿＿＿＿＿＿＿＿＿＿＿ 。

可～啦

解释 *Explanation*

强调程度比较深，用于感叹句。

Used in an exclamatory sentence to indicate a high degree.

例句 *Examples*

1. 今天的考试题目可容易啦。

   Today's exam is really easy.

2. 我哥哥的女朋友可讨人喜欢啦。

   My brother's girlfriend is really lovely.

3. 这条路坑坑洼洼的，可不好走啦。

   This road is too bumpy for walking.

4. 你看看我新买的电子词典，用起来可方便啦。

   Look, my new electronic dictionary. It's really convenient.

对话 *Dialogues*

1. A: 你这件大衣看上去是毛料的，不便宜吧?

   Your coat looks like woolen. Is it expensive?

   B: 别提了，可贵啦，花了我差不多一个月的工资。

   Don't mention it. I got screwed! It costs a month's salary.

2. A: 北京人对 2008 年奥运会可关心啦!

   Beijingers really care about the 2008 Olympic Games.

   B: 那当然，北京市民是最大的受益者。

   That's true. They benefit the most.

练习 *Exercises*

用"可～啦"完成句子。Complete the sentences with the pattern.

1. A: 黄山的风景怎么样?

   B: _____ 。

2. A: 现在这个季节你们那里的天气好吧?

   B: _____，晴空万里。

解释 *Explanation*

是"马上就要~"的意思，表示很快就会出现某种情况。

Used to indicate that something will happen soon.

例句 *Examples*

1. 天快亮了，鸡也快叫了，还能接着睡吗？

   It's almost dawn and the cock is about to crow. How can I continue to sleep?

2. 福利彩票快要抽奖了。

   The winning ticket in the welfare lottery will soon be drawn.

3. 我们朝夕相处快两年了，相互能不了解吗？

   We have been together for nearly two years. Certainly we understand each other.

4. 春天快来了，柳树也快发芽了。

   Spring is coming and willows are about to sprout.

对话 *Dialogues*

1. A: 您的女儿快要大学毕业了吧？

   Your daughter will soon graduate from university, right?

   B: 对，很快能挣钱了。

   Yes, she will be able to earn money soon.

2. A: 夕阳快要西下了，鸟儿就要归林了。

   The sun is setting and birds will go home.

   B: 万家灯火也快亮起来喽。

   A myriad of lights will soon be seen.

练习 *Exercises*

用"快 ~ 了"完成句子。Complete the sentences with the pattern.

1. _____，大家都在认真复习、备考。

2. _____，商场里好多人，都在购买年货。

解释 *Explanation*

"啦"是"了"和"啊"的合音，两个或几个连用，用于举例说明，相当于"~什么的"。

啦 is the combination in terms of pronunciation of 了 (le) and 啊 (a), used in reduplicated form for giving examples, similar to ~什么的.

例句 *Examples*

1. 她真是多才多艺，唱啦，跳啦，什么都行。

   She is really versatile. She can sing, dance and do many other things.

2. 出门在外，冷啦，热啦，自己要多当心。

   As you are away from home, you should take care of yourself against cold or heat.

3. 一般女孩子成了大姑娘之后，爱情啦，婚姻啦，五花八门的浪漫想法就都有了。

   When little girls grow up, they dream of love, marriage, and get various ideas of romance.

4. 办公室里电脑啦，传真机啦，现代化办公设备样样齐全。

   The office is equipped with modern office facilities such as computer and fax machine.

对话 *Dialogues*

1. A: 日常饮食必须讲究科学。

   We must have healthy diet.

   B: 是啊，粗粮啦，细粮啦，水果、蔬菜啦，得搭配起来吃。

   Yes. We should eat coarse grains, flour and rice, fruit and vegetables in good proportion.

2. A: 现在中国市场上进口商品多着呢。

   Now there are many imported commodities in the Chinese market.

   B: 可不，美国的啦、韩国的啦、意大利的啦，都有。

   True. There are commodities from the United States, South Korea, Italy and other countries.

练习 *Exercises*

用"~啦，~啦"完成句子。Complete the sentences with the pattern.

1. A: 你喜欢喝什么?

   B: ＿＿＿＿＿＿＿＿＿＿＿我都爱喝。

2. A: 你今天逛商场都买了些什么?

   B: ＿＿＿＿＿＿＿＿＿＿＿买了一大堆。

汉语常用格式330例

解释 *Explanation*

表示动作多次反复的意思，"来"、"去"前用动词。

Used each after a verb to indicate a repeated action.

例句 *Examples*

1. 别再犹豫来犹豫去了，时间不等人啊。

   Don't hesitate any more. Time waits for no man.

2. 我比来比去，还是我女朋友心灵手巧。

   I compare again and again and find out that my girlfriend is clever and deft.

3. 他们研究来研究去，也没找出事故发生的原因。

   They studied it again and again, but failed to find out the cause of this accident.

4. 天太热了，我躺在床上翻来覆去，怎么也睡不着。

   It's so hot that I toss from side to side in bed but cannot fall asleep anyway.

对话 *Dialogues*

1. A：他挑来挑去，怎么挑上了这么个人！

   He chose among many people, but how come he picked such a person?

   B：真没眼力！自找苦吃。

   He made a bad choice. He asked for it.

2. A：到底派谁去参加谈判呢？

   Who on earth should be sent to participate in the negotiation?

   B：领导们商量来商量去，还是决定不了。

   Leaders discussed it again and again but could not decide.

练习 *Exercises*

用"～来～去"和所给的动词造两个句子。Make sentences with the pattern and verbs in parentheses.

1. _____。（数）

2. _____。（考虑）

~来着

解释 Explanation

表示已经发生过的事情，常用来追问对方已经说过的话，用于句末。

Used at the end of a sentence to indicate what happened in the past and often to ask what the other speaker said.

例句 Examples

1. 他们要什么来着？你瞧瞧，我怎么给忘了。

   What did they want? Look, how come I forget it?

2. 你回老家这些天都干什么来着？

   What did you do those days at your hometown?

3. 你千万别告诉她我昨天喝酒来着。

   Never tell her that I drank yesterday.

4. 我昨天哪儿也没去，在家玩儿游戏来着。

   I didn't go any place yesterday. I played game at home.

对话 Dialogues

1. A: 刚才你说什么来着？

   What did you say just now?

   B: 怕是你记错了吧？我什么也没说呀。

   Maybe you remember it wrong. I said nothing at all.

2. A: 你叫什么名字来着？我记不清了。

   What's your name? I don't remember.

   B: 何怡。

   My name is He Yi.

练习 Exercises

用"～来着"完成句子。Complete the sentences with the pattern.

1. A: 我昨天陪新来的同事去故宫、雍和宫、天坛了。

   B: 对不起，我没听清。＿＿＿＿＿＿＿＿＿＿＿＿＿＿＿？

2. A: 你家人来探亲的这些天，你是怎么过的？

   B: ＿＿＿＿＿＿＿＿＿＿＿＿＿＿＿＿＿。

解释 *Explanation*

表示不想或不愿意做某事。

Used to indicate "not want to do" or "not feel like doing something".

例句 *Examples*

1. 我不是不想你，只是懒得写信。

   It's not that I don't miss you, but I am just tired of writing letters.

2. 这种人只考虑自己，自私自利，我懒得理他。

   Such kind of person is selfish, caring nothing but himself. I don't want to talk to him.

3. 这位郭师傅太啰嗦了，我真懒得再跟他打交道。

   Master Guo is too wordy. I am tired of dealing with him.

4. 就这么两行字，手写一下算了，懒得再开电脑了。

   There are only a few words. Use your handwriting. I don't feel like starting the computer.

对话 *Dialogues*

1. A: 你买的这个背包有毛病，得去换。

   There is something wrong with the backpack you bought. You have to change it.

   B: 凑合着用吧，我懒得再跑了。

   Make do with it. I don't want to go there again.

2. A: 深更半夜的，他们又吵起来了。你去看看吧。

   It's deep in the night and they quarrel again. Go to have a look.

   B: 我懒得管了。

   I'm tired of bothering about them.

练习 *Exercises*

用"懒得 ～"完成句子。Complete the sentences with the pattern.

1. 今天丈夫和孩子们都不回来吃饭，_____。

2. 他这个人这么不讲道理，_____。

解释 *Explanation*

前后用同样的动词，表示动作多次反复。

Used between two same verbs to indicate a repeated action.

例句 *Examples*

1. 妈妈叮嘱了又叮嘱，路上千万要小心。

   Mom asked me again and again to be careful on the way.

2. 爷爷把传家的宝玉包了又包，放在箱底。

   Grandpa wrapped the heirloom jade layer upon layer and put it at the bottom of the box.

3. 她穿上新警服，对着镜子照了又照，觉得自己更有魅力了。

   She put on the new police uniform, and looked into the mirror again and again, believing that she was more charming.

4. 出去要锁好门，这一点我是提醒了又提醒，可她还总是忘记。

   I warn her once and again to lock the door when going out, but she always forgets it.

对话 *Dialogues*

1. A: 老大娘，那人是什么模样，能告诉我们吗？

   Grandma, can you tell us what the man looks like?

   B: 我想了又想，还是想不起来。咳，老啦。

   I thought over and over but could not remember. Well, I'm old.

2. A: 你姐姐看了那张照片了吗？

   Did your elder sister look at that photo?

   B: 她看了又看，还是认不出那个人。

   She looked again and again but failed to recognize that man.

练习 *Exercises*

用 " ~ 了又 ~ " 和所给的动词造两个句子。Make sentences with the pattern and verbs in parentheses.

1. ＿＿＿＿＿＿＿＿＿＿＿＿＿＿＿＿＿＿＿＿＿。（检查）

2. ＿＿＿＿＿＿＿＿＿＿＿＿＿＿＿＿＿＿＿＿＿。（选）

解释 *Explanation*

表示包括前后两项内容，或表示两种动作同时发生，此时多和单音节动词一起用。

Used to indicate that two items are included, or used mostly with monosyllabic verbs to indicate that two actions occur almost simultaneously.

例句 *Examples*

1. 看来他是饿坏了，连饭带菜，三口两口就吃完了。

   It seems he was very hungry as he ate up rice and dishes in several mouthfuls.

2. 我这套职业妇女装连裙子带上衣一共才花了二百来块钱。

   My office suit, including jacket and skirt, only cost me some 200 yuan.

3. 一路上，我们连说带笑，一会儿就走到了。

   On the way, we talked and laughed, and it took just a while to walked there.

4. 他老远看到我，连奔带跑地就迎过来了，真是老朋友见面分外亲热。

   He saw me in the distance and ran all the way to me. We were beaming with joy and warmth, seeing old friends.

对话 *Dialogues*

1. A：你看朴太太真能干，连肉带菜，摆了满满一桌。

   Mrs. Piao is so capable. Look, there are so many dishes on the table, including meat dishes and vegetables.

   B：哟，真丰盛，咱们可以一饱口福啦。

   Oh, it's marvelous. We can satisfy our appetite!

2. A：邻居家的孩子，连哭带闹地吵了一夜。

   The child of our neighbor cried and made noises all night.

   B：这也难怪，妈妈出差了，爸爸怎么哄得了嘛。

   No wonder. The child's mom went on a business trip, and the dad cannot deal with it.

练习 *Exercises*

用"连～带～"和所给的词语造两个句子。Make sentences with the pattern and words in parentheses.

1. ＿＿＿＿＿＿＿＿＿＿＿＿＿＿＿＿＿＿＿＿＿＿。（家具　电器）

2. ＿＿＿＿＿＿＿＿＿＿＿＿＿＿＿＿＿＿＿＿＿＿。（跳　唱）

连 ~ 也/都 ~

汉语常用格式330例

解释 *Explanation*

通过突出的甚至极端的事例表示强调。含有"甚至"的意思。

Used to emphasize something surprising, outstanding or extreme, meaning "even".

例句 *Examples*

1. 孙子说的笑话，连病中的爷爷也给逗笑了。

   The boy told a joke and even his sick grandpa was amused.

2. 这消息连大街上都传开了，你怎么还不知道？

   This news has been spread even in the street. How could you not know it?

3. 她说出这样的话，连她自己都觉得可笑。

   She said such words, and even she herself found it funny.

4. 参加这样盛大的体育比赛，连她这样身经百战的老将都不免有点儿紧张。

   Even she, an experienced athlete having competed many times, felt a bit nervous when taking part in such a grand game.

对话 *Dialogues*

1. A: 这些娃娃围棋手们的水平提高得真快。

   The young players of go do improve quickly.

   B: 是啊，连老师都败在他们的手下了。

   Yes. They can even defeat their teacher.

2. A: 工作虽然紧张，但也要注意锻炼身体呀。

   Although your work is busy, you should do exercises.

   B: 连厕所也没时间去，还锻炼呢！

   I even have no time to go to the toilet, much less for exercises!

练习 *Exercises*

用"连~也/都~"完成句子。Complete the sentences with the pattern.

1. 功课实在太多了，忙得我_____。

2. 真没想到这里贫富差距这么大，穷人穷得_____。

连~也/都~，甭/别说~了

解释 Explanation

强调表示一般人最容易做到的或应该做到的，可某人做不到，其他的更不必说了。或相反的情况，一般人难以做到的某人都能做到，其他的当然更不在话下。

Used to emphasize that someone cannot do what ordinary people can do easily, let alone other things. Or on the contrary, someone can do what ordinary people cannot, let alone other things.

例句 Examples

1. 这孩子连他爸爸的话都不听，甭说你了。

   This child does not even obey his father, let alone you.

2. 连上千元的衣服她也嫌不好，甭说几百块钱的了。

   She even considers thousand-yuan clothes bad, let alone hundred-yuan clothes.

3. 他连高等数学题做起来都不困难，别说这么简单的题了。

   He can solve higher mathematics problems without difficulty, let alone such simple ones.

4. 她连冰上芭蕾舞、国标准舞都会跳，别说这一般的交谊舞了。

   She can even dance ice ballet and ballroom dance of international standard, let alone such an ordinary ballroom dance.

对话 Dialogues

1. A：我看妹妹这病，老不见好，给她吃点儿中药试试？

   Sister has not recovered for a while. Why not try some Chinese medicine?

   B：她连西药都不肯吃，别说那么苦的中药了。

   She is unwilling to take Western medicine, much less bitter Chinese medicine.

2. A：你父母都会用电脑吗？

   Can both your parents use a computer?

   B：他们连手机都不会用，甭说电脑了。

   They cannot even use a cell phone, let alone computer.

练习 Exercises

用"连~也/都~，甭/别说~了"完成句子。Complete the sentences with the pattern.

1. 他家在农村，_____。

2. 这个箱子太重了，_____。

连~也/都~，何况

解释 *Explanation*

"何况"表示更进一层的意思。

Used to indicate a furthering meaning.

例句 *Examples*

1. 连三层楼他都懒得爬，何况六层呢？

   He is too lazy even to walk up three storeys, much less six.

2. 连学本国语言都得下苦工夫，更何况学外语呢？

   It demands hard work to learn the native language, let alone a foreign one.

3. 我连啤酒也喝不了，何况白酒呢？

   I cannot drink beer, let alone liquor.

4. 她结婚前连方便面也不会煮，更何况炒菜做饭呢？

   Before getting married, she could not cook instant noodles, much less cooking dishes.

对话 *Dialogues*

1. A: 对不起，我迷路了，所以来晚了。

   Sorry, I'm late because I got lost.

   B: 没事儿，连本地人也会迷路的，何况你是外国人。

   It doesn't matter. Even a local person gets lost, and you are a foreigner.

2. A: 哎呀，刮风了。

   Whoops, wind blows.

   B: 紧张什么！连沙尘暴我们都碰上过，何况这风并不算大。

   Don't be nervous. We have met even a sand storm, besides, the wind is not strong.

练习 *Exercises*

用"连~也/都~，何况"完成句子。Complete the sentences with the pattern.

1. A: 她吃不吃牛肉？

   B: 她是素食主义者，＿＿＿＿＿＿＿＿＿＿＿＿＿＿＿＿＿。

2. A: 你有博客吧？常上 MSN 吗？

   B: 我是电脑盲，＿＿＿＿＿＿＿＿＿＿＿＿＿＿＿＿。

汉语常用格式330例

解释 *Explanation*

用双重否定的句式表示肯定，以加强语气，意思是在某种条件下所有的人或事都没有例外地会出现某种情况，处于某种状态。多用于口语。

Used as a double negative to indicate strong affirmation, it means that under certain conditions, there is no exception to a certain action or state. It is mostly used colloquially.

例句 *Examples*

1. 长期吃垃圾食品，身体没个不受影响的。

   Always having junk food do effect people's health.

2. 平时爱贪图小便宜的人，没个不上当的。

   Anyone out for small advantages is taken in.

3. 看到那个人那么无理取闹，没个不生气的。

   Seeing that man making trouble out of nothing, all got angry.

4. 在专家、教授面前进行论文答辩，没个不紧张的。

   Anyone defending thesis in front of experts and professors gets nervous.

对话 *Dialogues*

1. A: 她不远千里来到这里上学，实现了她的梦想，可是非常想家。

   She traveled a long distance to study here and fulfilled her dream. But she is homesick.

   B: 初离故乡，没个不思念亲人的。

   Everyone who leaves home for the first time grows homesickness.

2. A: 中国有句俗话："七八九，嫌似狗。"是什么意思啊？

   A Chinese saying goes, "Seven, eight and nine, as annoying as a dog." What does it mean?

   B: 就是说，半大不小的男孩儿，没个不讨厌的。

   It means that any boy at that age is annoying.

练习 *Exercises*

用"没个不～的"完成句子。Complete the sentences with the pattern.

1. 这么可爱的女孩子，＿＿＿＿＿＿＿＿＿＿＿＿＿＿＿＿＿＿＿。

2. 这么高强度的训练，＿＿＿＿＿＿＿＿＿＿＿＿＿＿＿＿＿＿＿。

没什么大不了的

汉语常用格式330例

解释 *Explanation*

表示没什么大问题，情况没那么严重。

Used to indicate something is not a big deal or nothing serious.

例句 *Examples*

1. 不就是丢了钱嘛，没什么大不了的，再挣呗。

   You only lost some money. It's no big deal. You can earn it back.

2. 这事没什么大不了的，由我来处理，你就放宽心吧。

   It's no big deal. I will handle it. Set your mind at rest.

3. 他觉得这次没被续聘也没什么大不了的，正好另谋高就。

   He did not take it serious when the contract was not renewed. He took the opportunity to find a better job.

4. 这点儿困难没什么大不了的，大风大浪都经历过了，还怕这个？

   Such a difficulty is no big deal. You are not afraid of it after going through great ups and downs.

对话 *Dialogues*

1. A: 哎呀，电脑出问题了，我昨天写的文章全丢啦！

   Alas! There is something wrong with the computer. I lost all the articles I wrote yesterday.

   B: 这没什么大不了的，重新写一下不就得了。

   Nothing serious. Rewrite them.

2. A: 爸，我不小心把花瓶打碎了，您会说我吗？

   Dad, I broke the vase accidentally. Will you blame me?

   B: 这没什么大不了的，以后小心就是了。

   It's no big deal. Be careful later.

练习 *Exercises*

用"没什么大不了的"完成句子。Complete the sentences with the pattern.

1. A: 车子坏了，这可怎么办呢？

   B: _____。

2. A: 这次作文比赛我没拿到第一，只拿了个第二名。

   B: _____。

解释 *Explanation*

用于否定，表示不必、用不着、不值得的意思。

Used as a negative form to indicate something is not necessary or worthwhile.

例句 *Examples*

1. 这个手续一定要补办，没什么好说的。

   You must go through the formalities afterwards. It's not negotiable.

2. 这事就这么定了，你愿意不愿意都得照办，没什么好商量的。

   It's done. You must act on it whether you like or not. No more discussion.

3. 算了，没什么可讨论的了，散会！

   That's all. There is nothing else for discussion. The meeting is over.

4. 我跟他真找不到什么共同语言，没什么可说的。

   I really have no common language with him. We have nothing to talk about.

对话 *Dialogues*

1. A：这个电影没什么好看的，你怎么这么感兴趣?

   This film is not good. Why are you so interested in it?

   B：这就是代沟啊!

   This is the generation gap!

2. A：咱们再去跟他谈谈，希望他能改变态度。

   Let's talk with him again. I hope he will change his attitude.

   B：跟这样蛮不讲理的人没什么好谈的。

   No need to talk with such an unreasonable person.

练习 *Exercises*

用"没什么好/可 ~ 的"完成句子。Complete the sentences with the pattern.

1. A：今天你去商场买了些什么?

   B：看了半天，_____，就空着手回来了。

2. A：这些 DVD 你都不感兴趣吗?

   B：都是老片子，_____。

没有比 A 更~的了

解释 Explanation

表示 A 的程度最高。

Used to indicate A is of the highest degree.

例句 Examples

1. 这孩子真伶俐，没有比她更讨人喜欢的了。

   This girl is really cute. Nobody else is more lovely than her.

2. 没有比今天的考试更容易的了。

   Today's exam could not be easier.

3. 当前没有比发展经济更重要的了。

   At present, nothing else is more important than economic development.

4. 没有什么比失去亲人更让人伤心的了。

   Nothing is more saddening than losing a family member.

对话 Dialogues

1. A: 这里的姑娘打扮得都非常时尚。

   Girls here are all dressed in fashion.

   B: 那还用说，没有比她们更新潮的了。

   It's no doubt. Nobody is more fashionable than them.

2. A: 这件休闲服式样不错，有再长一点儿的吗?

   This leisurewear has a good design. Is there a longer one?

   B: 对不起，没有比这件更长的了。

   Sorry, no longer ones.

练习 Exercises

用"没有比 A 更~的了"改写句子。Rewrite the sentences with the pattern.

1. 对我来说，数学是最难学的。→_____。

2. 我的家乡是世上最美的地方。→_____。

没有 ~，哪（能）有 ~

解释 *Explanation*

表示没有某种前提，就没有某种结果。

Used to indicate that the result won't appear without a certain premise.

例句 *Examples*

1. 没有播种，哪有收获呢？

   Without sowing, there will be no harvest.

2. 没有父母的辛勤养育，哪有我今天的成就？

   How come my achievements without my parents' hard work in raising me?

3. 没有创业的艰难，哪能有成功的喜悦？

   There will be no happiness of success without hard work in starting up the business.

4. 没有前人种的树，哪能有后人乘凉的好地方？

   Without trees planted by our predecessors, how can we enjoy the cool shade?

对话 *Dialogues*

1. A: 没有雄厚的经济实力，哪能有强大的国防？

   Without economic power, how will there be strong national defense?

   B: 可是，高科技才是国防的基础。

   But it is advanced science and technology that is the very foundation of national defense.

2. A: 唉，这次新抗癌药品实验又没成功。

   Well, the experiment on new anti-cancer drugs failed again.

   B: 别泄气，没有失败，哪有成功。

   Don't give up. Without failure, there is no success.

练习 *Exercises*

用"没有~，哪（能）有~"改写句子。Rewrite the sentences with the pattern.

1. 只有经历过才会有这样切身的感受。　→＿＿＿＿＿＿＿＿＿＿＿＿＿＿。

2. 有了健康的身体才能享受幸福的生活。→＿＿＿＿＿＿＿＿＿＿＿＿＿＿。

解释 *Explanation*

表示应该做某事以避免发生不希望发生的事。

Used to indicate that something should be done so as to avoid what is undesirable.

例句 *Examples*

1. 咱们先查一下交通图吧，免得跑冤枉路。

   To avoid a vain trip, let us check the map first.

2. 读书写字姿势要正确，不要总趴着，免得变成个小驼背。

   Read and write in a correct posture. Don't lean over the table, or you may become a little humpback.

3. 最好把最近要做的事都记下来，免得到时候忘了。

   You'd better write down what you need to do, or you may forget them.

4. 到了那里，常来电话，省得大家为你担心。

   Call back often when you are there, so that we won't worry about you.

对话 *Dialogues*

1. A: 喂，小丽，还生气吗？下了班我就来看你，好吗？

   Hello, are you still angry, Xiaoli? I will come to see you after work, OK?

   B: 你别来，免得我见你更生气。

   Don't come, or I will be even angrier.

2. A: 现在我去领事馆办签证。

   I'm going to the consulate to get a visa.

   B: 检查一下材料是否都带齐了，省得又白跑一趟。

   To avoid a vain trip, check your materials first.

练习 *Exercises*

用"~，免得/省得 ~"完成句子。Complete the sentences with the pattern.

1. 凡事要早做准备，_____。

2. 带上把雨伞吧，_____。

解释 *Explanation*

表示 A 和 B 比较。

Used to compare A with B.

例句 *Examples*

1. 拿孩子跟成人比，那怎么行呢？

   It's not reasonable to compare children with adults.

2. 拿凉面跟热面比，我觉得凉面爽口。

   Compared with hot noodles, I think cold noodles are more refreshing.

3. 拿古典音乐和流行音乐比，古典音乐高雅。

   Compared with pop music, classic music is more elegant.

4. 拿美国人和欧洲人比，在某些方面美国人算是比较保守的。

   Compared with Europeans, American people are more conservative in some aspects.

对话 *Dialogues*

1. A: 他特爱喝酒，常喝醉，你也是吧？

   He is especially fond of spirit, and often gets drunk. Is it the same with you?

   B: 他是他，我是我，你别拿我跟他比。

   We are different. Don't compare me with him.

2. A: 你看人家小妞妞多细心啊！

   Look, what a careful girl!

   B: 大姐，你怎么老拿我和女孩子比？

   Sister, why do you often compare me with girls?

练习 *Exercises*

用"拿 A 跟/和 B 比"完成第一个对话，改写第二个句子。Complete the first dialogue and rewrite the second sentence with the pattern.

1. A: 强强，健健这次考得又比你好。

   B: 妈，你怎么总是_____？

2. 我们现在的生活水平比以前好得多。

   →_____。

拿～来说

解释 *Explanation*

表示用某人、某事做例子。

Used to take someone or something as an example.

例句 *Examples*

1. 拿气候来说，韩国首尔和北京差不多。

   In terms of climate, Seoul is similar to Beijing.

2. 拿工资待遇来说，外企要比国企高很多。

   In terms of payment, foreign enterprises offer higher than state-owned ones.

3. 每个人口味都不同，拿我来说，就是不喜欢吃甜的。

   Each person has his own taste. Take me as an example, I don't like sweet things.

4. 我觉得住在农村比住在城里好，就拿空气来说，农村的空气新鲜多了。

   I think it's better to live in the countryside than in the city. Take air as an example, the air in the countryside is much fresher.

对话 *Dialogues*

1. A：对门邻居的那个女孩子真讨人喜欢。

   The girl in the opposite room is really adorable.

   B：对，拿性格来说，既活泼，又开朗。

   I agree. Regarding disposition, she is cheerful and lively.

2. A：近几年中国的知识分子待遇提高了不少。

   In recent years, intellectuals in China have enjoyed improved status and payment.

   B：没错儿，拿大学老师来说，一般都超过了"小康"水平。

   It's true. Take college teachers as an example, their living standard is above being well-off.

练习 *Exercises*

用"拿～来说"完成句子。Complete the sentences with the pattern.

1. A：这两块儿手表你喜欢哪块儿？

   B：＿＿＿＿＿＿＿＿＿＿＿＿＿＿＿。

2. A：每个人都有自己的优点。

   B：可不吗，＿＿＿＿＿＿＿＿＿＿＿＿＿。

解释 *Explanation*

"哪儿"用在动词前表示否定，没有处所意义，是反问句式。"哪儿呀"多用于答话，委婉地否定对方说话的内容。

哪儿 is used before a verb in a rhetorical question to indicate negation. It does not refer to any place. While 哪儿呀 is mostly used in a reply to politely decline what the other said.

例句 *Examples*

1. 这么多人，一辆车哪儿坐得下？

   How could this bus hold so many people?

2. 大家相处得这么融洽，分别后哪儿能不想？

   We get along so well with each other. How can we not miss each other after departure?

3. 不爱开口，哪儿能学好外语？你非张口不行！

   How can you learn a foreign language well without speaking? You must open your mouth!

4. 自由惯了的人，一下子被管得死死的，哪儿受得了。

   Such a free person is suddenly strictly restricted. How can he bear that?

对话 *Dialogues*

1. A：听说你被解聘了？

   I heard you were fired, weren't you?

   B：哪儿呀，是我自己辞职的。

   No. I quit.

2. A：他说他们学校挺大的。

   He said his school was very big.

   B：哪儿大呀，他瞎吹，就这么几座楼。

   How can it be possible? He exaggerated. There are only several buildings.

练习 *Exercises*

用"哪儿（呀）"完成句子。Complete the sentences with the pattern.

1. A：你这条大围巾是新买的吗？挺好看的。

   B：＿＿＿＿＿＿＿＿＿＿＿＿＿＿＿＿。（哪儿呀）

2. A：今天的活动我就不参加了，你们好好玩儿吧。

   B：＿＿＿＿＿＿＿＿＿＿＿＿＿＿，那我们也不去了。（哪儿 行）

~哪儿，~哪儿

解释 *Explanation*

两个"哪儿"泛指同一地方，表示前后相关。

The two 哪儿 refer to the same place in general to indicate the connection between the two actions.

例句 *Examples*

1. 这个烟鬼，走到哪儿，抽到哪儿。

   This heavy smoker smokes wherever he goes.

2. 他是个助人为乐的人，走到哪儿，好事做到哪儿。

   He is ready to help others and does good deeds wherever he goes.

3. 你放心吧，他是个言行一致的人，从来都是说到哪儿，做到哪儿。

   Set your mind at rest. He is a man practicing what he preaches. He always does as he says.

4. 他的枪法可准了，指哪儿打哪儿，百发百中。

   He has a good marksmanship. He can hit every target you point to.

对话 *Dialogues*

1. A: 你姐姐真爱聊天。

   Your elder sister really loves to chat.

   B: 是啊，她走到哪儿聊到哪儿。

   It's true. She chats wherever she goes.

2. A: 明天我去同学家聚会。

   Tomorrow I will go to my classmate's for a gathering.

   B: 周末嘛，你想去哪儿，就去哪儿。

   It's weekend. You can go wherever you want.

练习 *Exercises*

用"～哪儿，～哪儿"完成句子。Complete the sentences with the pattern.

1. 他是个酒鬼，_____。

2. 他很好学，_____。

解释 *Explanation*

表示随时的意思。

Used to indicate "at any time".

例句 *Examples*

1. 这里叫出租车很方便，哪会儿叫哪会儿到。

   It's very convenient to call a taxi here. Whenever you call, it will arrive.

2. 蔡老板既精明，又很了解情况，公司哪会儿有问题，他就哪会儿出现。

   The boss, Mr. Cai, is smart and familiar with the company. He will be there whenever the company has problems.

3. 我家买了成箱的牛奶和饮料，我哪会儿想喝就哪会儿喝。

   I bought boxes of milk and beverage. I can drink whenever I want.

4. 我平时生活没什么规律，哪会儿饿了就哪会儿吃。

   My hours are not regular. I eat when I feel hungry.

对话 *Dialogues*

1. A: 王先生，我们以后怎么联系呢？

   Mr. Wang, how can I contact you later?

   B: 这是我的手机号码，哪会儿要找我，您就哪会儿给我打个电话。

   This is my cell phone number. Call me when you need.

2. A: 你什么时候再来呢？

   When will you come again?

   B: 你哪会儿想我了，我就哪会儿来看你，怎么样？

   I will come to see you when you miss me, alright?

练习 *Exercises*

用"哪会儿 ~ 哪会儿 ~"完成句子。Complete the sentences with the pattern.

1. A: 你什么时候去夏威夷度假？

   B: 现在太忙了，_____ 。

2. A: 咱们什么时候去看电影？

   B: 什么时候都可以，_____ 。

解释 *Explanation*

表示条件关系，泛指一个地方有某种条件，就会出现相应的结果。

Used in a conditional statement to indicate in general that where there is some condition, some result will occur correspondingly.

例句 *Examples*

1. 哪里交通便利，哪里经济发展就快。

   Where there are transport facilities, economy develops fast.

2. 哪里价廉物美，哪里顾客就多。

   Where products are cheap and good, it will attract many customers.

3. 哪里有梦想，哪里就有未来。

   Where there is a dream, there is the future.

4. 哪里有需要，哪里就有陆工程师的身影。

   Engineer Lu will show up wherever he is needed.

对话 *Dialogues*

1. A: 哪里老师好，哪里学生质量高。

   Where there are great teachers, there are good students.

   B: 对，有道理。

   I agree. It's true.

2. A: 建公寓必须注意绿化。

   Trees and lawns should go with newly built flats.

   B: 是啊，哪里空气好，哪里的房子就卖得快。

   True. Where the air is good, the flats sell fast.

练习 *Exercises*

用"哪里 ~ ，哪里 ~"改写句子。Rewrite the sentences with the pattern.

1. 有压迫的地方就有反抗。→＿＿＿＿＿＿＿＿＿＿＿＿＿＿＿。

2. 人多的地方就热闹。→＿＿＿＿＿＿＿＿＿＿＿＿＿＿。

解释 *Explanation*

表示不管客观情况如何，也不管遇到多少困难都要做某事。常用于口语。

Used often in oral Chinese to indicate the determination to do something in spite of difficulties.

例句 *Examples*

1. 哪怕路途再遥远，春节我也得回家跟父母团聚。

   Even it's far, I must go home to reunite with my parents in the Spring Festival.

2. 要想学好外语就得多听，哪怕听不懂，硬着头皮也要听下去。

   To learn a foreign language, you must listen more, even though you don't understand.

3. 当官的要多听老百姓的意见，哪怕有些意见考虑不周也没什么。

   Officials must listen more to ordinary people, even some points are not thorough.

4. 只要电视转播足球比赛，哪怕半夜三更，我家小钟都要看。

   Whenever there are live football matches on TV, my Xiaozhong will watch it even it's late night.

对话 *Dialogues*

1. A: 这孩子很有音乐天分。

   The child is talented in music.

   B: 是啊，哪怕再难的曲子，他都能又快又熟练地弹出来。

   True. He can play music quickly and skillfully, even difficult pieces.

2. A: 那个钻戒太贵了，别买了。

   That diamond ring is too expensive. Don't buy it.

   B: 不行！哪怕借钱，也要给你买。

   No way. I must buy it for you, even if I have to borrow money.

练习 *Exercises*

用"哪怕~，也/都~"完成句子。Complete the sentences with the pattern.

1. A: 早点儿睡吧，明天再写吧。

   B: 不，_____。

2. A: 你算了吧，他不会同意你这么干的。

   B: 我一定要干，_____。

解释 *Explanation*

表示做某事得考虑一定的条件，或表示能否做成某事取决于一定的条件。

Used to indicate that a certain condition must be taken into consideration when doing something, or the success of something depends on a certain condition.

例句 *Examples*

1. 我想明天就走，不过那得看能否买到票。

   I want to leave tomorrow, but it depends on whether I can get the ticket.

2. 这种红木家具我是想买，不过那得看价钱怎么样。

   I do want to buy this kind of rosewood furniture. But it depends on the price.

3. 明天能不能去长城那要看天气如何。

   It depends on the weather whether we can go to the Great Wall tomorrow.

4. 能不能说服他，那要看你的口才了。

   It depends on your eloquence to persuade him.

对话 *Dialogues*

1. A: 看样子你很喜欢狗?

   It seems you like dog very much, right?

   B: 那得看是什么狗。

   It depends on what kind of dog.

2. A: 最好跟谁都不要伤和气。

   You'd better not to hurt your relationship with anyone.

   B: 那要看对方是什么人。

   It depends on what kind of person he is.

练习 *Exercises*

用"那得/要看 ~"完成句子。Complete the sentences with the pattern.

1. 一个人事业能否成功＿＿＿＿＿＿＿＿＿＿＿＿＿＿＿＿＿＿。

2. 这孩子很挑食，吃多吃少＿＿＿＿＿＿＿＿＿＿＿＿＿＿＿＿＿。

解释 *Explanation*

表示不可能发生某种情况或出现某种状态，用反问的句式来强调。

Used as a rhetorical question for emphasis to indicate it's impossible that something or some situation occurs.

例句 *Examples*

1. 这孩子从小父母就这样惯，长大那还好得了？

   Spoiled like this by his parents, the child won't be good when growing up!

2. 这次考试，她毫无准备，分数那还高得了？

   She was totally unprepared for the exam. No wonder her remarks were not high.

3. 现在的人天天用电脑，手写的汉字那还好看得了？

   Nowadays people use computer every day. Their handwritings cannot be good.

4. 你看你，什么都尽挑名牌的买，钱那还够花得了？

   You buy famous brands for everything. How could your money suffice?

对话 *Dialogues*

1. A: 听说温家铺子快倒闭了。

   I heard that the Wen's shop was about to close down.

   B: 对顾客的态度那么坏，生意那还好得了？

   Their attitude to customers is so bad. No wonder the shop would close down.

2. A: 她怎么还是这么瘦？

   Why is she still so thin?

   B: 吃得这么少，又不注意营养，那还胖得了？

   She eats a little and pays no attention to nutrition. Of course she won't get fat.

练习 *Exercises*

用"那还～得了"完成句子。Complete the sentences with the pattern.

1. A: 这苹果怎么不太好吃啊？

   B: 都放了快一个月了，＿＿＿＿＿＿＿＿＿＿？

2. A: 我的脚好痛，真不舒服。

   B: 你穿的鞋跟儿那么高，＿＿＿＿＿＿＿＿＿＿。

解释 *Explanation*

表示已经很清楚，不用多说。用于答话。

Used in a reply to indicate a certainty unnecessary of further explanation.

对话 *Dialogues*

1. A：这次大赛，大姚肯定会得奖的。

    Da Yao will certainly take the cake in this competition.

    B：那还用说！他的水平比别人高多了。

    You bet! He is much better than others.

2. A：没有车，那我们就去不了啦?

    We have no car. So we cannot go there?

    B：那还用说！二十里的路，怎么走啊?

    That goes without saying. How can we walk ten km?

3. A：孔英玉同学即使进不了北大，也能考上别的重点大学。

    Even though Kong Yingyu cannot go to Peking University, she can enter another key university.

    B：那还用说，她的高考分数那么高！

    You bet! She got such high marks in the university entrance exam!

4. A：这场比赛要是再输了，他们连亚军也得不了啦！

    If they lose this match again, they cannot even get the second place!

    B：那还用说！

    That goes without saying.

练习 *Exercises*

用"那还用说"完成句子。Complete the sentences with the pattern.

1. A：你看他越来越瘦了，一定是学习太辛苦了。

    B：_____。

2. A：朋友们为你开了这么大的生日晚会，你肯定很兴奋吧?

    B：_____。

解释 *Explanation*

反问句式，表示否定或怀疑。"莫非"多用于书面语。

Used in a rhetorical question to indicate negation or doubt. 莫非 is often used in written language.

例句 *Examples*

1. 这么明显的错误我都没看出来，难道我真的老眼昏花了？

   I did not see such an obvious mistake. Am I dim-sighted from old age?

2. 孩子已经承认错误了，难道一定还要打他一顿不成？

   The child has admitted his mistake. Is there any need you beat him?

3. 总裁让秘书打电话约你都不行，莫非要他亲自去请你？

   The president asked his secretary to make an appointment with you and you refused. Is it that you want the president to invite you personally?

4. 我已经向你道歉了，你怎么还不依不饶的，莫非要我下跪不成？

   I have apologized to you. Why do you keep pestering me? Do I need to kneel?

对话 *Dialogues*

1. A: 吴教授，按照规定，这封信不能由别人转交。

   Professor Wu, according to our rules, this letter cannot be passed on by others.

   B: 怎么？莫非要我亲自来取不成？

   What? I must come to pick it up by myself?

2. A: 对不起，现在已经下班了。

   I'm sorry, but we are off work now.

   B: 什么？难道下午我还要再来一趟不成？

   What? Do I have to come here again this afternoon?

练习 *Exercises*

用"难道/莫非 ~（不成）"和所给的词语完成句子。Complete the sentences with the pattern and words in parentheses.

1. 小石还没有来？他可是一向守时的，_____？（病了）

2. 他怎么会知道这件事的？_____？（告诉）

汉语常用格式330例

解释 *Explanation*

说明决心已下，不管事情发展到什么程度也不改变。

Used to indicate the determination will not be changed in spite of anything.

例句 *Examples*

1. 不及格就是不及格，闹到天也没用。

   Failure is failure. It's no use whatever you do.

2. 这是规定，我必须按规定办，你就是闹到天也没用。

   I must act according to rules. It's no use whatever you do.

3. 你发这么高的烧，闹到天我也不能让你出门。

   You're having such a high fever. I won't let you out whatever you say.

4. 他利用职权，随心所欲，闹到天我也要反映到上边去。

   He abuses power and does as he wishes. I must report this to higher authorities anyway.

对话 *Dialogues*

1. A: 他说要到法院告你，跟你打官司。

   He said he would take you to court.

   B: 他是无理取闹，闹到天我也不怕。

   He's pestering unreasonably. I'm not afraid whatever he does.

2. A: 他说，一定得跟你见个面，当面和你谈。

   He said he must see you and talk to you face to face.

   B: 这种人，闹到天我也不会跟他见面的。

   I won't see such kind of person whatever he does.

练习 *Exercises*

用"闹到天也 ~"完成句子。Complete the sentences with the pattern.

1. A: 孩子又哭又闹，不肯去上幼儿园。

   B: 那怎么行，＿＿＿＿＿＿＿＿＿＿＿＿＿＿＿＿＿。

2. A: 你是不是得罪他了，他去老板那里告你的状了。

   B: 我只不过是坚持原则，＿＿＿＿＿＿＿＿＿＿＿＿＿＿＿＿＿。

解释 *Explanation*

表示对对方的行为不甚满意，或认为对方不必这样做。

Used to indicate dissatisfaction with the other's action, or express the view that the other doesn't have to do so.

例句 *Examples*

1. 你看你，这么点儿小事都办不好，还能干什么大事。

   How could you accomplish important matters while unable to handle such a little thing?

2. 你看你，每次考试都是临时抱佛脚。

   You always make a frantic last-minute effort for exams.

3. 你看你，年纪轻轻的，记性怎么这么差。

   You're young but have such a bad memory.

4. 你看你，来就来吧，干吗还带东西来呀。

   . Well, why bring gifts with you? Just come as you are.

对话 *Dialogues*

1. A: 老肖，这是我的一点儿心意，请收下。

   Lao Xiao, this conveys my regard. Please take it.

   B: 你看你，这么客气干吗?

   Well, why such formality?

2. A: 我可不买这么贵的东西。

   I won't buy such expensive goods.

   B: 你看你，总是不舍得给自己花点儿钱。

   You're always loath to spend money for yourself.

练习 *Exercises*

用"你看你，～"完成句子。Complete the sentences with the pattern.

1. A: 对不起，我迟到了。

   B: _____。

2. A: 哎呀，我拿错课本了。

   B: _____。

你 ~ 你的（~）

解释 *Explanation*

表示让对方继续做正在进行的事或打算要做的事，不必受干扰。

Used to let the other person continue what he/she is doing or planning to do and not need to be interrupted.

例句 *Examples*

1. 你忙你的，我随便看看。

   Continue your work. I'm just looking around.

2. 你们玩儿你们的，我先告辞了。

   You continue playing. I shall say goodbye first.

3. 你写你的作业，我去买菜做饭。

   You do your homework, and I will go to buy and prepare food.

4. 你搞你的研究，这种应酬的事我来负责。

   You do your reserch, and I'll take care of social intercourse.

对话 *Dialogues*

1. A：你回来啦，快洗洗手吃饭。

   You're back. Wash your hands and have some food.

   B：你吃你的，我现在不饿，一会儿再吃。

   You have the meal first. I'm not hungry now and will have it later.

2. A：我把电视关了，陪你说说话。

   I'll turn off the TV and chat with you.

   B：不用，不用，你看你的。

   No need to do that. Enjoy watching TV, please.

练习 *Exercises*

用"你~你的（~）"完成句子。Complete the sentences with the pattern.

1. A：我弹琴影响你睡觉吗？

   B：不碍事，_____。

2. A：家里出了这么大的事儿，我怎么能放心走呢？

   B：_____，家里有我呢。

汉语常用格式330例

解释 *Explanation*

"你"、"我"并不是实指，表示人多，有的人这样，有的人那样。

Used to indicate a lot of people, among whom some are doing this, some are doing that. 你 and 我 are indefinite.

例句 *Examples*

1. 一家人你说我笑，家里洋溢着欢乐的气氛。

   All family members talk and laugh. The home is full of happiness.

2. 办公室里常常你来我往的，怎么能静下心来写报告。

   There are often people coming and going in the office. How can I calm down to write the report?

3. 你瞧这些运动员，你追我赶的，都憋着股劲儿拿第一呢。

   Look, these athletes vie with each other. All are bursting with energy and ready to take the first prize.

4. 这真是你方唱罢我登场，那叫一个热闹。

   When you have sung your part, I take the stage. What a din!

对话 *Dialogues*

1. A: 你怎么刚来就要走啦?

   Why are you going? You just got here.

   B: 你打我闹的，吵死人了。

   They are kicking up a din. It's too noisy.

2. A: 怎么? 看不惯，生气啦?

   What? You don't like it? Are you angry?

   B: 这些人你拉我扯的，能不生气吗?

   How could I not get angry? These people are pulling at each other.

练习 *Exercises*

用"你~我~"和所给的词语完成句子。Complete the sentences with the pattern and words in parentheses.

1. 晚会上大家_____，热闹极了。(弹　唱)

2. 游乐场里孩子们_____，玩得高兴极了。(蹦　跳)

解释 *Explanation*

表示多个人轮流进行同一动作。"你"、"我"后接数量短语。

Used with quantifying phrases to indicate that several people act the same in turn.

例句 *Examples*

1. 你一杯，我一杯，一壶茶很快就喝光了。

   With all drinking, they soon drank up a pot of tea.

2. 大伙儿你一言，我一语，越聊越高兴。

   We chatted with everyone joining in. The more we chatted, the happier we were.

3. 听到这个惊人的消息，同学们你一句，我一句，讨论了起来。

   Hearing the surprising news, students started discussion with everyone joining in.

4. 这里卖的珍珠项链真漂亮，价格也合理，游客们你一条，我一条，抢购一空。

   The pearl necklaces were beautiful and the price was reasonable. With all tourists buying some, the necklaces sold out soon.

对话 *Dialogues*

1. A: 她怎么哭了？

   Why is she crying?

   B: 你一句，我一句的，这么批评，她哪能受得了！

   All criticized her. How could she bear that?

2. A: 那篇社论已经翻译完了？

   Have you finished translating the editorial?

   B: 是啊，大家你一段，我一段，很快就完稿了。

   Yes. All took part in the translation and finished it quickly.

练习 *Exercises*

用"你 ~ 我 ~"完成句子。Complete the sentences with the pattern.

1. A: 这次给灾区捐款，同学们捐得多不多？

   B: 多，_____，很快就捐了上万元。

2. A: 那么大个西瓜，这么快就吃完了？

   B: 是啊，这么多人，大家_____，很快就吃光了。

解释 *Explanation*

表示说话人在比较了两个都不如意的情况后，选择前者。强调后者是说话人最不情愿的事。

Used to indicate that the speaker chooses the former one after comparing two unsatisfactory conditions, which emphasizes that the latter one is the last thing the speaker would do.

例句 *Examples*

1. 她本性善良，宁可自己吃亏、受委屈，也不愿伤害别人。
   She is kind in nature. She'd rather suffer losses or be wronged herself than harm others.

2. 我宁可砸锅卖铁，也不能让孩子辍学。
   I would rather sacrifice everything than let my child drop out of school.

3. 我宁可一辈子独身，也不嫁给这样窝囊的人。
   I'd rather stay single all my life than marry such a weak and cowardly man.

4. 古人说：宁可不吃肉，也不能住在没有竹子的地方。
   Ancient man said, "I'd rather give up eating meat than live in a house without bamboo."

对话 *Dialogues*

1. A：老夏这人可真厚道。
   Lao Xia is really good-hearted.

   B：是啊，他宁可自己吃亏，也不愿对不起朋友。
   I agree. He would rather suffer losses himself than do any disservice to friends.

2. A：假如因特殊情况考前未做好准备，考试时你会偷看别人的吗？
   Will you peep at other's paper at exam if you're not well prepared for special reasons?

   B：绝不会，我宁可没好成绩，也不能没人格。
   Absolutely no. I'd rather get poor marks than lose my dignity.

练习 *Exercises*

用"宁可 ~ ，也不 ~"完成句子。Complete the sentences with the pattern.

1. 上下班时公交车实在太挤了，_____。

2. 虽然他是我的领导，但这是原则问题，_____。

解释 *Explanation*

表示某人要做某事的决心，并为此情愿接受前面所说的不利的情况或条件。

Used to indicate someone is determined to do something and thus would accept the bad situation or condition that has been mentioned.

例句 *Examples*

1. 全村的人意见一致，宁可少分红甚至不分红，也要把学校建起来。

All villagers have reached the consensus that in order to set up a school they would rather get less or even no bonus.

2. 我宁可被人嘲笑为傻子，也要按照自己想好的路子走下去。

Following my own way, I would rather be laughed at as a fool.

3. 她是那种宁可放弃事业，也要保全爱情的女人。

She is that kind of woman who would rather sacrifice career for love.

4. 有些人特好面子，宁可借钱，也要办个体面的婚事。

Some people are especially concerned about face-saving, and they would rather borrow money so as to hold a decent wedding ceremony.

对话 *Dialogues*

1. A: 你觉得 GDP 重要，还是环境重要？

   Which one do you think is more important, GDP or environment?

   B: 当然环境重要，宁可牺牲 GDP，也要保护环境。

   Environment, of course. We would rather sacrifice GDP for environmental protection.

2. A: 你说如果我现在把股票卖了，会不会踏空啊？

   If I sell the share now, will it be the case that the price goes up and I earn nothing?

   B: 宁可踏空，也要回避风险。

   We would rather earn no money than take risks.

练习 *Exercises*

用"宁可 ~，也要 ~"完成句子。Complete the sentences with the pattern.

1. 人的生命是第一重要的，_____。

2. 孩子是父母的心头肉，父母_____。

解释 *Explanation*

表示多或多而杂乱。

Used to indicate multiplicity or disorder.

例句 *Examples*

1. 他写字从来不认真，总是七扭八歪的。

   He never writes carefully. He always writes scribbles.

2. 我爸七弄八弄，居然把这玩具修好了。

   My father tried several times, and to our surprise, he finally repaired the toy.

3. 这里的路太复杂，车七拐八拐，都把我拐糊涂了。

   The road system here is very complicated. The car turned so many times that I finally got lost.

4. 大家七手八脚地，很快就把汉语演讲比赛的会场布置好了。

   With everyone joining in, the room was soon ready for the Chinese speech competition.

对话 *Dialogues*

1. A: 这篇论文质量实在太差了，根本无法通过。

   This quality of the thesis is really poor. We simply cannot pass it.

   B: 是，七拼八凑的，毫无自己的见解。

   I agree. It is a scissors-and-paste stuff and the author has no idea of his own.

2. A: 主任，你为什么不让大家说了？

   Why don't you allow us speak, Director?

   B: 七嘴八舌的，我听谁的？

   So many people talked all at the same time. Who should I listen to?

练习 *Exercises*

选词填空。Choose the right phrases to fill in the blanks.

七搞八搞　　七拼八凑　　七上八下　　七嘴八舌

1. 听说要提高印花税，股民们心里＿＿＿＿＿＿＿＿的。

2. 一听说在校园里发生了这样的事，大家＿＿＿＿＿＿＿＿地议论开了。

汉语常用格式330例

千~万~

解释 *Explanation*

表示很多的意思，有时也表示强调或加重语气。

Used to indicate multiplicity, and sometimes used for emphasis or in a stronger mood.

例句 *Examples*

1. 经过千辛万苦的训练，这次比赛他终于拿到了金牌。

   After going through untold hardships of training, he finally won the gold medal in this competition.

2. 现在我认识到，千错万错，出了这样的事我不该瞒着她。

   Now I realize that I made many mistakes, but I should let her know when it occurred.

3. 外面的世界千好万好，也不如家里好。

   No matter how good the outside world is, it is not as good as home.

4. 千不该万不该，我不该搞这行，真是后悔莫及。

   I regret a thousand times over it. I should not engage in this business. Now my remorse is too late.

对话 *Dialogues*

1. A: 想开公司？哪儿有那么容易！

   You want to start a company? It's not so easy!

   B: 即使千难万难，我也要试试。

   I will have a try in spite of all the difficulties.

2. A: 人人都说，世上只有妈妈好。

   Everyone agree that mom is the best in the world.

   B: 可不是，妈妈的恩情，千言万语说不尽。

   It's true. No words can describe mom's deep affection.

练习 *Exercises*

选词填空。Choose the right phrases to fill in the blanks.

千叮万嘱	千恩万谢	千山万水	千真万确

1. 出门前，妈妈＿＿＿＿＿＿＿＿＿＿＿＿＿＿＿＿＿＿，一定要注意安全。

2. 这个消息是＿＿＿＿＿＿＿＿＿＿＿＿＿＿＿的，我绝不会搞错。

解释 *Explanation*

"前"和"后"呼应，用来加重语气。表示两种事物或行为在时间或空间上一先一后，或表示反复。

Used for emphasis to indicate the sequential connection in space or time between two things or two actions, or to indicate repetition.

例句 *Examples*

1. 应该了解事情的前因后果，再做判断。
   Make judgment after getting to know the entire matter.
2. 真不巧，方会计前脚走，田主任后脚就来了。
   As luck would have it, Director Tian arrived the moment Accountant Fang left.
3. 这个相声真有意思，大家都笑得前仰后合的。
   This crosstalk is really interesting. All of us are shaking with laughter.
4. 这个地方前不着村后不着店的，哪里去弄吃的呢？
   This place is in the middle of nowhere. Where can we get food?

对话 *Dialogues*

1. A：你到底去不去？
   Are you going or not?
   B：我前思后想，觉得还是不去好。
   I have thought of it over again and decided that I'd better not go.

2. A：这件事还得考虑考虑。
   I must ponder over it.
   B：别前怕狼后怕虎的，这样什么事也干不成。
   You must banish all unnecessary fears, otherwise you will achieve nothing.

练习 *Exercises*

选词填空。Choose the right phrases to fill in the blanks.

前因后果	前思后想	前摇后晃	前呼后拥

1. 他是大明星，出门总是_____的。

2. 他非常谨慎，不管干什么都要_____才做决定。

汉语常用格式330例

181

解释 *Explanation*

用于答话。表示客气地否定或纠正对方所说的。或用于受别人称赞时，表示谦虚。或用于别人向自己道谢或说客气话时，表示不必。

Used in an answer to politely negate or correct what the other speaker said, or often to express modesty when praised, or to indicate "it doesn't matter" when accepting gratitude or apology.

对话 *Dialogues*

1. A：回到美国以后，别忘了我们啊！

   Don't forget us when you return to America!

   B：瞧你说的，怎么会呢？

   Fancy your talking like that. How can that be possible?

2. A：你的字和书法家写的一样。

   Your handwriting is the same as a calligrapher's.

   B：瞧你说的，我的字还差得远呢。

   You flatter me! Mine is much inferior.

3. A：你唱歌在我们全公司是数一数二的。

   Your singing is one of the best in our company.

   B：瞧你说的，我哪儿有那么棒啊。

   You flatter me! I couldn't be that good.

4. A：实在是太感谢了，我们在这里的这段日子，人生地不熟的，多亏有你帮忙。

   Thank you very much. We are strangers here. But owing to your help, we could have a good time.

   B：瞧你说的，咱们是什么关系！

   Don't mention it. We are on good terms!

练习 *Exercises*

用"瞧你说的，~"完成句子。Complete the sentences with the pattern.

1. A：你现在可是个知名人士了。

   B：_____。

2. A：你看上去真年轻，哪里像这么大年纪的人啊！

   B：_____。

解释 *Explanation*

表示别人愿意怎样就怎样，或原来怎样就怎样，不必去管。

Used to indicate to let somebody do as he likes or to let it go.

例句 *Examples*

1. 他已经长大成人了，让他自己闯去吧！

   He has grown up. Let him temper himself.

2. 只有两个名额，让他们争去吧，我不想去凑热闹。

   There are only two for the quota. Let they compete. I don't want to join in.

3. 随他折腾去吧，反正就这么点儿家产。

   Let him do as he likes. After all, there is only such a little family fortune.

4. 房间随它乱去吧，我也不想收拾了。

   The room is disorderly. Let it go. I don't want to tidy it up.

对话 *Dialogues*

1. A: 作为领导人，他怎么能对大家的要求置之不理？

   He is a leader. How could he totally disregard our demands?

   B: 随他去吧，说也没用。

   Let him go. It's no use blaming him.

2. A: 有的人老爱在背后说别人的坏话。

   Some people like to speak ill of others behind their back.

   B: 让他们说去吧，这种人没什么市场。

   Let them gossip. Such people are not appreciated.

练习 *Exercises*

用"让/随 ~ 去吧"完成句子。Complete the sentences with the pattern.

1. A: 说了她多少次了，不能老这么晚回家，不安全。

   B: _____。

2. A: 哎呀，几件衬衣都脏了，也没时间洗。

   B: _____。

如果 ~ , 就 ~

解释 *Explanation*

表示假设有了某种条件，就会出现相应的情况或相关的结果。

Used to indicate a thing or result would occur on a presumed condition.

例句 *Examples*

1. 如果连放五天假，我就去西藏旅游。

   If the holiday lasted five consecutive days, I would go for a trip in Tibet.

2. 她如果身高一米七五，就会去当服装模特。

   If she were 1.75 meters tall, she would make herself a model.

3. 如果环境污染得不到有效的治理，企业发展后劲儿就会不足。

   If environmental pollution cannot be effectively controlled, enterprises will have no sustainability for development.

4. 如果出现通货膨胀，政府就一定会进行宏观调控。

   If inflation occurs, the government will certainly exercise macroeconomic control.

对话 *Dialogues*

1. A: 谢谢你帮了我的大忙，问题解决了。

   Thank you very much. You did me a big favor. My problem has been solved.

   B: 如果以后还有问题，就请随时来找我。

   Come to me at any time when you have problems later.

2. A: 今天又是黑色星期一，大盘下跌了190点。

   Today is another black Monday. The large-cap index dropped by 190 points.

   B: 如果政府再不救市，股民们就会失去信心，出现赎回潮。

   If the government still does not rescue the stock market, stockholders will lose confidence, which in turn will result in a wave of redemption.

练习 *Exercises*

用"如果 ~ , 就 ~"完成句子。Complete the sentences with the pattern.

1. A: 你们明天去不去郊游?

   B: _____。

2. A: 我同屋迷上了玩儿游戏，一天至少有七八个小时坐在电脑前。

   B: _____。

如果说 ~，那（么）~ 则/就 ~

解释 *Explanation*

假设某种说法成立或某种情况存在，那另一种说法或情况也肯定有理由存在。"则"多用于书面语。

Used to indicate that if some statement is true, then another statement is true as well; or if a situation exists, then another situation will naturally exist. 则 is often used in written language.

例句 *Examples*

1. 如果说你是一本书，那我就是一首诗。

   If you were a book, I would be a poem.

2. 如果说人生是一首优美的乐曲，那痛苦则是一个不可缺少的音符。

   If life is a piece of melodious music, misery will be an indispensable note.

3. 如果说政治关系是两国关系的核心，那么经贸、人文交流则是双边关系的两翼。

   If political relationship is the core, then economic and trade exchanges and cultural and educational exchanges will be the two wings for bilateral relations.

4. 如果说各种规章制度是规范员工行为的"有形规则"，那么企业文化就作为一种"无形规则"存在于员工的意识中。

   If various rules and regulations are "visible rules" for employees, corporate culture exists in their minds as an "invisible rule".

对话 *Dialogues*

1. A: 德语太难学了，我没信心学下去。

   German is difficult to learn. I lack the confidence to continue learning it.

   B: 如果说德语难学，那么中文就是难上加难了。

   If German is difficult, then Chinese is much more difficult.

2. A: 这也算经典小说啊？

   This should not be called a classic novel.

   B: 如果说这都不算经典小说，那就没什么经典的了。

   If this is not a classic, then there will be no classics at all.

练习 *Exercises*

用"如果说 ~，那（么）~ 则/就 ~"完成句子。Complete the sentences with the pattern.

1. A: 你说减肥有什么好办法吗？

   B: 如果说减肥有什么好办法的话，＿＿＿＿＿＿＿＿＿＿＿＿＿＿。

2. A: 我是个没什么文化的人。

   B: 如果说你是个没文化的人，＿＿＿＿＿＿＿＿＿＿＿＿＿＿。

解释 *Explanation*

表示数目不多或间隔时间短。

Used to indicate a small number or a short interval.

例句 *Examples*

1. 这事说起来话长，三言两语说不完。

   It is a long story and I cannot explain it in a few words.

2. 上课铃响了，学生们才三三两两地往教室走。

   When the bell rang, students walked toward the classroom by twos and threes.

3. 她手脚特麻利，三下两下就把厨房收拾得井井有条。

   She did things deftly and soon tidied up the kitchen.

4. 看来他真是饿坏了，这么一大碗面条，他三口两口就吃完了。

   It seems he was really hungry. He ate up such a big bowl of noodles in a few mouthfuls.

对话 *Dialogues*

1. A：一般女孩子出嫁了，也老惦着妈妈。

   Girls always miss their mom after marriage.

   B：可不，我表姐也是三天两头往娘家跑。

   It's true. My cousin returns to her parents' home almost every day.

2. A：做什么事情，都不能三天打鱼两天晒网。

   You cannot work off and on for anything.

   B：当然，要不然一事无成。

   Certainly. Otherwise, you will achieve nothing.

练习 *Exercises*

选词填空。Choose the right phrases to fill in the blanks.

> 三言两语　　三天两头　　三三两两　　三天打鱼两天晒网

1. 他们这帮中学同学关系可真亲密，＿＿＿＿＿＿＿＿＿＿＿地聚会。

2. 他的发言十分简短，＿＿＿＿＿＿＿＿＿＿就说完了。

解释 *Explanation*

表示很干脆，动作很快。

Used to indicate to act or move neatly and quickly.

例句 *Examples*

1. 一大堆垃圾，大家三下五除二，一会儿就清理干净了。

   They finished clearing off this big pile of rubbish in a jiffy.

2. 无论做什么，她从来都是三下五除二，一下子就干完了。

   Whatever she does, she always finishes it quickly.

3. 你看我多利索，这么多图书卡片，三下五除二，半天工夫就抄写完了！

   Look, how quick I am! I finished copying so many catalog cards in half a day!

4. 因为赶着去上班，两大块儿面包他三下五除二就塞进肚子里了。

   As he was hurrying to work, he soon ate up two big pieces of bread.

对话 *Dialogues*

1. A：秦部长作风泼辣，处理任何问题都很干脆。

   Minister Qin works in a bold and vigorous style. He handles everything with decision.

   B：真的。多么复杂的问题到他手里，三下五除二，就能提出解决方案。

   I agree. He can quickly propose a solution to even a very complicated problem.

2. A：经理助理小郝很能干。来了什么事，三下五除二，就处理妥当了。

   Manager Assistant Xiao Hao is very capable. She can handle anything well in a jiffy.

   B：怪不得老板总夸奖她呢。

   That's why the boss often praises her.

练习 *Exercises*

用"三下五除二"写两个句子。Make two sentences with the pattern.

1. _____ 。

2. _____ 。

解释 *Explanation*

用在数量词后，表示大概是这个数量。意思同 " ~ 左右"。

Used after a quantifier to indicate a rough quantity, same as ~ 左右。

例句 *Examples*

1. 她钓上来的这条鱼可真不小，有五斤上下呢。

   The fish she trolled is really big. It's about five *jin*.

2. 我们的校长才三十岁上下，真是年轻有为。

   Our schoolmaster is only about 30 years old, young and promising.

3. 考古队新发现的这个地下古城估计有两千年上下的历史。

   The underground city discovered by the archeological team has a history of about 2,000 years.

4. 这种小巧玲珑的笔记本电脑重量只有一公斤上下。

   This kind of small and exquisite laptop weighs only about one kilogram.

对话 *Dialogues*

1. A: 你们学校有多少学生?

   How many students are there in your school?

   B: 两千上下吧。

   Around 2,000.

2. A: 你提一下看看这箱子有多重?

   You carry this box, to see how heavy it is.

   B: 我看，三十斤上下。

   Well, it's about 30 *jin*.

练习 *Exercises*

用 " ~ 上下" 完成句子。Complete the sentences with the pattern.

1. 他的年龄在_____ 。

2. 我的力气可大了，能拿动_____的东西。

解释 *Explanation*

表示估计数目的最小限度，常用于口语。

Used often in oral Chinese to indicate the minimum of an estimated numeral.

例句 *Examples*

1. 这礼堂少说也能坐两千人上下。

   This auditorium can hold at least 2,000 people.

2. 我这次去上海、新疆考察，少说也得个把月才能回来。

   I'm going to Shanghai and Xinjiang on an inspection tour and will be back at least one month later.

3. 那次参加反战示威游行的队伍，少说也有两三万人。

   There are at least 20,000 to 30,000 people joining in that anti-war demonstration.

4. 这次义演筹得的善款少说也有上百万人民币。

   The fund raised at that charity performance totaled at least one million yuan.

对话 *Dialogues*

1. A: 你看这副翡翠手镯值多少钱？

   How much does this pair of green jade bracelets cost?

   B: 少说也得上万。

   At least 10,000 yuan.

2. A: 去美国私立学校留学，我看一年得要两万美金。

   I think it costs 20,000 US dollars per year to study at a private school in the United States.

   B: 不止，不止，少说也得三万出头。

   More than that amount. I think it's at least over 30,000.

练习 *Exercises*

用"少说（也）~"完成句子。Complete the sentences with the pattern.

1. A: 整理完这些听课笔记，需要多长时间？

   B: _____。

2. A: 当法官、律师一个月能挣多少钱？

   B: _____。

解释 *Explanation*

表示否定、不同意。常与动词、形容词连用。与动词连用有时带有不满的意味。

Used often with a verb or an adjective to indicate negation or disagreement, and sometimes dissatisfaction when used with a verb.

例句 *Examples*

1. 大家都休息了，你嚷嚷什么！

   All have rested. Why are you shouting?

2. 雨下得这么大，还散什么步！

   Take a stroll? Don't you see it's raining so hard?

3. 生什么气！小孩子淘气很正常。

   Why do you get angry? Children are naturally naughty.

4. 他就是作案嫌疑人，证据确凿，还犹豫什么？

   He is the criminal suspect, and there is sufficient evidence. Why do you hesitate?

对话 *Dialogues*

1. A: 你这身儿打扮，我真看不惯，太难看了！

   I don't like your dress. It's too ugly!

   B: 难看什么！懂吗？这叫新潮。

   Ugly! It's fashion. Understand?

2. A: 你好好跟他谈谈嘛，也许他会改变态度的。

   You do have a good talk with him, maybe he will change his attitude.

   B: 谈什么！跟这种人没什么好谈的！

   A good talk! I have nothing to talk with such kind of person!

练习 *Exercises*

用"～什么"完成句子。Complete the sentences with the pattern.

1. A: 快走！快走！来不及了！

   B: ＿＿＿＿＿＿＿＿＿＿＿＿＿＿！再等五分钟。

2. A: 他要是当个作家也许还行。

   B: ＿＿＿＿＿＿＿＿＿＿＿＿＿＿！他这个人缺少想象力。

解释 *Explanation*

表示不同意或不必去考虑的意思，多用于引述别人的话。有"什么 A 不 A 的"和"什么 A 呀 B 的"两种形式。

Used mostly in quoting the other's words to indicate disagreement or taking no account. There are two forms：什么 A 不 A 的 and 什么 A 呀 B 的.

例句 *Examples*

1. 想吃就吃，什么钱不钱的！

   Eat as you wish. Don't mention money!

2. 管谁说什么好看不好看的，自己觉得适合自己就行。

   It's OK as long as you think it fits you, whether others say it's pretty or not.

3. 拿着吧，什么你呀我的，咱们是铁哥们儿。

   Don't mention it. Just take it. We are sworn friends.

4. 什么大呀小的，有得吃就不错了。

   Don't be choosy. It's OK as long as we have something to eat.

对话 *Dialogues*

1. A：大家都说你是帅哥，你一定要交个漂亮的女友。

   Everybody thinks you are very handsome. You should have a beautiful girlfriend.

   B：什么漂亮不漂亮的，心眼好、性格好最重要。

   I don't think so. Good nature and personality are most important.

2. A：这套结婚礼服质量、式样都不错，可价钱太贵了。

   This wedding dress has a high quality as well as a good design, but it's too expensive.

   B：什么贵不贵的，买！

   Price is not important. Buy it!

练习 *Exercises*

用"什么～不～的"完成句子。Complete the sentences with the pattern.

1. A：我的男朋友什么都好，就是个子有点儿矮。

   B：_____。

2. A：你给我买了这么多东西，让你破费了。

   B：_____。

解释 *Explanation*

"什么"用在名词前，表示在所说的范围内没有例外。

Used to indicate that there is no exception within the limits mentioned, with a noun used after 什么.

例句 *Examples*

1. 我刚回国，什么情况都不了解。

   I just returned from overseas and am still in the dark.

2. 在我们单位，杜会计什么人都认识，而且都能谈得来。

   In our company, Accountant Du knows everyone and gets along well with everyone.

3. 这些天她累得够呛，回家来什么话也不想说。

   She has been so exhausted these days that she didn't want to say anything after coming home.

4. 孩子到了逆反年龄，什么事也不愿意告诉父母。

   The child is at an age of rebellion, and is unwilling to tell anything to his parents.

对话 *Dialogues*

1. A: 没见你看报纸，怎么什么消息都知道？

   How can you know everything since I haven't seen you read newspaper?

   B: 我上网啊。

   I do get on the Internet.

2. A: 你见多识广，什么事情都懂。

   You're well-read and well-informed, and know everything.

   B: 哪里，哪里，我也是一知半解。

   Not at all. I just have a smattering of knowledge.

练习 *Exercises*

用"什么 ~ 都/也 ~"完成句子。Complete the sentences with the pattern.

1. A: 上周末你回学校都见到谁了？

   B: 除了孔老师，＿＿＿＿＿＿＿＿＿＿＿＿＿＿＿ 。

2. A: 刚来这里的时候，你感觉怎么样？

   B: 很不好，因为＿＿＿＿＿＿＿＿＿＿＿＿＿，没有朋友。

解释 *Explanation*

表示没必要、不值得。用在"看、唱、学、吃、喝、玩、买"等动词后边。

Used after a verb such as 看, 唱, 学, 吃, 喝, 玩, 买 to indicate to be unnecessary or not worthwhile.

例句 *Examples*

1. 这些节目没意思，看什么劲儿呀！

   The programs are not interesting. Why watch it?

2. 这事和我根本没关系，你和我说个什么劲儿！

   It has nothing to do with me. Why are you talking about it with me?

3. 他既然不想说，你还老问个什么劲儿！

   Why do you keep asking since he is unwilling to say?

4. 这么老掉牙的歌，还听个什么劲儿！

   The song is too old. Why listen to it?

对话 *Dialogues*

1. A: 他年纪这么大了，还学什么劲儿！

   He is so old. Why still study?

   B: 俗话说：活到老，学到老嘛。

   As the saying goes, it's never too old to learn.

2. A: 这种牌，太简单了，玩儿个什么劲儿！

   This kind of cards is too simple. It's not interesting!

   B: 反正没事，消磨时间呗。

   Just to kill time. Anyhow, we have nothing to do.

练习 *Exercises*

用"~什么劲儿"完成句子。Complete the sentences with the pattern.

1. 你看你，这鸡翅也没什么肉，＿＿＿＿＿＿＿＿＿＿＿＿＿＿＿＿。

2. 这种无聊的电视剧，＿＿＿＿＿＿＿＿＿＿＿＿＿＿＿ 。

~什么，~什么

解释 *Explanation*

"什么"是泛指，前后所指相同，前者决定后者。

Two 什么, referring to the same unspecific things, used one after another to indicate that the first one determines the second.

例句 *Examples*

1. 快开学了，你还缺什么，就买什么。

   A new semester will begin. Buy whatever you lack.

2. 今天我做东，你们想吃什么，我就请什么。

   Today I will treat you. You can order whatever you want to eat.

3. 高考就像个指挥棒，高考常考什么，老师就教什么。

   The college entrance exam is a baton. Teachers teach what are often tested.

4. 孩子小，没有判断力，大人教什么，他就学什么。

   The boy is too little to judge things. He learns whatever adults teach him.

对话 *Dialogues*

1. A：这个箱子装什么好呢？

   What shall I place in this box?

   B：想装什么，装什么呗。

   Whatever you want.

2. A：你要我说些什么呢？

   What do you want me to say?

   B：你想说什么就说什么，我都洗耳恭听。

   Whatever you want. I am all ears.

练习 *Exercises*

用"~什么，~什么"完成句子。Complete the sentences with the pattern.

1. 今天放假，不用上课，我可以_____。

2. 有些独生子女真成了"小皇帝"了，他们_____。

解释 *Explanation*

表示任指，指所说的、所涉及的都包括在内。

Used to refer to things in general, and what's mentioned or involved is inclusive.

例句 *Examples*

1. 心情不好时，我什么都干不下去。

   When in bad mood, I can hardly do anything.

2. 这位总理脑子真快，记者提什么问题都难不倒他。

   The premier has a quick mind, and can answer all the questions reporters raise.

3. 我困死了，现在你跟我说什么也是白说。

   I'm too sleepy to respond to whatever you talk.

4. 真是初生牛犊不怕虎，年轻人常常什么也不怕，敢闯敢干。

   As newborn calves are not afraid of tigers, young people often fear nothing and dare do anything.

对话 *Dialogues*

1. A: 你这次可是出远门，再想想，该带的还缺什么？

   You're going to travel far. Think about it. What else should you take along?

   B: 别担心，该带的都带了，什么也不缺了。

   Don't worry. I've taken all that should be taken. I need nothing else.

2. A: 难得来一回，还要买些什么吗？

   You don't come very often. What else to buy?

   B: 都全了，什么也不用买了。

   No, nothing else.

练习 *Exercises*

用"什么也/都 ~"完成句子。Complete the sentences with the pattern.

1. 你别问我，昨天我不在办公室，＿＿＿＿＿＿＿＿＿＿＿＿ 。

2. 你是怎么搞的，学了半天，＿＿＿＿＿＿＿＿＿＿＿＿。

解释 *Explanation*

用"甚至"来举出极端事例，表示突出、强调。前面常和"不但"、"不仅"连用，后面常用"也"、"都"。

Used often in conjunction with 不但 or 不仅 before it, and 也 or 都 after it for emphasis to indicate an extreme example.

例句 *Examples*

1. 这次颁奖会不但他的家长来了，甚至一些亲朋好友也来了。

   Not only his parents but also some of his relatives and friends attended that award ceremony.

2. 世界上竟会有这样稀奇古怪的事！我甚至连听都没听说过。

   There is such a bizarre thing in the world! I never hear of it.

3. 她这么个年纪轻轻的姑娘，真受不了这样的打击，甚至都不想活了。

   She is too young to stand such a blow. She even doesn't want to live.

4. 他爷爷得了失忆症，甚至自己的名字都忘了。

   His grandpa has got amnesia and even forgets his own name.

对话 *Dialogues*

1. A：现在，不少儿童智商都很高。

   Many children are very intelligent now.

   B：是啊，甚至三岁的娃娃也会玩儿电脑游戏。

   It's true. Even a three-year-old child can play computer games.

2. A：不管是东方国家还是西方国家，不少孩子都喜欢孙悟空。

   Many children, whether in the East or West, like the Monkey King.

   B：岂止孩子，甚至大人也喜欢。

   Even adults like him.

练习 *Exercises*

用"~，甚至~"完成句子。Complete the sentences with the pattern.

1. 这两天实在是太忙了，忙到＿＿＿＿＿＿＿＿＿＿＿＿＿＿ 。

2. 好久没写汉字了，差不多都忘了，＿＿＿＿＿＿＿＿＿＿＿＿＿ 。

汉语常用格式330例

解释 *Explanation*

表示有时这样，有时那样，常出现完全相反的现象。

Used to indicate the difference from time to time, more often two opposite statuses.

例句 *Examples*

1. 这电视的图像时隐时现，真气人。

   The television picture appears one moment and disappears the next. It's annoying.

2. 现在是梅雨季节，在我们南方牛毛细雨时下时停。

   It's now the rainy season. In South China, one moment it drizzles, the next it stops.

3. 前面的那辆车开得是时快时慢，让我超也不是，不超也不是。

   The car in front is sometimes fast, sometimes slow. I don't know whether I should overtake it.

4. 主机的风扇是不是出毛病了? 怎么声音时大时小?

   Is there anything wrong with the host fan? Why is the sound now loud, and then low?

对话 *Dialogues*

1. A: 她每天什么时候来?

   When does she come every day?

   B: 没准儿，时早时晚。

   Not at a fixed time. She is sometimes early, sometimes late.

2. A: 这孩子的成绩不错嘛，几门主科都是优。

   The child has a good performance. He got A on all the major subjects.

   B: 哪儿呀，不稳定，时好时坏。

   Not really. His marks are sometimes good, sometimes bad.

练习 *Exercises*

选词填空。Choose the right phrases to fill in the blanks.

> 时好时坏　　时快时慢　　时明时暗　　时左时右

1. 她的病情不稳定，_____。

2. 灯光一闪一闪的，前面的建筑物也_____。

汉语常用格式330例

时而~时而~

汉语常用格式330例

解释 *Explanation*

表示一会儿是某种情况，一会儿又是另一种情况，时常变换。

Used to indicate a changeable status.

例句 *Examples*

1. 近来气候反常，时而刮黄沙风，时而又下泥雨。

   The climate is abnormal recently：one moment it blows wind with sand, the next rains with mud.

2. 躺在草原上，听到远处传来悠扬的歌声，时而高，时而低。

   Lying on the grassland, I heard melodious song from the distance, rising and falling from time to time.

3. 这位扬名天下的运动员，最近情绪时而高涨时而低迷。

   This athlete, famous around the world, recently has been cheerful this moment and depressed the next.

4. 你注意到了吗？她的神情时而欢快，时而忧郁。

   Have you noticed that she looks sometimes happy, sometimes depressed?

对话 *Dialogues*

1. A：她的精神好些了吗？

   Is she better now?

   B：还不稳定。时而兴奋异常，时而泪流满面。

   Still not stable. She is very excited one moment, but cries the next.

2. A：目前中东地区形势如何？

   How is the situation in the Middle East now?

   B：情况依旧，时而紧张，时而缓和。

   It's just as before, sometimes tense, sometimes eased.

练习 *Exercises*

用"时而~时而~"改写句子。Rewrite the sentences with the pattern.

1. 孩子的表情变化很快，一会儿哭，一会儿笑。

   →_____。

2. 这里的天气阴晴不定，一会儿狂风大雨，一会儿艳阳高照。

   →_____。

解释 *Explanation*

"好像是~"的意思，用在名词、代词或动词后面。常和"跟"、"像"一起用。

Used after a noun, pronoun or verb and often in conjunction with 跟 or 像 to indicate to be similar to or in the manner of.

例句 *Examples*

1. 她深深地爱着你，离开你就像鱼儿离开水似的。

   She loves you deeply. And when she leaves you, it's as fish leaves water.

2. 你看他狼吞虎咽的，简直跟个饿狼似的。

   Look, he's wolfing down food, just as a hungry wolf.

3. 你这么个大小伙子怎么也扭扭捏捏的，像个小姑娘似的。

   You are a boy. Why are you mincing like a little girl?

4. 他突然发病，脑袋疼得像针扎似的。

   He was suddenly taken ill, and his head hurt so much that it seemed to be pricked by a needle.

对话 *Dialogues*

1. A: 他的官不大，架子怎么那么大?

   His position is not high. Why has he got such airs?

   B: 是啊，像多大的官似的，没人喜欢他。

   Yes. He looks like a high-ranking official. Nobody likes him.

2. A: 这小伙子，运动员似的。

   This young man looks like an athlete.

   B: 嗯，结实、健美、高高大大，挺像个篮球运动员!

   Yes. He's tall and sturdy, just as a basketball player!

练习 *Exercises*

用"~似的"完成句子。Complete the sentences with the pattern.

1. 你看这女孩子多漂亮啊，_____。

2. 你怎么那么任性，像个_____。

解释 *Explanation*

用于强调某个已发生事件的时间、地点、方式、施事等方面，或是说话人用来强调自己的态度、看法等。"是"常可以省略。

Used to emphasize when, where, how or who, or to emphasize the attitude or opinion of the speaker. 是 is often omitted.

例句 *Examples*

1. 我的汉语是在北大学的。

   It was at Beida (Peking University) that I learned Chinese.

2. 我今天开车来的，你可以搭我的车回家。

   I drive today, so I can drive you home.

3. 那照相机是他借来的，弄坏了当然要赔。

   The camera was borrowed. Of course he had to compensate if it was damaged.

4. 你别一脸不高兴，这是机密，我是不会告诉你的。

   Don't be unhappy. It's a secret, and I won't tell you.

对话 *Dialogues*

1. A: 你买到去海南三亚的火车票了?

   Did you buy a train ticket to Sanyan, Hainan?

   B: 对，是昨天下午买到的。

   Yes. I bought it yesterday afternoon.

2. A: 你病成这样，我看明天的会你就别去了。

   You are so sick. Don't attend tomorrow's meeting.

   B: 那哪儿成啊，我还得发言呢，非参加不可的。

   It won't do. I must attend it, because I have a speech to deliver.

练习 *Exercises*

用"是~的"完成句子。Complete the sentences with the pattern.

1. A: 你是什么时候知道这件事的?

   B: _____。

2. A: 你说他会不会食言啊?

   B: _____，他是最守信用的人。

解释 *Explanation*

意思和"虽然~可是~"相近，表示虽然承认一种事实，但有另一种事实需要考虑。"是/归"的前后用同一词语。

With a similar meaning to 虽然~可是~, the pattern is used to indicate that although one fact is acknowledged, another fact still needs consideration. 是/归 is used between identical words.

例句 *Examples*

1. 这份工作累归累，但能学到不少东西。
   Although the work is tiring, you can learn quite a bit from it.
2. 养孩子辛苦归辛苦，可是孩子也给父母带来很多快乐。
   Although it is hard to be a parent, you can find great joy in raising children.
3. 学外语难是难，可是还得学。
   Although it's difficult, we still have to learn foreign languages.
4. 这种进口车贵是贵，但质量确实好，还是有不少人买。
   Although they are expensive, these imported cars are of good quality. So quite a few people have bought them.

对话 *Dialogues*

1. A: 我知道你喜欢喝这种酒，今天让你喝个够。
   I know you like to drink this kind of wine. Today you can drink to your heart's content.
   B: 喜欢归喜欢，但为了身体，还得少喝。
   Although I like it, I have to drink less for the sake of my health.

2. A: 她长得那么漂亮，你怎么跟她分手了呢?
   She is so pretty. Why did you break up with her?
   B: 漂亮是漂亮，可是缺少共同语言。
   Although she's attractive, we don't have a common language.

练习 *Exercises*

用"~是/归~，可是/但~"完成句子。Complete the sentences with the pattern.

1. A: 我看你这工作太累了，要把身体搞垮的，换个工作吧。
   B: _____。我不打算换。

2. A: 这个区的房子便宜多了，咱们买这里的吧。
   B: _____。还是买离单位近点儿的好。

解释 *Explanation*

表示发生某种情况正合心意，或时间正合适。否定时用"不是时候"。

Used to indicate that something happens as the speaker wishes or at a proper time. The negative form is 不是时候.

例句 *Examples*

1. 你来的是时候，我刚从农贸市场采购回来，可以做一顿丰盛的午餐。

   You can't have come at a better time. I just came back from the market. We can make a marvelous lunch.

2. 我来的真是时候，能见到你说的比天使还好的姨妈。

   I come just in the nick of time and can see your auntie, who as you said is better than angel.

3. 现在买股票可不是时候，股价已经太高了，说不定还有泡沫呢。

   It's not a good time to buy stock. The price is too high and probably the market has bubbles.

4. 你这会儿跟他说这样的事可不是时候，他正为提职称的事烦着呢。

   It's not a good time to talk with him about such things now. He is worried about the upgrading of his professional title.

对话 *Dialogues*

1. A: 崔医生，您的那笔稿费来了。

   Doctor Cui, the remuneration for the article you wrote arrived.

   B: 哈，这笔钱来的是时候，我正缺钱用呢。

   Aha, it came just in the nick of time. I'm short of money now.

2. A: 清明节你和他们去扫墓啦?

   Did you go to sweep graves with them on the Tomb-sweeping Day?

   B: 是，不过走的不是时候，半路上遇到大雨，都淋了个落汤鸡。

   Yes. But we started at a bad time. It rained heavily halfway and we all got soaked.

练习 *Exercises*

用"～是时候"完成句子。Complete the sentences with the pattern.

1. A: 同学们，水来了!

   B: 这水＿＿＿＿＿＿＿＿＿＿＿＿＿＿＿＿，我正渴得要命呢。

2. A: 我昨天向爸爸要零花钱，他一脸不高兴。

   B: ＿＿＿＿＿＿＿＿＿＿＿＿＿＿＿＿，昨天他心情不好。

解释 *Explanation*

表示 A 和 B 是不同的人或事物，彼此没有关系。

Used to indicate that A and B are different people or things, and are unrelated.

例句 *Examples*

1. 他是他，我是我。别把我们扯一块儿。

   He and I are different. Don't put us together.

2. 去年是去年，今年是今年，哪儿能年年都是一个样儿呢。

   Last year was last year and this year is this year. Each year is different from the others.

3. 送礼是送礼，行贿是行贿，不能混为一谈。

   Giving a present is different from bribery and you shouldn't confuse them.

4. 说是说，做是做。能说会道的人，事情未必能办得漂亮。

   Speech and action are different. An eloquent person doesn't necessarily do things well.

对话 *Dialogues*

1. A：鱿鱼是不是就是章鱼？

   Is squid octopus?

   B：哪儿呀，鱿鱼是鱿鱼，章鱼是章鱼。

   No. The two are different.

2. A：这桩婚事你妈都同意了，你还反对？

   Your mother has given her consent to this marriage. Why do you still oppose it?

   B：我妈是我妈，我是我。

   My mother has her stand and I have mine.

练习 *Exercises*

用"A 是 A，B 是 B"完成句子。Complete the sentences with the pattern.

1. _____，别在工作中混入太多感情色彩。

2. _____，她不能代表我。

~是他/你，~也是他/你

解释 *Explanation*

表示两种完全相反或多个类似的令人不能理解的行为都是同一个人做的。

Used to indicate that two actions that are completely different or several similar things that are hard to understand are done by the same person.

例句 *Examples*

1. 疼人的是他，气人的也是他。

It's he who loves me dearly; and it's also he who annoys me.

2. 哭着喊着要去的是她，去了又说没意思的也是她。

She made a scene to go there; but when arriving there, she said that it's uninteresting.

3. 帮我的人是你，给我添麻烦的人也是你，叫我说你什么好。

It's you who help me; it's also you who bring trouble to me. What shall I say?

4. 哭的是你，闹的是你，打人骂人的也是你。

It's you who cry, stir up trouble, beat me and call my name.

对话 *Dialogues*

1. A：她怎么啦？把自己关在房间里。

   Why does she shut herself in the room?

   B：别理她，笑的是她，恼的也是她。

   Leave her alone. She smiles one moment but gets angry the next.

2. A：干吗把眼睛瞪得那么大，是谁惹你啦？

   Why do you glaring at me? Who annoys you?

   B：这东西说要买的是你，买来不要的也是你！

   It's you who wanted to buy it and you who don't like it now.

练习 *Exercises*

用"~是他/你，~也是他/你"和所给的词语完成句子。Complete the sentences with the pattern and words in parentheses.

1. 他的成绩忽上忽下，_____。（第一　倒数第一）

2. 我对他爱恨交加，_____。（爱　恨）

解释 *Explanation*

用于列举事项。

Used to list items.

例句 *Examples*

1. 想学好外语，首先要多听，其次要多说。

   To learn a foreign language well, one should first listen to it more; and secondly speak it more.

2. 我买东西，首先考虑质量，其次才考虑价格。

   When I go shopping, my first concern is the quality, then the price.

3. 我觉得喝酒有好处，首先能让人忘记烦恼，其次使人容易交朋友。

   I believe drinking can do people good. First of all it helps them forget their troubles. Secondly it makes it easy for them to make friends.

4. 首先我要感谢王老师的指导，其次我还要感谢家人的支持。

   Firstly I would like to thank Teacher Wang for her guidance. Secondly I would like to say how grateful I am for the support of my family.

对话 *Dialogues*

1. A: 为什么你觉得汉语比英语难学？

   Why do you think Chinese is a more difficult language than English?

   B: 首先，汉字很难写；其次，汉语有声调，这也很难掌握。

   Firstly Chinese characters are hard to write. Secondly it has tones, which are difficult to master.

2. A: 你觉得怎样才算是好朋友？

   What do you think makes a good friend?

   B: 好朋友首先要能互相理解，其次在困难的时候能帮助你。

   Firstly a good friend really understands you. Secondly he/she is always willing to help you out of difficulties.

练习 *Exercises*

用"首先 ~ , 其次 ~"完成句子。Complete the sentences with the pattern.

1. A: 当你的意见和父母的意见不一样时，你怎么办？

   B: _____。

2. A: 你为什么那么喜欢旅行？

   B: _____。

谁 ~ , 谁 ~

解释 *Explanation*

前后的"谁"是任指的同一个人；两个"谁"也可指不同的人，多用于否定句，有互相如何的意思。

Used to refer to the unspecified same person; or different persons, mostly in a negative form to express a mutual understanding or a mutual feeling.

例句 *Examples*

1. 下午开全体大会，谁要是不能来，谁就得请假。

   This afternoon we will hold a general meeting. Anyone unable to attend must ask for a leave.

2. 这里是禁烟区，谁要抽烟，谁就到外边去抽。

   It's a non-smoking area. Those who want to smoke please go outside.

3. 我们过去谁也不认识谁，可现在是好朋友。

   We did not know each other in the past. But now we are good friends.

4. 他们俩虽是同班同学，可谁也不喜欢谁，谁也看不起谁。

   Although the two are classmates, they dislike and despise each other.

对话 *Dialogues*

1. A: 今天谁请客?

   Who will treat us today?

   B: 谁要请，谁请，反正我不掏钱。

   Whoever wants to treat may do so. I won't pay anyway.

2. A: 明天我也可以去看安防新仪器展览吗?

   Can I go to the Exhibition of New Security Devices tomorrow?

   B: 当然可以，谁想去谁报名。

   Yes. Those who wish to go please sign up.

练习 *Exercises*

用"谁 ~ , 谁 ~"完成句子。Complete the sentences with the pattern.

1. 这些糖是小李拿来的，大家_____。

2. 这些衣服我都穿不下了，你们_____。

解释 *Explanation*

指任何人都这样，没有例外。

Used to indicate there is no exception.

例句 *Examples*

1. 我说的全是真的，怎么谁也不相信呢。

   What I said is all true. Why nobody believes me?

2. 不是我们不肯帮她，是谁也帮不了她。

   It's not that we don't want to help her, but that nobody can help her.

3. 在那种情况下，大家都拼命干，谁都不愿意落后。

   Under such circumstances, all worked hard and didn't want to lag behind.

4. 像他这样两面三刀的人，谁都不喜欢。

   Nobody will like such kind of person given to duplicity as him.

对话 *Dialogues*

1. A: 求你了，别说了，太恐怖了！

   Don't say it any more, please! It's too horrible!

   B: 我知道，你们谁都不爱听，可这是铁的事实！

   I know all of you don't like it. But it's an indisputable fact!

2. A: 白小姐怎么还不回来，去哪儿啦？

   Why is Miss Bai still not back? Where has she gone?

   B: 谁也不知道她上哪儿去了。

   Nobody knows.

练习 *Exercises*

用"谁也/都~"改写句子。Rewrite the sentences with the pattern.

1. 没有人想在环境这么糟糕的地方吃饭。

   → _____。

2. 没有人喜欢跟脾气这么坏的人交往。

   → _____。

解释 *Explanation*

表示按照某条线路或某种情况继续进行。

Used to indicate to go on along a certain route or follow with something.

例句 *Examples*

1. 顺着马路右边往前走，五分钟就到了。

   Walk on along the right side of the road, and you will arrive in five minutes.

2. 这些花籽儿，就顺着墙根儿往前撒吧。

   Sow these flower seeds along the root of the wall.

3. 你是新手，别走快车道，就顺着慢车道往前开吧。

   You're a beginner. Don't take the fast lane; drive on along the slow lane.

4. 既然丁处长提到了这个问题，那我就顺着他的话题再往下说两句。

   Since Director Ding mentioned this problem, I will take this opportunity to talk more about it.

对话 *Dialogues*

1. A: 快告诉我，后来那个孩子找到他亲妈了吗？

   Tell me! Did the child find his mom later?

   B: 别急，你顺着这篇报道往下看，就知道了。

   No hurry. Continue reading this report, and you will know the result.

2. A: 文章后半部分怎么写呢？

   How to write the later half of the article?

   B: 顺着刚才说的思路往下想，不就行了。

   Just follow with what you spoke of right now.

练习 *Exercises*

用"顺着 ~ 往 ~"完成句子。Complete the sentences with the pattern.

1. A: 请问北京大学怎么走？

   B: _____。

2. A: 现在我要不要把车并到左道去？

   B: 不用，咱们不往左拐，_____。

解释 *Explanation*

表示某种巧合，或者一谈到某事就常会出现某种情况。

 Used to indicate a coincidence, or that some situation arises while talking about something.

例句 *Examples*

1. 说到她孙子，张奶奶就会乐得合不上嘴。

   Talking about her grandson, Grandma Zhang always grins from ear to ear.

2. 小马来啦！真是说到曹操，曹操就到。

   Xiao Ma has come. Speak of the devil.

3. 说到过去的那段经历，她就会伤心流泪。

   Every time she talks about that experience, she will be reduced to tears.

4. 刚说到炒股，咱们赚钱的机会就来了，你们看，"抄底"的时候到了。

   We're talking of speculating in stocks, and now comes our opportunity to earn money. Look, it's time we bought stocks at this lowest level.

对话 *Dialogues*

1. A: 哈哈！我们刚说到你，你就到了。

    Aha! We were just talking of you and you have come.

   B: 你们是不是在背后说我的坏话呢？

    Are you speaking ill of me behind my back?

2. A: 你最近老愁眉苦脸的，为什么事烦恼啊？

    You have been pulling a long face recently. What are you worried about?

   B: 人家都说我谈的是马拉松式恋爱，可我只要一跟他说到结婚，他就转移话题。

    People say my love affair is a marathon. But the moment I mention marriage, he will change the topic.

练习 *Exercises*

用"说到 ~ ，就 ~ "完成句子。Complete the sentences with the pattern.

1. 说到动画片，人们_____ 。

2. 怎么这么巧，说到想吃蛋糕，_____。

解释 *Explanation*

客气话，委婉地表示不是前面提到的情况，或不同意对方的说法。用于答话的开头。

Used at the beginning of a reply to politely express disagreement.

对话 *Dialogues*

1. **A:** 你送这么重的礼，真叫我过意不去。

   You give me such a generous gift. I feel uneasy.

   B: 说到哪儿去了，一点点心意。

   What are you saying? It is just a token of my appreciation.

2. **A:** 你帮了我这么大的忙，真不知道怎么谢你！

   Thank you so much for helping me a lot!

   B: 说到哪儿去了，这只不过是举手之劳。

   Don't mention it, it's nothing.

3. **A:** 今天还让你掏腰包，怎么好意思呢?

   I feel sorry for letting you pay today.

   B: 说到哪儿去了，没几个钱。

   Don't mention it, it's not much.

4. **A:** 让你花了那么多时间陪我东逛西逛，太不好意思了。

   I'm sorry that you spent so much time showing me around.

   B: 说到哪儿去了，老乡嘛，应该的。

   You are welcome. We are from the same place and I should do so.

练习 *Exercises*

用"说到哪儿去了"完成句子。Complete the sentences with the pattern.

1. **A:** 多亏你帮忙，真不知怎么感谢才好。

   B: _____。

2. **A:** 你告诉我的这些信息太有用了，非常感谢！

   B: _____。

解释 *Explanation*

指说话的一会儿时间，表示时间很短，有"马上"、"立刻"的意思。

Used to indicate a short time, meaning "in a minute" or "right away".

例句 *Examples*

1. 都五月了，说话就要热了。

   It's May, and it will be hot soon.

2. 刚才还是大太阳呢，说话就下起雨来了。

   It's sunny just now, but rains in a minute.

3. 孩子长得可真快，说话就长成大姑娘了。

   Children grow up quickly; she has become a young lady.

4. 他们俩一直说说笑笑的，怎么说话就大吵起来了呢？

   They two have been talking while laughing. How come they quarreled in a minute?

对话 *Dialogues*

1. A：服务员，这么半天了，怎么还不给我们上菜呀！

   Waiter, why not serve our dishes for such a long time?

   B：说话就得，说话就得。

   They will be ready in a jiffy.

2. A：真是光阴似箭，日月如梭啊！

   Time flies.

   B：可不，一年说话就又要过去了。

   Yes, another year will go by soon.

练习 *Exercises*

用"说话就 ~"完成句子。Complete the sentences with the pattern.

1. 他做事真是麻利，甭管多费功夫的事儿，＿＿＿＿＿＿＿＿＿＿＿＿＿＿＿＿＿＿。

2. 他跑得可真快呀，＿＿＿＿＿＿＿＿＿＿＿＿＿＿＿＿＿＿。

解释 *Explanation*

表示行为、动作发生得很突然、很快或情况很容易发生变化。前后用相同的动词。

Used with the same verb to indicate a sudden, swift action or easily changing situation.

例句 *Examples*

1. 北京的春天，说刮风就刮风。

   In spring in Beijing, wind blows all of a sudden.

2. 山区的天气说变就变，早晚多穿点儿。

   The weather in mountainous areas changes quickly. Wear more in the morning and evening.

3. 中国的股市说暴涨就暴涨，说暴跌就暴跌，是什么原因？

   The Chinese stock market rises and drops suddenly and quickly. What's the reason?

4. 你怎么说辞职就辞职了？难道去哪个单位已经确定啦？

   Why do you suddenly quit? Have you already got a new offer?

对话 *Dialogues*

1. A: 今后咱们一块儿打羽毛球吧！得注意锻炼身体了。

   From now on, let's play badminton together. We have to do some exercises.

   B: 好，说干就干，从今天下午开始。

   OK, let's start from this afternoon.

2. A: 我们的车间主任老蒋人挺好，就是脾气不太好。

   Our workshop director Lao Jiang is a good man, but has a bad temper.

   B: 是啊，说发脾气就发脾气。

   It's true. He gets angry all of a sudden.

练习 *Exercises*

用"说 ~ 就 ~"和所给的词语完成句子。Complete the sentences with the pattern and words in parentheses.

1. 当演员就得能_____。（哭　笑）

2. 这人太没人情味儿了，_____。（翻脸）

（把话）说开了~

解释 *Explanation*

把心里的真实想法讲出来。

Used to express real feelings or thoughts.

例句 *Examples*

1. 说开了，老百姓就是对缺少民主不满意。

   Frankly speaking, people are not satisfied with the lack of democracy.

2. 很多问题都是由误会引起的，说开了，问题也就解决了。

   Many problems are caused by misunderstandings. If things are clearly explained, problems will be solved.

3. 把话说开了，我不想跟他这种人打交道。

   Frankly speaking, I don't want to deal with people like him.

4. 我看你们之间并没什么大矛盾，两个人把话说开了，还可以是好朋友。

   I don't think the differences between you two are all that big. You can still be good friends as long as you show your real feelings.

对话 *Dialogues*

1. A: 最近她心情极坏，连班都懒得去上了。

   Recently, her mood is so bad that she doesn't even want to go to work.

   B: 劝劝她，有什么意见，说开了就完了，不要老压在心上。

   It's better to talk to her about it. That way if she has something to say, she will be able to get off her mind.

2. A: 为什么不让我们做总代理呢？

   Why don't you make us the agency of choice?

   B: 把话说开了，你们公司的实力还不够。

   Frankly speaking, your company isn't capable.

练习 *Exercises*

用"（把话）说开了~"完成句子。Complete the sentences with the pattern.

1. A: 你前段时间对小李很有意见，现在没事了吧？

   B: 上周他来找我，＿＿＿＿＿＿＿＿＿＿＿＿＿＿＿，发现原来是一场误会。

2. A: 你说美国那时为什么要打伊拉克？

   B: ＿＿＿＿＿＿＿＿＿＿＿＿＿。

解释 *Explanation*

表示说话人对做某事的态度很坚决。有"无论如何"的意思。

Used to indicate the speaker's resolute attitude, meaning "in any case" or "in no case".

例句 *Examples*

1. 都这么晚了，说什么也不能让她一个人回家。

   It's so late that she cannot go home alone on any account.

2. 这孩子太小，身体又弱，说什么也要保证她的营养。

   The child is so young and weak that we must guarantee she has a good nutrition anyhow.

3. 我说什么也不愿再过这种平淡无聊的生活了。

   In no case will I lead such a boring life of milk and water.

4. 基金市值一路下滑，我损失惨重，以后说什么也不买了。

   The market values of funds have been dropping, and I lost a lot. In no case will I buy funds.

对话 *Dialogues*

1. A：这次毕业考试，你得好好复习了。

   You must have a good review of your lessons to prepare for the graduation exam.

   B：是，说什么也要考个高分。

   Yes, I must have good marks anyhow.

2. A：金老板老借钱不还。

   Mr. Jin borrows money but never returns.

   B：说什么也别和这种人打交道了。

   Never deal with such kind of person under any circumstances.

练习 *Exercises*

用"说什么也 ~"完成句子。Complete the sentences with the pattern.

1. 他常常说话不算数，我＿＿＿＿＿＿＿＿＿＿＿＿＿＿＿＿＿＿＿＿。

2. 最近天天吃方便面，吃得我倒胃口，以后＿＿＿＿＿＿＿＿＿＿＿＿＿＿＿。

解释 *Explanation*

好像是又好像不是。中间常常用相同的单音节名词、形容词或动词。

Used often with the same monosyllabic noun, adjective or verb to indicate to look like … but not quite.

例句 *Examples*

1. 我根本没睡着，只是似睡非睡地躺了一会儿。

   I did not fall asleep at all. I just lay for a while in a half-sleeping state.

2. 她这么打扮，似男非男，似女非女。

   She dresses in such a way that she looks like half-man, half-woman.

3. 这种似酒非酒，似水非水的是什么饮料？

   It looks like half-wine, half-water. What kind of beverage is it?

4. 她的话似真非真、似假非假，我还真难以判断。

   Her words are half true. I can hardly judge it.

对话 *Dialogues*

1. A: 听说总经理辞职，另谋高就了？

   I heard that our general manager quitted and found a better job. Is it true?

   B: 对于这个消息，大家都还似信非信呢。

   We cannot really believe it.

2. A: 科学院陆院士的这篇文章你看懂了吗？

   Have you read the article by Academician Lu of the Academy of Sciences?

   B: 老实说，似懂非懂。

   To be frank, I cannot understand all.

练习 *Exercises*

选词填空。Choose the right phrases to fill in the blanks.

似梦非梦　　似懂非懂　　似睡非睡　　似信非信

1. 我问她相信不相信闹鬼的事，她脸上现出一副_____的样子。

2. 老师讲完以后，学生都是_____的表情。

解释 *Explanation*

表示用退让一步的办法来解决问题，不再计较，或干脆不再考虑了。

Used to indicate a concession for solving the problem or giving no more consideration.

例句 *Examples*

1. 大雪天的，在家随便吃点儿算了，别出去了。

   It's snowing. Just have something at home. Don't eat out.

2. 算了，红茶没有了，喝绿茶吧。

   There is no black tea. Let's just drink green tea.

3. 既然你那么不情愿合作，那我们就各干各的算了。

   Since you are reluctant to cooperate, we might do without each other.

4. 他对你不冷不热的，你又何必对他如此钟情，干脆分手算了。

   He is lukewarm to you. Why are you still captivated by him? Break up with him.

对话 *Dialogues*

1. A: 因为雾大，下午的航班也取消了，怎么办?

   The flight of this afternoon is also canceled due to thick fog. What shall we do?

   B: 算了，算了，退票吧。

   Let it be. Refund the tickets.

2. A: 他连着开了两天夜车，现在还在呼呼大睡呢。

   He worked late into the night for two days, and now is still fast asleep.

   B: 那算了，别叫醒他了。

   Then let him sleep. Don't wake him up.

练习 *Exercises*

用"算了"完成句子。Complete the sentences with the pattern.

1. 家里没有菜了? 那就_____。

2. 这公交车等半天也不来，_____。

解释 *Explanation*

表示转折关系。前面说的尽管是事实，可后面的情况也存在。

Used to indicate an adversative relation that the former one is true, but the following situation is also true.

例句 *Examples*

1. 那幢别墅虽然是精装修，但是设计不当。

   This villa is exquisitely decorated, but the design is not proper.

2. 虽然中国社会还存在这样那样的问题，但是经济的发展速度是有目共睹的。

   Although there are still problems in the Chinese society, the speed of China's economic development is obvious to all.

3. 我们虽然住在同一个公寓小区，可是来往并不多。

   Although we live in the same residential block, we don't have much contact.

4. 他虽然想在国外开个贸易公司，可是又怕风险太大，承受不了。

   Although he wants to start a trading company overseas, he is afraid that he cannot tolerate the high risk.

对话 *Dialogues*

1. A：那个新来的年轻设计师一看就知道是个精明强干的人。

   That new young designer looks smart and competent.

   B：虽然能干，但是有些狂妄自大。

   Competent as he is, he is somewhat swaggering.

2. A：这两天天气还行，不怎么太热。

   It's not so hot in the past two days.

   B：虽然不算热，可是挺闷的，一点儿风都没有。

   But it's sultry; there is even no breeze.

练习 *Exercises*

用"虽然 ~ ，但是/可是 ~"完成句子。Complete the sentences with the pattern.

1. A：我觉得住在大城市好，就业机会比较多。

   B：_____。

2. A：和父母一起住，生活有人照顾，多好！

   B：_____。

虽说~，可~

解释 *Explanation*

意思和"虽然~，但是~"一样，多用于口语。

Used often in oral Chinese to mean the same as 虽然~，但是~.

例句 *Examples*

1. 当老师虽说工资不算高，可受人尊敬。

Teachers are not well paid, but are respectable.

2. 田师傅这个人哪，遇到事情，虽说嘴上不讲，可心里有数。

When something happens, Master Tian says nothing but knows exactly about it.

3. 她虽说算不上美女，可很有风度，也很有魅力。

Although she's not very pretty, she is elegant and charming.

4. 他这人虽说有点儿懒，可为人真诚、坦率、值得信赖。

A bit lazy as he is, he is honest, frank and trustworthy.

对话 *Dialogues*

1. A: 你的衣服不少啦，衣柜都放不下了，怎么还买呀？

   You have so many clothes that even your wardrobe cannot hold them. Why do you still buy?

   B: 虽说不少，可连一件像样的也没有。

   But I don't have a decent dress for important occasions.

2. A: 这种苹果可不便宜呀。

   This kind of apple is not cheap.

   B: 虽说有点儿贵，可味道很好。

   A bit expensive as it is, it tastes good.

练习 *Exercises*

用"虽说~，可~"完成句子。Complete the sentences with the pattern.

1. 他们俩虽说是亲兄弟，_____。

2. 虽说他对我很好，_____。

解释 *Explanation*

表示 A 变化了，B 也跟着变化。

Used to indicate that B changes as A changes.

例句 *Examples*

1. 随着经济的发展，大陆的各个方面都发生了很大的变化。

   With economic development, great changes have taken place in many aspects on mainland.

2. 随着国际油价的不断攀升，国际石化产品的价格也不断上涨。

   Alongside growing world oil price, the prices of world petrochemical products grow, too.

3. 随着相处时日的增多，我渐渐地喜欢上了这个朴实的小伙子。

   As I got along with him more, I was gradually taken by this sincere and honest young man.

4. 随着城市化进程的加快，粮食紧张状态可能日益加剧。

   With accelerated urbanization, grain shortage may become increasingly worse.

对话 *Dialogues*

1. **A：**随着收入和财富总量的增长，分配的公平性将越来越受到社会的关注。

   With increasing income and total wealth, the fairness of distribution will attract more and more social attention.

   B：是啊，国家钱多了，大家当然要关心怎么分配。

   I agree. The state has more money, and people surely care how the money will be distributed.

2. **A：**现在我们的社会还有不少阴暗面。

   Our society still has a few seamy sides.

   B：是的。不过我相信随着时代的发展，这个社会肯定会越来越美好。

   It's true. But I believe with the development of the times, the society will be better and better.

练习 *Exercises*

用"随着 A 的 ~，B ~"完成句子。Complete the sentences with the pattern.

1. _____，跟中国人交往变得越来越容易。

2. _____，我们的生活越来越方便。

挺～的

解释 *Explanation*

表示程度比较高，常用于口语。

Used often in oral Chinese to indicate a high degree.

例句 *Examples*

1. 我得了过敏性鼻炎，挺难受的。

   I've got an allergic rhinitis, and feel rather bad.

2. 在中国市场，诺基亚、摩托罗拉和三星手机都挺受欢迎的。

   In the Chinese market, Nokia, Motorola and Samsung cell phones are quite popular.

3. 南方三月是鲜花盛开的季节，而北方这时还挺冷的呢。

   In the south, March is a season of blossoming flowers. But in the north, it is still very cold.

4. 《甜蜜蜜》、《月亮代表我的心》这两首歌你都不知道？挺经典的。

   Don't you know "Almost a Love Story" and "The Moon Represents My Heart"? The two songs are quite classic.

对话 *Dialogues*

1. A: 你们的班主任徐老师怎么样？

   What is your class advisor Teacher Xu like?

   B: 不但课讲得好，人也挺亲切、随和的。

   She does well in giving lessons, and is very kind and amiable.

2. A: 听说许经理对下级员工很不错？

   I hear that Manager Xu treats employees very well. Is it true?

   B: 是，他对下属的生活小事也挺关心的。

   Yes. He also takes care if we need help in our life.

练习 *Exercises*

用"挺～的"完成句子。Complete the sentences with the pattern.

1. 妈妈，你不用担心，我＿＿＿＿＿＿＿＿＿＿＿＿＿＿＿＿＿＿。

2. 你别说，他做的菜＿＿＿＿＿＿＿＿＿＿＿＿＿＿＿＿＿＿。

解释 *Explanation*

表示目的。

Used to indicate a purpose.

例句 *Examples*

1. 张总裁后天得去一趟香港，为的是参加合作签字仪式。

   President Zhang will go to Hong Kong the day after tomorrow to attend the signing ceremony for cooperation.

2. 她常在夏季购冬装，为的是能买到物美廉价的服装。

   She often buys winter clothing in summer, so that she can buy cheap but good clothes.

3. 他故弄玄虚，为的是掩盖事实真相。

   He is deliberately mystifying the matter to cover up truth.

4. 父母起早贪黑地工作，为的是给子女幸福的生活。

   Parents work from dawn to night, so as to grant children a happy life.

对话 *Dialogues*

1. A: 你姑妈怎么老陪她女儿去健身房？

   Why does your aunt always accompany her daughter to the gym?

   B: 为的是让她的胖妞减肥。

   To let her fat daughter lose weight.

2. A: 想要自助游，就得每到一个地方都买张地图。

   If you want to travel by yourself, buy a map on arriving at any place.

   B: 对，为的是了解交通情况，要不东西南北都不清楚，怎么游啊。

   I agree. You buy the map to get to know the traffic; otherwise you may have no sense of direction and cannot travel by yourself.

练习 *Exercises*

用"为的是 ～"完成句子。Complete the sentences with the pattern.

1. 我现在努力学习，＿＿＿＿＿＿＿＿＿＿＿＿＿＿＿＿＿＿＿＿。

2. 我小妹出门老喜欢紧跟着我，＿＿＿＿＿＿＿＿＿＿＿＿＿＿＿＿＿＿。

解释 *Explanation*

表示为某个原因或目的去做某事。

Used to indicate to do sth. with a certain reason or purpose.

例句 *Examples*

1. 他们正在为祖国的存亡而战。

   They are fighting for the survival of the motherland.

2. 政府要想方设法让老百姓不会为物价上涨而感到不安。

   The government tries every means to make people not feel uneasy about rising prices.

3. 父亲为给孩子凑足教育费而到处奔波。

   The father ran about to gather enough money for his child's tuition.

4. 表演艺术家们正在为这场义演而加紧排练。

   Performing artists lose no time in rehearsing for this charity performance.

对话 *Dialogues*

1. A: 孙悟空为什么三打白骨精?

   Why did the Monkey King beat the White Bone Demon three times?

   B: 他是为保护师傅唐僧而战。

   He fought to protect his master.

2. A: 韩国不少公务员在学习汉语上可真下工夫。

   Many civil servants of South Korea work hard to learn Chinese.

   B: 他们是为去中国留学或工作而拼命学习。

   They work so hard as to study or work in China.

练习 *Exercises*

用"为~而~"完成句子。Complete the sentences with the pattern.

1. A: 你知道音乐家的这首曲子是为谁而写的吗?

   B: _____。

2. A: 我是为得到我心上人的爱而活着。

   B: 我不是,我觉得人应该是_____。

解释 *Explanation*

表示目的，和"为了 ~"意思相同。多用于书面语。

Used mostly in written Chinese to indicate purpose, meaning the same as 为了 ~ .

例句 *Examples*

1. 为节电起见，请随手关灯。

   To save electricity, turn off lights when leaving, please.

2. 为安全起见，必须时刻注意防火。

   To ensure safety, we must always guard against fire.

3. 为提高国民文化素质起见，政府需增加教育经费。

   To improve cultural awareness and knowledge among society, the government needs to spend more on education.

4. 专家建议，为孩子健康成长起见，八岁以下儿童应少打手机。

   As experts suggest, children under the age of eight should use less cell phones for the sake of their health.

对话 *Dialogues*

1. A：这个文件要留副本吗？

   Shall I keep a copy of this file?

   B：为保险起见，留一份吧，以防万一。

   To be on the safe side, keep a copy just in case.

2. A：这次出国访问，还有什么事要做准备？

   What else shall I prepare for this visit abroad?

   B：为联络方便起见，最好准备点儿礼品。

   You'd better prepare some gifts for the convenience of making contacts.

练习 *Exercises*

用"为 ~ 起见"完成句子。Complete the sentences with the pattern.

1. 为国际贸易公平起见，_____ 。

2. 报刊为方便读者起见，_____ 。

解释 *Explanation*

用于说话的开头，以提醒对方注意，后面表示说话人的看法或态度。多和对听话人的称呼连用。

Used at the beginning of a sentence as a reminder to express the speaker's opinion or attitude, mostly in conjunction with the form of address for the listener.

例句 *Examples*

1. 我说老王，今天别去了，有什么事明天再说吧。

   Lao Wang, don't go today. Let's deal with it tomorrow.

2. 我说李总，这是原则问题，我是不会轻易让步的。

   General Manager Li, it's an issue of principle and I will not give in easily.

3. 喂，我说，还是带上伞吧，有备无患嘛。

   Well, I think we should take our umbrellas with us. Preparedness averts peril.

4. 我说你有完没完了，不就是芝麻大点儿破事，至于嘛。

   Enough is enough! It's only a trivial thing!

对话 *Dialogues*

1. A：我说老公，这封投诉信什么时候写？

   Hubby, when shall I write the letter of complaint?

   B：过几天吧，听说有关部门要进行调查了。

   In few days. I've heard that departments concerned are going to investigate it.

2. A：我说阿姨，汤里得洒点儿胡椒粉吧。

   Auntie, will you add some pepper into the soup?

   B：对，我给忘了。

   Oh, I forgot.

练习 *Exercises*

用"我说 ~"写两个句子。Make two sentences with the pattern.

1. _____。

2. _____。

汉语常用格式330例

解释 *Explanation*

表示事实证明自己原有的估计或看法正确，用于答话的开头。

Used at the beginning of a reply to indicate that the speaker's estimation or opinion is right as proved by facts.

对话 *Dialogues*

1. A: 老吴没参加会，是脚扭伤了。

   Lao Wu did not come to the meeting because he sprained his ankle.

   B: 我说嘛，他怎么会无故缺席呢。

   What did I say? He wouldn't be absent without reason.

2. A: 老武说他昨天没来参加，是他太太忘了告诉他。

   Lao Wu said that he did not attend the meeting because his wife forgot to tell him.

   B: 我说嘛，小许不会不通知他的。

   I told you, Xiao Xu definitely had informed him of it.

3. A: 她知道这个不幸的消息后，挺伤心的。

   She was very sad hearing that unfortunate news.

   B: 我说嘛，她不会不伤心的。

   I told you that she would not be indifferent.

4. A: 对不起，我迟到了，我的这辆破车在半路上又抛锚了。

   I'm sorry that I'm late. My battered car broke down halfway.

   B: 我说嘛，没原因你不会晚来的。

   I know that you won't be late without a reason.

练习 *Exercises*

用"我说嘛，~"完成句子。Complete the sentences with the pattern.

1. A: 我刚才说今天停课，是说着玩儿的。

   B: ＿＿＿＿＿＿＿＿＿＿＿＿＿＿＿。

2. A: 班长的那辆自行车是 650 块钱买的，不是 50 块钱。

   B: ＿＿＿＿＿＿＿＿＿＿＿＿＿＿＿。

解释 *Explanation*

表示曾产生疑问，现在恍然大悟，多用于对话。

Used mostly in a dialogue to indicate the speaker had doubts but understands now.

对话 *Dialogues*

1. A: 报上说，今天气温 38 摄氏度。

   The newspaper says that it's 38 degree centigrade today.

   B: 我说呢，坐着什么都没干，怎么还一直淌汗呢。

   That's why I keep sweating though I just sit here doing nothing.

2. A: 她可是当过模特、上过电视的人物啊。

   She was once a model and appeared on TV.

   B: 我说呢，怎么好多人都认识她。

   Oh, then I know why so many people know her.

3. A: 王副市长因为贪污受贿被送上了法庭。

   Deputy Mayor Wang was taken to court because of the graft and corruption.

   B: 我说呢，最近他没在电视上露面。

   That's why he has not appeared on TV recently.

4. A: 这孩子一顿要吃三碗饭。

   The boy eats three bowls of rice for a meal.

   B: 我说呢，他怎么这么壮。

   Oh, that's why he is so strong.

练习 *Exercises*

用"我说呢，~"完成句子。Complete the sentences with the pattern.

1. A: 我家莉莉谈恋爱了！

   B: _____。

2. A: 林林的爸爸是数学老师，常常辅导他。

   B: _____。

解释 *Explanation*

表示说话人向对方提出看法或建议，有时略含不满情绪。"你"也可以换成对对方的称呼。

Used to express an opinion or suggestion, and sometimes indicate a slight dissatisfaction. 你 can also be changed into a form of address for the other.

例句 *Examples*

1. 我说你，都有啤酒肚了，得抽时间锻炼了。

   You have already had a beer belly; you must set aside time for exercises.

2. 我说你，还是把烟戒了的好，别让我们吸二手烟了。

   I think you'd better give up smoking. Don't expose us to passive smoking.

3. 我说小林，别真像林妹妹一样，老那么多愁善感的。

   Xiao Lin, don't always be so sentimental like Lin Daiyu.

4. 我说贾哥，话可不能这么说，到底谁欺负谁呀？

   Brother Jia, you cannot say so. Who on earth bullies the other?

对话 *Dialogues*

1. A: 今天学校开家长会，咱们都忙，不去了。

   The school will hold a parents' meeting today. Since we are both busy, we won't go.

   B: 我说孩子他爸，这是第一次召开家长会，怎么能不去听听呢。

   Daddy, it's the first parents' meeting. How could we not attend?

2. A: 明天的聚会，我穿什么衣服好？

   What shall I wear for tomorrow's gathering?

   B: 我说你，穿什么衣服还要问我，让人烦不烦哪！

   Well, you ask me about what to wear? I have had enough of you.

练习 *Exercises*

用"我说你，~"和所给的语境写两个句子。Make sentences with the pattern according to the context.

1. 丈夫整天在外应酬，越来越胖。妻子可能说：

   _____。

2. 同事老岳整天埋头工作，还老加班，身体越来越差，你可能说：

   _____。

解释 *Explanation*

表示说话的人开始对某种情况不理解，后来知道了原因，清楚了。

Used to indicate that the speaker did not understand first but now is aware of the reason and fact.

例句 *Examples*

1. 我说他怎么这么糊涂呢，原来是喝醉了。

   So I know why he was so silly—he's drunk.

2. 我说房间里怎么这么冷呢，是停暖气了。

   Then I know why it's so cold in the room; it's because the central heating was stopped.

3. 我说你这两天怎么回来得这么晚呢，原来是在赶写实验报告。

   Then I know why you came back late for two days; it's because you were dashing out your lab report.

4. 奶奶中了福利大奖了？我说她怎么那么开心呢。

   Is it true that Grandma won a big prize in the welfare lottery? Then I know why she is so happy.

对话 *Dialogues*

1. A: 昨晚我妹妹一人在家，听到有人敲门，把她给吓坏了。

   My younger sister stayed at home alone last night. And she was scared when hearing someone knocking at the door.

   B: 我说房里灯亮着怎么没人给我开门呢。

   Well, then I know why the light was on in the room, but nobody opened the door for me.

2. A: 江先生不打算回美国了，留在中国社会科学院工作了。

   Mr. Jiang isn't going back to America. He will work at the Chinese Academy of Social Sciences.

   B: 我说他怎么还没走呢。

   That's why he hasn't left.

练习 *Exercises*

用"我说 ~ 怎么 ~ 呢"完成句子。Complete the sentences with the pattern.

1. A: 小丽结婚了，现在不住这儿了。

   B: _____。

2. A: 我半年前就开始参加了英语口语辅导班。

   B: _____。

汉语常用格式330例

解释 *Explanation*

表示不管有什么情况或理由，都必须这样。跟"无论如何"差不多。

Used to indicate in any case or whatever happens, similar to 无论如何.

例句 *Examples*

1. 无论怎么说，他也不应该撒谎骗钱啊。

   In no case should he, as a man, tell lies to get money.

2. 无论怎么说，他也不该干那种伤天害理的事。

   In no case should he do such an inhuman thing.

3. 无论怎么说，公司也应该留有足够的流动资金。

   In any case, the company should keep adequate liquidity.

4. 无论怎么说，你也不能先动手打人，有理讲理嘛。

   In no case should you hit others first. Be reasonable.

对话 *Dialogues*

1. A: 关于这个问题我已经多次表明了我的观点，不想再谈了。

   I have stated my opinion many times about this issue. I don't want to say more.

   B: 无论怎么说，也得和他们再沟通一下。

   Anyhow, we should communicate with them again.

2. A: 反正我已经拿到了公司的聘书，没必要再到学校去了。

   Since I have got the letter of appointment from the company, I don't need to go to school any more.

   B: 无论怎么说，你也该把这学期的课上完哪。

   Anyhow, you should finish this term.

练习 *Exercises*

用"无论怎么说，也 ~"完成句子。Complete the sentences with the pattern.

1. A: 明明是爸说错了，为什么我不可以反驳他？

   B: _____。

2. A: 我的头真的有点儿晕，今天能不能不去上学了？

   B: _____。

无论 ~ ，只要 ~

解释 *Explanation*

表示不管什么地方、什么人或什么情况，有了某种条件，就会有某种结果。

Used to indicate a result occurs under a certain condition no matter where or how.

例句 *Examples*

1. 无论是到天涯还是海角，只要你去哪里，我就去哪里。

   I will go with you wherever you go.

2. 无论是法国、意大利还是瑞士，只要有钱，有时间，我都想去看看。

   As long as I have money and time I want to visit some place, be it France, Italy or Switzerland.

3. 无论是赢是输，只要能参加这次奥运比赛，就算圆了我的梦。

   I will fulfill my dream as long as I can take part in the Olympic Games, no matter I win or lose.

4. 无论遇到多强的谈判对手，只要吴部长参加谈判，都能搞定。

   However strong the rival is, we can succeed in the negotiation as long as Minister Wu takes part.

对话 *Dialogues*

1. A: 没想到朱总经理是这么幽默的人。

   I did not know that General Manager Zhu is so humorous.

   B: 没错。无论在哪儿，只要他讲话，笑声就不断。

   It's true. Wherever he is, he evokes laughter the moment he speaks.

2. A: 新来的乔部长很严肃？

   Is the new Minister Qiao a serious man?

   B: 嗯，无论是谁，只要一见到他，都有点儿紧张。

   Yes. Anyone will feel a bit nervous when seeing him.

练习 *Exercises*

用"无论 ~ ，只要 ~"改写句子。Rewrite the sentences with the pattern.

1. 做任何事情用心了的话，就一定会成功。

   → _____。

2. 别人说什么都没关系，我认准的事一定会干到底。

   → _____。

解释 *Explanation*

表示"始终、一直"的意思。多用于书面语。

Used mostly in written Chinese to indicate "always" and "all the time".

例句 *Examples*

1. 有些人无时无刻不想发财，而且是不择手段。

   Some people always think of making a fortune, by fair means or foul.

2. 这孩子真是淘气得出奇，无时无刻不让人操心。

   This child is extremely naughty, and his parents always worry about him.

3. 她只身一人在国外，无时无刻不在思念故乡和亲人。

   She is abroad alone and misses her homeland and family all the time.

4. 交通真是糟糕透顶，白天几乎无时无刻不在堵车。

   The traffic is terrible. There is always traffic jam in daytime.

对话 *Dialogues*

1. A: 公司开发新产品，遇到了技术难题。

   Our company encounters a technological problem in developing new products.

   B: 听说工程师们无时无刻不在研究如何解决这个难题。

   I've heard that engineers are studying how to solve it all the time.

2. A: 小王近来好像心神不定的。

   It seems that Xiao Wang has been uneasy recently.

   B: 妈妈病了，她无时无刻不惦记着。

   Her mother is ill and she worries about her all the time.

练习 *Exercises*

用"无时无刻不 ~"完成句子。Complete the sentences with the pattern.

1. 他是个工作狂，_____，甚至吃饭的时候都在考虑问题。

2. 你怎么好像_____？我每次上网都能看见你。

解释 *Explanation*

表示对所谈的内容，没有不涉及的，"无所不"后面常用单音节动词。

Used often with a monosyllabic verb to indicate that all the content being discussed is included.

例句 *Examples*

1. 现在的年轻人拼车、拼房、拼吃、拼玩儿、拼购、拼卡，真是无所不拼！

   Nowadays, young people carpool, co-rent apartments, co-pay for food and entertainment, co-shop and co-use cards. Everything can be pooled.

2. 他自称万事通，这世上的事，无所不知、无所不通。

   He calls himself a jack-of-all-trades and claims to know and master everything in the world.

3. 他总是夸夸其谈，让人觉得他无所不能。

   He is always boasting, and thus makes others believe he is capable in everything.

4. 这本书内容丰富，历史、地理、政治、艺术……，几乎是无所不包。

   This book covers a wide range of topics: history, geography, politics, art, etc. It's almost all-embracing.

对话 *Dialogues*

1. A：有些中国人好像动物的什么部位都吃。

   It seems that some Chinese eat all the parts of animals.

   B：对啊，什么猪蹄、牛筋、鸡爪，可以说是无所不吃。

   Yes. They eat almost everything: pig trotters, beef tendon, chicken feet, etc.

2. A：现在有了网络真方便，什么都可以查到。

   The Internet makes our life convenient. You can find everything online.

   B：可不是吗？网络上真是无所不有。

   I agree. The Internet has everything on it.

练习 *Exercises*

用"无所不 ~"改写句子。Rewrite the sentences with the pattern.

1. 听说很多人什么神都拜。→＿＿＿＿＿＿＿＿＿＿＿＿＿＿＿＿ 。

2. 这样的现象生活中到处都存在着。→＿＿＿＿＿＿＿＿＿＿＿＿＿ 。

解释 *Explanation*

"无"分别用在两个意义相同或相近的词或语素前面，强调没有。

Used before two parallel characters or morphemes, similar or identical in meaning to emphasize the absence of something.

例句 *Examples*

1. 一转眼，那孩子已经跑得无影无踪了。

   In a second, the child ran away, disappeared without a trace.

2. 经理无缘无故地发什么火呀? 谁惹他啦?

   Why did the manager get angry for no reason? Who provoked him?

3. 她无时无刻不在牵挂着灾区的亲人们。

   She worries about her relatives in the disaster-hit area all the time.

4. 谁不怀念童年时代那种无拘无束、无忧无虑的日子。

   Everyone cherishes the memory of carefree childhood.

对话 *Dialogues*

1. A: 小朋友们，什么东西是无色无味的?

   What has no color and no smell, boys and girls?

   B: 水。

   Water.

2. A: 这帮流氓大白天的竟敢这样为非作歹。

   These gangsters dare to do evil in broad daylight.

   B: 简直是无法无天。

   They're absolutely lawless.

练习 *Exercises*

选词填空。Choose the right phrases to fill in the blanks.

无声无息	无依无靠	无穷无尽	无怨无悔

1. 鹅毛大雪_____地飘落下来。

2. 亲人们都在地震中丧生了，这个孩子现在_____。

解释 *Explanation*

表示先进行某事或某行为动作，然后马上进行别的。有时也表示某种情况紧接着另一种情况出现。

Used to indicate to have something done first and then have other things done immediately. Sometimes used to indicate one thing follows another closely.

例句 *Examples*

1. 先把作文写好，接着把数学题做完，明白吗？

First write your composition, and then finish maths problems. Understand?

2. 我这次先去四川九寨沟旅行，接着去云南大理考察。

This time I will travel to Jiuzhaigou in Sichuan first, and then make an inspection tour to Dali in Yunnan.

3. 我每次生病都是先流鼻涕、咳嗽，接着就是喉咙红肿。

Every time I get sick, I have a running nose first, then cough and then have an inflamed throat.

4. 她们先洗桑拿浴，接着美容，然后又做了足底按摩，用了一整天时间。

They spent a whole day first on sauna, then beauty treatment, and finally foot massage.

对话 *Dialogues*

1. A: 服务员，快给我们上饺子，我们要赶火车。

   Waiter, hurry up. Our dumplings, please. We have to catch the train.

   B: 好，好，您二位先吃点儿凉菜，接着就上饺子。

   OK. You two have some cold dishes first, and then dumplings will be served.

2. A: 贺顾问，请对这个议题发表你的意见。

   Advisor Gu, please air your opinion on this topic.

   B: 我和主任商议过。他先说，我接着说。

   I discussed with the director. He will speak first and I'm after him.

练习 *Exercises*

用"先~，接着~"完成句子。Complete the sentences with the pattern.

1. A: 昨天早上你干了些什么？

   B: _____ 。

2. A: 听说今天上午你有两门考试？

   B: 对，_____ 。

解释 *Explanation*

表示先进行一项活动，再继续进行别的活动。或表示在一件事情之后，又发生另一件事情。

Used to indicate to have something done first and then proceed with other things, or that one thing follows another.

例句 *Examples*

1. 我打算先在国内学点儿外语，然后再去国外留学。

   I plan to learn a foreign language in China and then go abroad to study.

2. 你得先通过留学考试，然后再考虑申请哪所大学。

   You must first pass the exam for overseas study and then think over which university to apply to.

3. 这个问题很复杂，我们得先了解一下情况，然后再考虑如何处理。

   This problem is very complicated. We must get to know the matter first and then work out how to handle it.

4. 我们进入山区后，那里先是刮了一阵狂风，然后又下了倾盆大雨。

   After we entered the mountainous area, strong wind blew and then it rained cats and dogs.

对话 *Dialogues*

1. A: 你拿到考题时千万别慌，先做容易的题，然后再思考难的题。

   Don't be nervous when getting your paper. Work on easy problems first, then on difficult ones.

   B: 这是宝贵的经验，我得好好记住。

   It's a precious experience. I must remember it.

2. A: 这些都是美味，咱们先尝尝饺子、包子、馄饨，然后再吃锅贴。

   These are all delicious. Let's first eat some dumplings, steamed stuffed buns and wontons, and then fried dumplings.

   B: 好，一样样地品尝，哈哈，就怕把肚子撑破了。

   OK. Let's taste them one by one. Aha, I'm afraid we will be too full.

练习 *Exercises*

用"先～，然后～"完成句子。Complete the sentences with the pattern.

1. A: 这次接待单位都给你们安排了什么活动?

   B: _____。

2. A: 我想去美国探亲，都要办哪些手续?

   B: _____。

先~着，~

解释 *Explanation*

"先~着，~"表示次序在前，也表示暂时的意思。

Used to indicate that the action comes first in order, or just for the moment.

例句 *Examples*

1. 大伙儿先认真地听着，然后再提意见。

   You listen carefully first, and then offer your comments.

2. 你们俩先在这儿等着，我马上就把车子开过来。

   You two stay here and wait. I will drive the car here at once.

3. 他建议你先在那里干着，以后再想办法跳槽。

   He suggested you work there temporarily, and try to find another employment later.

4. 你们先聊着、喝着，我再去弄两个下酒菜来。

   You chat and drink first, and I go to cook some dishes for going with wine.

对话 *Dialogues*

1. A: 哥哥，我也想玩儿一会儿电脑。

   Brother, I also want to play a while on the computer.

   B: 你先看着，一会儿就让你玩儿。

   You watch first, and I will let you play in a moment.

2. A: 售货员小姐，让我们进去吧，外边冷着呢!

   Miss, let us in. It's cold outside.

   B: 对不起，先等着吧，还没开始营业呢。

   I'm sorry, but please wait for a while. It's not open yet.

练习 *Exercises*

用"先~着，~"完成句子。Complete the sentences with the pattern.

1. 这队排得这么长啊，这样吧，_____，我过半个小时来替你。

2. 我的这个 MP3 你_____，我暂时不用。

解释 *Explanation*

有"好像~一样"的意思。

Used to indicate the same meaning as 好像~一样.

例句 *Examples*

1. 她装得真像，跟什么事都没发生过似的。

   She does well in pretending that nothing had happened.

2. 怎么跟你说什么你都没反应，跟个傻子似的。

   You have no response whatever I said, like a fool.

3. 你怎么那么没精打采的，像寒霜打了的茄子似的。

   Why are you as languid as frost-bitten eggplant?

4. 你看他在专家面前还这么指手画脚的，像行家似的，真是不知天高地厚。

   Look, he criticizes this and condemns that before experts, as if he is a proficient. He does think too much of himself.

对话 *Dialogues*

1. A: 她身材苗条，穿着又讲究，很是迷人。

   She's slim and well-dressed, looking charming.

   B: 有人说她像个模特似的。

   Someone says she looks like a model.

2. A: 你看小李接到录取通知书后的高兴劲儿。

   Look, Xiao Li is so happy after receiving the letter of admission.

   B: 又唱又跳的，像个孩子似的。

   He's singing and dancing like a child.

练习 *Exercises*

用"像/跟 ~ 似的"完成句子。Complete the sentences with the pattern.

1. 今天你们家怎么这么热闹，_____。

2. 他只是五岁的孩子，可说话的口气 _____ 。

解释 *Explanation*

表示向对方提供选择或建议，意思跟"或者"相近。

Used to offer a choice or suggestion for the other, with a meaning similar to 或者.

例句 *Examples*

1. 大家累得都抬不起腿来了，要不就在这里休息吧。

   All are too tired to walk on. Shall we have a rest here?

2. 时间还早，去看场电影怎么样？要不到公园走走。

   It's still early. What about going to a movie? Or have a walk in the park?

3. 不知怎么回事，我今天特想见你，你能来吗？要不我去你那儿？

   I don't know why, but I'm eager to see you today. Will you come? Or I go to your place?

4. 你不想做饭？那出去吃吧，要不你歇着，我做辣子鸡丁给你吃。

   You don't want to cook, right? Let's eat out. Or you have a rest and I will cook chicken dices with chili for you.

对话 *Dialogues*

1. A：哟，都这时候了，我该回家了。

   Well, it's late. I should go home.

   B：太晚了，别走了，要不我送你回去。

   It's too late. Don't go, or let me take you home.

2. A：我的第一志愿选哪个专业好呢？

   Which major shall I choose for my first choice in university?

   B：经济？要不选企业管理专业？都是热门。

   Economics? Or business management? The two are both popular.

练习 *Exercises*

用"~，要不~"完成句子。Complete the sentences with the pattern.

1. 我们去听音乐会吧，＿＿＿＿＿＿＿＿＿＿＿＿＿＿＿＿＿。

2. 国内旅游点咱们几乎都游遍了，＿＿＿＿＿＿＿＿＿＿＿＿＿＿＿。

解释 *Explanation*

表示"如果不这样"、"否则"，多用于口语。也说"要不然"。

Used mostly in oral Chinese to indicate otherwise or else, 要不然 can also be used.

例句 *Examples*

1. 少在路边小摊上乱吃，要不容易拉肚子。

   Don't eat anything at roadside stalls, or else you are prone to have loose bowels.

2. 夫妻之间首先应相互信任，要不关系怎么能好呢！

   Husband and wife should trust each other in the first place. Otherwise how can they get along with each other?

3. 我这次考前要踏踏实实地认真准备，要不然还会名落孙山。

   I must make careful preparations for this exam, or else I will fail again.

4. 你也抽上烟了？趁还没上瘾，赶快别抽了，要不然就难戒了。

   Did you start smoking? Stop it before you get addicted, otherwise it will be hard to quit.

对话 *Dialogues*

1. A: 你给家里打个电话，要不他们会不放心的。

   Call your home, or they will worry about you.

   B: 你说得对。

   You're right.

2. A: 政府首先要把经济搞上去。

   The government should first develop the economy.

   B: 当然，要不然老百姓会一百个不满意。

   Of course. Otherwise people won't be satisfied.

练习 *Exercises*

用"~，要不~"完成句子。Complete the sentences with the pattern.

1. 现在我们要改变发展道路和发展模式，＿＿＿＿＿＿＿＿＿。

2. 你的腿都肿成这样了，必须得上医院，＿＿＿＿＿＿＿＿＿。

要不是 ~

解释 *Explanation*

表示假设，意思是指如果不是某种情况，就不会有后面的结果。

Used to indicate an assumption, meaning that the result won't occur without some condition.

例句 *Examples*

1. 要不是你耐心地给我说事实摆道理，我怎么能明白过来。

   If you had not set out facts and reason things out for me, I would not have understood.

2. 要不是老师的帮助，我根本考不上大学，更别说是名牌学校了。

   Without my teacher's help, I wouldn't have been able to enter university at all, let alone a prestigious one.

3. 要不是你提醒我，我就把明天要开会的事忘得一干二净了。

   If you had not reminded me, I would have forgotten all about tomorrow's meeting.

4. 要不是有那么多好心人捐钱给那孩子治病，可怜的他很可能已经见上帝去了。

   Without the money donated by so many kind people, the poor boy might have died.

对话 *Dialogues*

1. A: 要不是你，哪儿有我的现在？

   Without you, I wouldn't have my present life.

   B: 不要这么说，其实我也没做什么。

   Don't say so. Actually I did nothing.

2. A: 您好，任主任，还没下班哪。

   Hello, Director Ren. You haven't gone off work, have you?

   B: 要不是下雨，我早就回家了。

   I would have gone home if it hadn't rained.

练习 *Exercises*

用"要不是 ~"完成句子。Complete the sentences with the pattern.

1. _____，我不可能到美国留学。

2. _____，他哪能那么长寿？

解释 *Explanation*

表示某事或某种情况较晚才会发生，用于将发生的事件。

Used to indicate that something or some situation will not happen until later.

例句 *Examples*

1. 要到考试后的第二周，我们才能查成绩。

   We won't be able to check our marks until the second week after the exam.

2. 中央气象台预报说，要到三月初冰雪灾情才能缓和。

   According to the forecast of the Central Meteorological Observatory, the snow disaster will not abate until early March.

3. 我们要到拿到硕士学位，找到工作后，才考虑结婚的事。

   We won't consider marriage until we both get the master's degree and get employed.

4. 难道要到事情发展到不可收拾的地步，领导才出面干预？

   Don't tell me that the leadership won't interfere until things get out of hand.

对话 *Dialogues*

1. A: 你说孩子怎么才算是长大了？

   Tell me, when a child is truly grown up?

   B: 要到能理解父母、体谅父母和尊重父母时，才算是真正长大了。

   He's truly grown up when he can understand, be considerate to and respect parents.

2. A: 听说你丈夫出国进修了，什么时候回来？

   I heard your husband went to study abroad. When will he come back?

   B: 早呢，要到明年夏天才能回来。

   A long time from now. He won't come back until next summer.

练习 *Exercises*

用"要到 ~，才 ~"完成句子。Complete the sentences with the pattern.

1. A: 你什么时候有时间，咱们聚聚？

   B: 我平时比较忙，＿＿＿＿＿＿＿＿＿＿＿＿＿＿＿＿。

2. A: 这里天黑得很晚！

   B: 对，＿＿＿＿＿＿＿＿＿＿＿＿＿＿＿＿。

要多~有多~

解释 Explanation

表示程度极高。

Used to indicate a very high degree.

例句 Examples

1. 我特别喜欢那部戏里的女主角，要多漂亮有多漂亮。

   I'm particularly fond of the leading actress in that movie. She's so beautiful!

2. 在炎热的夏天，游过泳后，喝瓶冰镇啤酒，要多爽有多爽。

   In hot summer, it's very refreshing to drink a bottle of iced beer after a swim.

3. 他们举行婚礼时，摆了上百桌酒席，要多热闹有多热闹。

   At their wedding ceremony, they entertained guests to a sumptuous banquet at a-bout one hundred tables. It was bustling with excitement.

4. 办美国签证手续极其复杂，可以说要多麻烦有多麻烦。

   It's very complicated and troublesome to go through the formalities for getting a US visa.

对话 Dialogues

1. **A:** 你看这款手机样子挺不错的吧？功能也多。

   What do you think of this cell phone? It looks good and has many functions.

   B: 棒极了，要多酷有多酷。

   Great! It's so cool.

2. **A:** 他的枪法怎么样？

   What about his marksmanship?

   B: 百发百中，要多准有多准。

   His every shot hits the bull's eyes. How precise!

练习 Exercises

用"要多~有多~"完成句子。Complete the sentences with the pattern.

1. 这孩子_____，谁见了都喜欢。

2. 她丈夫对她可体贴了，_____。

解释 *Explanation*

表示某事能否成功取决于某人。

Used to indicate that the success of something depends on somebody.

例句 *Examples*

1. 我没能说服她，现在要看你的了。

   I failed to persuade her. Now it depends on you.

2. 小欣是最后一个出场的，我们队能不能拿冠军要看她的了。

   Xiaoxin is the last to enter the arena. It depends on her whether our team can get the first place.

3. 这位老科学家对年轻人说："以后要看你们的了。"

   This old scientist told young people, "It will depend on you in the future."

4. 父辈们已经完成了他们的历史使命，现在要看我们的了。

   Our elder generation has fulfilled their historic missions, and now it depends on us.

对话 *Dialogues*

1. A：你看这场比赛北京队能不能赢?

   Do you think the Beijing team will win the match?

   B：那要看 11 号的了。

   It depends on player No. 11.

2. A：你说我们公司这次投标有戏没戏?

   Do you think our company can win this bidding?

   B：这事是梁总负责的，要看他的了。

   General Manager Liang is responsible for it, so it all depends on him.

练习 *Exercises*

用"要看 ~ 的了"完成句子。Complete the sentences with the pattern.

1. 小雷去买火车票了，今天能不能走_____。

2. 小顾和这家宾馆的经理认识，能不能拿到最低折扣_____。

解释 *Explanation*

表示选择，有时也可以用一个"要么"。

Used to indicate an option. Sometimes only one 要么 is used.

例句 *Examples*

1. 要么她来，要么我去，总得见面解决吧。

   Either she comes or I go. We have to meet and solve the problem.

2. 要么支持小孟，要么支持大康，模棱两可不太好吧。

   Support either Xiao Meng or Da Kang. It's not so good as to support both.

3. 企业要发展下去，要么有足够的知名度，要么产品能走近千家万户。

   To develop itself, an enterprise should either enjoy high fame, or get access to numerous households for its products.

4. 数码时代，柯达公司如遇劫难，要么创新，要么关门。

   In the digital era, Kodak will have to either make innovations or go bankruptcy in face of any crisis.

对话 *Dialogues*

1. **A:** 别跟这种人计较了，要么你换个单位怎么样？

   Don't argue with such kind of person. How about finding another job?

   B: 没那么简单，为了养家糊口我还得忍哪。

   It's not so simple. I have to support my family, so I must put up with him.

2. **A:** 你怎么什么任务都完成得那么出色？

   How can you do so well in any task?

   B: 对任何事情我的态度是要么全力以赴，要么索性不干。

   My attitude is either to go all out or do nothing.

练习 *Exercises*

用"要么 ~，要么 ~"完成句子。Complete the sentences with the pattern.

1. 面对困难，你只有两个选择，_____。

2. "不进则退"的意思是人生像逆水行舟，_____。

解释 *Explanation*

表示条件不好，需要的或希望的都没有。常两个连用。

Used often in reduplicated form to indicate bad condition—without what's needed or expected.

例句 *Examples*

1. 这里要什么没什么，怎么开展工作！

   Anything we need is not available. How can we possibly start our work?

2. 现在我的工作很难做，要钱没钱，要人没人。

   I find it difficult to carry on my task now：no money, no helping hands.

3. 这种企业，要技术没技术，要服务没服务，是兔子尾巴——长不了。

   Such kind of enterprises that have neither technology nor after-sale services won't last long.

4. 长辈们经历的"一穷二白"的那段时期，要吃没吃，要穿没穿。

   Our older generation experienced the hard times when they had nothing to eat and wear.

对话 *Dialogues*

1. A: 上边布置你写的那篇文章写好了吧?

   Have you finished the article that your superior assigned?

   B: 早着呢，要时间没时间，要材料没材料。

   No, a long way off. I have no time, no material.

2. A: 他老婆对他照顾得无微不至，他为什么对她还不满意?

   His wife takes meticulous care of him. Why is he still unsatisfied with her?

   B: 他认为她呀，要模样没模样，要文化没文化。

   He thinks that she is not pretty and she is not well-educated.

练习 *Exercises*

用"要 ~ 没 ~"完成句子。Complete the sentences with the pattern.

1. 十年前，他还是个穷小子，_____。

2. 唉，人老啦，_____ 。

要是 ~ 就 ~

解释 *Explanation*

表示假设。意思是如果在某种情况下，将会产生某种结果。多用于口语。

Used mostly in oral Chinese to indicate assumption, meaning that some result will be produced under a certain condition.

例句 *Examples*

1. 要是再过半小时他还不来，咱们就不等了。

   If he cannot come in half an hour, we won't wait.

2. 董事会要是没什么再讨论的，我就先告辞了。

   If the board of directors has nothing else for discussion, I will take leave first.

3. 要是他不同意就算了，不能一相情愿。

   We might as well do without him if he doesn't agree. It's of no use that only we have wishful thinking.

4. 做买卖的要是对人和气，生意就好做些，和气生财嘛。

   If you do business with a kind and friendly attitude, you will make more money. As the saying goes, amiability begets riches.

对话 *Dialogues*

1. **A:** 明天的运动会照常进行吗?

   Will tomorrow's sports meeting be held as scheduled?

   B: 要是下大雨，就开不成了。

   It won't be held if it rains heavily.

2. **A:** 你要是没什么事情，我们就去看场电影。

   If you have nothing to do, let's go to the cinema.

   B: 好的。

   OK.

练习 *Exercises*

用"要是 ~ 就 ~"完成句子。Complete the sentences with the pattern.

1. 我得改变一下生活习惯了，_____。

2. 你快离开这里吧，_____。

解释 *Explanation*

表示说话人的一种愿望，多为假设的情况。

Used to express the speaker's wish, mostly assumptions.

例句 *Examples*

1. 要是一家人都能在一起就好了，特别是过年过节的时候。

   It would be wonderful if family members could get together, particularly during the Spring Festival and other holidays.

2. 要是大陆开车来就好了，我们可以搭他的车。

   If only Da Lu drove his car here, we could ask him for a lift.

3. 人要是真能返老还童就好了，那一切都可以从头来过。

   It would be great if only man could turn young, then one could start everything again from the very beginning.

4. 要是你早点儿告诉我就好了，我一定会奉陪的。

   If only you could tell me earlier, I would certainly accompany you.

对话 *Dialogues*

1. A: 小方，我在国外太寂寞了。

   I'm so lonely abroad, Xiao Fang.

   B: 要是你跟我们在一起就好了，可以说说心里话。

   If only you could be with us, you would speak out your mind.

2. A: 当时要是他跟父母在一起就好了，那样就不会出事了。

   If only he had been with his parents, nothing would have happened to him.

   B: 咳，后悔也没用了。

   Well, it's no use regretting.

练习 *Exercises*

用"要是～就好了"完成句子。Complete the sentences with the pattern.

1. _____，你看，走晚了，车堵得这么厉害。

2. _____，老了的感觉真不好。

解释 *Explanation*

表示如果说到某人、某事、某种情况会如何。

Used to indicate what will happen if somebody, something, or some situation is referred to.

例句 *Examples*

1. 要说你的学历和工作经历，也不比他差多少啊。

You are not inferior to him, in terms of education and work experience.

2. 乔博士正在南美洲呢，要说他能赶回来，那是不可能的。

Doctor Qiao is now in South America. It's impossible that he can come back.

3. 要说我对这工作是百分之百的满意，那是假话。

It's not true that I'm one hundred percent satisfied with the job.

4. 要说私心啊，人人都有。可是说"人不为己，天诛地灭"，那不对。

Everyone has selfish motives. But it's not right to say "every man for himself, and the devil takes the hindmost."

对话 *Dialogues*

1. A: 你说，你们为什么选他当学生会主席而不选我?

You tell me. Why did you elect him chairman of the Student Union, not me?

   B: 要说活动能力，他比你强多了。

He is much better than you, speaking of the ability of planning and organizing activities.

2. A: 你觉得他能帮我吗?

Do you think he will help me?

   B: 他可是个热心肠的人，要说找他帮忙，他一定会尽力而为的。

He is a warmhearted man. And he will surely try his best to help if asked.

练习 *Exercises*

用"要说 ~"完成句子。Complete the sentences with the pattern.

1. A: 你说我是在学校当老师好呢，还是去公司工作?

   B: _____。

2. A: 你看老黄这人能力怎么样?

   B: _____。

解释 *Explanation*

表示如果想达到某个目的，必须具备某种条件才可以实现。

Used to indicate that certain conditions are required to achieve one's purpose.

例句 *Examples*

1. 要想提高国民的素质，得重视教育才行。

   The qualities of our citizens can only be enhanced if we emphasize the importance of education.

2. 要想改变这里的环境，得综合治理才行。

   The environment here can be improved only by taking comprehensive measures.

3. 要想得到别人的信任，得不说假话才行。

   A person will only be trusted if he/she tells the truth.

4. 你要想考上名校，还得更加努力才行。

   If you want to enter a prestigious university, you have to work harder.

对话 *Dialogues*

1. A: 怎样才能互相理解呢？

   How can we understand each other?

   B: 要想互相理解，得多接触多交流才行。

   Only through more contact and communication, can we improve mutual understanding.

2. A: 为什么一定要等我来呢？

   Why do you have to wait for me?

   B: 要想解决这个问题，得您出马才行。

   Because some problems can only be solved by you.

练习 *Exercises*

用"要想 ~，得 ~ 才行"完成句子。Complete the sentences with the pattern.

1. A: 怎样才能使身体健康？多吃点儿补品行吗？

   B: 不，_____。

2. A: 我怎么打不了汉语拼音？

   B: 你这台电脑装的是英文系统，_____。

解释 *Explanation*

表示需要的或想要的都有，意思是条件很好。

Used to indicate that there is all that is needed or expected, implying good conditions.

例句 *Examples*

1. 现在城市里的不少孩子可以说是要什么有什么。

   It might be fair to say, many children in cities have whatever they want nowadays.

2. 这小伙子真棒，要人品有人品，要本事有本事。

   This young man is truly outstanding. He has an excellent character, and is competent.

3. 你呀，太幸福了，要爱情有爱情，要事业有事业。

   You're so happy. You have found your love and have a successful career.

4. 要设备有设备，要资金有资金，要人才有人才，什么都不缺了。

   There are equipment, capital and human resources. Everything we need is here.

对话 *Dialogues*

1. A: 你知道吗，我很想去美国深造。

   You know what? I have a good mind to go to the United States for further study.

   B: 那完全不成问题，你要钱有钱，要学问有学问。

   It's no problem. You're well off and well-educated.

2. A: 我们公司很想到中国拓展业务。

   Our company has a great mind to expand our business in China.

   B: 没问题，你们要钱有钱，要关系有关系。

   No problem. You have money and connections.

练习 *Exercises*

用"要 ~有 ~"完成句子。Complete the sentences with the pattern.

1. 他出生在一个富裕的家庭，_____。

2. 你现在是什么也不缺了，_____。

解释 *Explanation*

有即使或无论怎么做也不能有某种结果的意思，"也"前后重复同一动词。

Used to indicate even if something is done or whatever to be done, certain result cannot be produced, with the same verb used before and after 也.

例句 *Examples*

1. 哎呀，这字这么小，看也看不清楚，还是你说给我听吧。

   Well, the characters are so small and I cannot read them. You tell me about it.

2. 这件新衣服弄上了果汁，洗也洗不干净。

   The new dress is stained with fruit juice and cannot wash clean.

3. 我这把年纪了，学什么也学不进去，还是算了吧。

   I'm too old to learn anything. Just forget about it.

4. 他留下的这些阿拉伯文书，我们看也看不懂，捐给图书馆算了。

   We don't understand these Arabic books he left. Just donate them to the library.

对话 *Dialogues*

1. A: 唉，老了，想多吃点儿也吃不动了。

   Ah, I'm old. I'm unable to eat more even if I want.

   B: 这话说得太早了吧！你离老还远着呢。

   It's too early to say so! You have many years to go to become old.

2. A: 你怎么不去学学游泳？对减肥特有效。

   Why don't you learn to swim? It's especially effective for losing weight.

   B: 我是旱鸭子，学也学不会，趁早拉倒吧。

   I'm a non-swimmer, and cannot get it anyway. I'd better give it up as early as possible.

练习 *Exercises*

用"A 也 A 不 ~"完成句子。Complete the sentences with the pattern.

1. A: 这次的会计师资格考试你参加吗？

   B: 我根本没准备，_____，还是下次再考吧。

2. A: 你跟他好好解释解释。

   B: 这事_____，算了吧。

解释 *Explanation*

表示按常理应该进行的动作未进行，就进行了后面的动作。"也不/没"前后用相同的词。

Used to indicate that somebody makes the latter action instead of what should be done according to common sense, with the same verb used before and after 也不/没.

例句 *Examples*

1. 当时我想也没想就答应了，现在觉得太草率了。

   I agreed without thinking about it, but now I find myself too hasty.

2. 撞伤行人后，肇事车停也不停就飞速逃走了。

   After hitting a pedestrian, the car did not stop but ran away quickly.

3. 今天我起晚了，早饭吃也没吃就出门了。

   I got up late today and went out without having breakfast.

4. 这么大一笔钱，齐经理问也不问就签字同意支付了。

   Manager Qi signed to approve the payment of such a big sum of money without inquiring about it.

对话 *Dialogues*

1. A：这黄瓜你怎么洗也没洗就吃了？

   Why didn't you wash the cucumber before eating?

   B：俗话说，不干不净，吃了没病。

   As the saying goes, unclean food won't cause disease.

2. A：我觉得北方人做菜比较粗。

   I think people in the north are not meticulous about cooking.

   B：是的，有时候整棵菜切也不切就下锅了。

   It's true. Sometimes they even don't cut a vegetable before putting it into the pan.

练习 *Exercises*

用"A 也不/没 A 就 ~"完成句子。Complete the sentences with the pattern.

1. 今天回到家时实在是累坏了，＿＿＿＿＿＿＿＿＿＿＿＿＿＿就睡了。

2. 我花了一晚上工夫给领导写了封信，没想到＿＿＿＿＿＿＿＿＿＿＿＿。

汉语常用格式330例

~ 也不是，~ 也不是

解释 *Explanation*

表示对某人、某事不知该如何对待或处理才好，感到十分为难。

Used to indicate that somebody is in a dilemma for not knowing how to deal with somebody or something.

例句 *Examples*

1. 听她这么说，我真是哭也不是，笑也不是。

   Hearing what she said, I don't know whether to cry or smile.

2. 我坐在那儿走也不是，留也不是，尴尬极了。

   I felt embarrassed because neither leaving nor staying was right.

3. 大盘持续下跌，我手里的股票卖也不是，不卖也不是。

   The large-cap index continues to drop. I have some shares but don't know whether to sell them or not.

4. 后妈难当啊，孩子做错了事，说也不是，不说也不是。

   It's hard to be a stepmother. When the child makes mistakes, you will be in a dilemma, not knowing whether to blame him or not.

对话 *Dialogues*

1. A: 你这人真怪，为什么怕别人请你吃饭？

   You're so strange. Why are you afraid of being invited to a meal?

   B: 我喝不了酒，饭桌上有人给我敬酒，我喝也不是，不喝也不是。

   I cannot drink. When someone toasts to me at table, I will feel uneasy.

2. A: 我妈怕冷，我爸怕热。这空调我开也不是，不开也不是。

   My mother is afraid of cold while my father is afraid of heat. I don't know whether to turn on the air-conditioner or not.

   B: 我们家也有一样的问题。

   Our family has the same problem.

练习 *Exercises*

用"~ 也不是，~ 也不是"完成句子。Complete the sentences with the pattern.

1. 我知道这事不该帮她，可是她老来求我。＿＿＿＿＿＿＿＿＿＿＿＿。

2. 我浑身酸疼，＿＿＿＿＿＿＿＿＿＿＿＿。

汉语常用格式330例

253

解释 *Explanation*

表示在某种情况下，不管有关人是否愿意，都必须要这样做，没有选择的余地。"~也得~"前后嵌入相同的动词。

Used to indicate that on certain conditions something must be done in a certain way regardless people's wishes. ~也得~ is used between the same verb.

例句 *Examples*

1. 今天可由不得你，去也得去，不去也得去。

   It's not up to you today. You have to go whether you want to or not.

2. 我是给老板打工的，老板让做的事，我做也得做，不做也得做。

   I work for the boss. I have to do what the boss asks me to do, whether I want to or not.

3. 都病成这样了，这药你是吃也得吃，不吃也得吃。

   You're so sick. You must take the medicine whether you want to or not.

4. "交情深，一口闷"，上了饭桌，这酒你是喝也得喝，不喝也得喝。

   "You must drink up in one mouth to show you're a real friend." At table you have to drink whether you want to or not.

对话 *Dialogues*

1. A: 你留学回来，英语口语真有明显的进步。

   Your spoken English has improved remarkably after you studied abroad.

   B: 是啊，在国外，这英语你是说也得说，不说也得说，怎么能没进步。

   Sure. When abroad, you have to speak English whether you want or not. No wonder I made some progress.

2. A: 我还没睡够呢，真不想起床啊。

   I haven't had enough sleep. I really don't want to get up.

   B: 时间到了，想起也得起，不想起也得起。

   It's time to get up. You have to get up whether you want to or not.

练习 *Exercises*

用"~也得~，不~也得~"和所给的动词写两个句子。Make two sentences with the pattern and verbs in parentheses.

1. ＿＿＿＿＿＿＿＿＿＿＿＿＿＿＿＿＿＿＿＿＿ 。（写）

2. ＿＿＿＿＿＿＿＿＿＿＿＿＿＿＿＿＿＿＿＿＿ 。（干）

汉语常用格式330例

解释 *Explanation*

两个或几个连用，表示在提及的情况下都是这样。

Used in reduplicated form (two or more) to indicate that it's the same under any circumstances.

例句 *Examples*

1. 孩子也好，成人也好，谁都有自己的个性。

   Either child or adult has his own individuality.

2. 让我下车间也好，坐办公室也好，只要能发工资就行。

   It's OK with me whether to work at the workshop or in an office, as long as I get paid.

3. 到北京也好，到上海也好，只要能去中国就谢天谢地了。

   I'd count myself lucky as long as I can go to China, either to Beijing or Shanghai.

4. 高级干部也好，普通公务员也好，都应该是为人民服务的。

   Either high-ranking officials or ordinary civil servants should serve the people.

对话 *Dialogues*

1. A：你想找什么样的对象？跟我说说，我想当红娘呢。

   Tell me, what kind of person do you like to date? I'd like to be a go-between.

   B：大学生也好，白领也好，只要心地善良、身体健康就行。

   Either college student or white-collar will be OK, as long as the person is kind and healthy.

2. A：哎，坐下来，聊聊咱们的旅行计划，想去哪里？

   Hi, sit down. Let's talk about our travel plan. Where do you want to go?

   B：欧洲也好，美国也好，只要有你跟我做伴儿，去哪里都愿意。

   I'd either go to Europe or America, as long as you accompany me.

练习 *Exercises*

用"~也好，~也好"完成句子。Complete the sentences with the pattern.

1. 他特别喜欢吃肉，＿＿＿＿＿＿＿＿＿＿＿＿＿＿＿＿，他都吃起来没够。

2. 我们是真心相爱，＿＿＿＿＿＿＿＿＿＿＿＿＿＿＿，我们都要一辈子在一起。

解释 *Explanation*

表示在某种情况下，自然会有某种结果或行动。

Used to indicate a result or action will be caused under a certain condition.

例句 *Examples*

1. 想想销售人员说的也有一定的道理，老板也就同意了。

   Finding what salespersons said was reasonable to some degree, the boss gave his consent.

2. 现在我家虽然不是很富裕，但是想起以前的穷日子，也就满足了。

   Our family is still not rich now. However, recalling the poor life in the past, we are content.

3. 我很想买新家具，但考虑过一段时间要搬家，也就打消了这种想法。

   I really want to buy new furniture. But I give up the thought considering that I will move soon.

4. 我自知理亏，既然对方给了个台阶下，我也就借坡下驴了。

   I know that I'm in the wrong. Now that the other side has given me a chance, I shall certainly grasp it.

对话 *Dialogues*

1. A: 现在谈判陷入了僵局。

   The negotiation is now in a deadlock.

   B: 要是双方都做些让步，僵局也就会打破了。

   It will be broken if both sides make some concessions.

2. A: 你不是说要去德国创办公司吗？

   Didn't you say that you would go to Germany and start a company?

   B: 但是后来想到父母年老体弱，也就打消了这个念头。

   But thinking of my aging parents, I gave up the idea.

练习 *Exercises*

用"也就 ~"完成句子。Complete the sentences with the pattern.

1. 看到他们转变了态度，我_____。

2. 孩子是看样学样，父母怎么做，_____。

解释 *Explanation*

表示"仅仅是"的意思。常限定了范围，有往小处说的意味。

Used often to set limits to indicate "only", implying understatement.

例句 *Examples*

1. 他们的公司不算大，也就是几十个人吧。

   Their company is not big, employing only several dozen people.

2. 一般的公寓不太贵，也就是五六十万一套吧。

   Ordinary apartments are not too expensive, only costing 500,000 to 600,000 yuan each.

3. 在我们看过的房子中，也就是这所房子还比较好。

   Among all the houses we have seen, only this one is reasonably good.

4. 其实那里并不算远，开车也就是二十分钟的路程吧。

   That place is not very far, only 20 minutes' drive from here.

对话 *Dialogues*

1. A：你找吕经理有事吗？

   Why do you ask for Manager Lv?

   B：没什么重要的事，也就是想和他聊聊而已。

   Nothing important. I just want to chat with him.

2. A：这位公司经理汉语怎么说得这么好，在哪里学的？

   The manager of the company speaks Chinese so well. Where did he learn it?

   B：据说是在国内学的，到中国学习也就是两三个月吧。

   It's said he learned Chinese in his country. And he studied in China for only two or three months.

练习 *Exercises*

用"也就是 ~"完成句子。Complete the sentences with the pattern.

1. 他们两个人从相识到结婚，也就是_____。

2. 这本书我写得很慢，一天_____ 。

解释 *Explanation*

表示时间短或数量小，常用在两个同义词或近义词前。

Used separately before synonyms or near-synonoyms, meaning not many (or much) or very soon.

例句 *Examples*

1. 要掌握一门外语不容易，一年半载可不行。

   It's not easy to master a foreign language. You can't do it in a short time.

2. 那个地方很偏僻，交通不方便，一天半天到不了。

   That place is out of the way with poor transportation. You cannot arrive there very soon.

3. 高手过招，输赢就在那一招半式之间。

   The competition between master-hands is decided by a few moves.

4. 既然想当公务员，谁不希望在政府机关谋个一官半职呢？

   Those who hope to become a civil servant all want to get a position in a government organ.

对话 *Dialogues*

1. A：你要盐，我这里有，要多少？

   You need salt, and I have some. How much do you want?

   B：一星半点儿就够。

   A little is enough.

2. A：你是这方面的专家！

   You're an expert in this field!

   B：哪里，我也只是一知半解。

   Thank you. I only have a smattering of knowledge.

练习 *Exercises*

选词填空。Choose the right phrases to fill in the blanks.

一星半点儿	一官半职	一知半解	一天半天

1. 咱俩认识也不是＿＿＿＿＿＿＿＿了，还那么客气！

2. 我并没有完全搞明白这个原理，还是＿＿＿＿＿＿＿。

一边 ~ 一边 ~

解释 *Explanation*

表示两个动作同时进行。口语常说 "一边儿 ~ 一边儿 ~"。

Used to indicate two actions taking place at the same time. 一边儿 ~ 一边儿 ~ is often used in oral Chinese.

例句 *Examples*

1. 学生们一边专心听老师讲一边认真记笔记。

   Students listened to the teacher attentively while making notes carefully.

2. 他一边看着笔记一边听着摇滚，能专心学习吗？

   He reads his notes while listening to disco music. How can he concentrate on study?

3. 他一边弹钢琴一边哼着曲子，自我陶醉。

   Playing piano while humming, he is enjoying himself.

4. 多年不见的朋友们欢聚一堂，一边慢慢品茶一边尽情说笑。

   Friends who have not seen each other for a long time gather together and drink tea slowly while talking and laughing to their hearts' content.

对话 *Dialogues*

1. A: 你觉得那个广播节目怎么样？

   What do you think of that radio program?

   B: 挺好的，我常常一边儿做饭一边儿听。

   Very good. I often listen to it while cooking.

2. A: 你这个单身汉，晚上都怎么过呢？

   How do you spend the evening, as a single man?

   B: 我嘛，一杯咖啡相伴，一边儿嗑点儿瓜子、花生一边儿看些有趣的电视节目，自得其乐啊。

   Me? With a cup of coffee, I eat melon seeds and peanuts while watching interesting TV programs, and I'm happy and content.

练习 *Exercises*

用 "一边 ~ 一边 ~" 完成句子。Complete the sentences with the pattern.

1. 我可以＿＿＿＿＿＿＿＿＿＿＿＿＿＿＿＿＿＿。

2. 他因为＿＿＿＿＿＿＿＿＿＿＿＿＿＿＿＿被警察罚了款。

一 ~ 不 ~

解释 Explanation

"一"和"不"可分别用在名词和动词前，表示强调或夸张；或是分别用在两个动词前，表示动作或情况一经发生就不改变。

— and 不 are either followed respectively by a noun and a verb which indicates emphasis or exaggeration, or they are followed by two verbs to indicate that actions or conditions can not be changed once they are occurred.

例句 Examples

1. 任何事物都是不断发展变化的，不是一成不变的。
   Everything is in a state of constant change and development. Nothing is immutable.

2. 人称他是吝啬鬼、铁公鸡，对赈灾活动也一毛不拔。
   He is called a miser, a tight wad. Even for this disaster relief he donated nothing.

3. 钱拿到手后，他就再没了音信，一去不返了。
   When he got the money, he disappeared.

4. 五年前他做生意失败，赔了一大笔钱，从此后就一蹶不振。
   Five years ago his business failed and he lost a large sum of money. Since then he has been in decline.

对话 Dialogues

1. A：我刚打扫过房间，怎么样，干净吧？
   I have just swept the room. How is it, clean?

   B：干净，真干净，简直是一尘不染。
   It is spotlessly clean.

2. A：局长最欣赏马秘书做事认真这点。
   The Bureau Chief appreciates the meticulosity of Secretary Ma.

   B：没错，可以说是一丝不苟。
   Yes, he deserved it for being such a conscientious person.

练习 Exercises

选词填空。Choose the right phrases to fill in the blanks.

> 一声不响　　一言不发　　一字不差　　一窍不通

1. 我是学文的，对机械构造方面_____。

2. 我很想听听你的意见，可是开会时你_____。

解释 *Explanation*

表示同时否定两个方面，并列关系。还可以接着说"三不 ~ ，四不 ~"等，否定多个方面。

Used to negate two coordinate aspects at the same time. 三不 ~ ，四不 ~ can be used to negate more aspects.

例句 *Examples*

1. 一不做，二不休，咱们一定得干到底。

   Since we have started, we must carry it through at all cost.

2. 他一不怕苦，二不怕累，工作勤勤恳恳、任劳任怨。

   Fearing neither hardship nor tiredness, he works hard and has no complaint.

3. 大家都认为他一不为名，二不为利，只是踏踏实实地做好本职工作。

   All believe he just does his own duty steadfastly, for neither fame nor money.

4. 我这样做又怎么了？一不违法，二不缺德，三不坑人！

   What's wrong with my behavior? I did not break the law, was not vicious, and did not cheat others.

对话 *Dialogues*

1. A: 小康真是个好学生。

   Xiao Kang is really a good student.

   B: 当然，他一不说谎，二不逃学，三不打架斗殴，学习认真，而且助人为乐。

   Sure. He neither tells lies, plays truant nor fights. He studies hard and is ready to help others.

2. A: 那里情况有些异常，警察突然增多了，你要小心点儿！

   Something is wrong there. More policemen suddenly show up. Be careful.

   B: 我一不偷，二不抢，怕什么！

   I neither steal nor rob. And I have nothing to fear.

练习 *Exercises*

用"一不 ~ ，二不 ~"完成句子。Complete the sentences with the pattern.

1. 四川菜的特点就是麻辣，你这菜做得＿＿＿＿＿＿＿＿＿＿＿，还是川菜吗？

2. 他＿＿＿＿＿＿＿＿＿＿＿，没有任何不良嗜好。

解释 *Explanation*

表示如果有一天或忽然有一天有了某种条件或出现了某种情况，那么某种结果就会随之发生。常和"就"一起用。

Used often with 就 to indicate that a result will be produced some day under a certain condition.

例句 *Examples*

1. 毒品很可怕，一旦沾染上，正常生活就彻底结束了。

   Drugs are terrible. Once you take drugs, your normal life will end completely.

2. 这座楼没有消防设备，一旦发生火灾，问题可就大了。

   There is no fire-fighting equipment in this building. Once fire breaks out, it will cause a big problem.

3. 你把所有的钱都投入股市，风险太大了，一旦股市崩盘，你会急疯的。

   It's too risky to put all your money into the stock market. Once the market crashes, you will go crazy.

4. 他这人很固执，一旦下了决心，就是十头牛也拉不回来。

   He is very stubborn. Once he makes the decision, nobody can talk him out of it.

对话 *Dialogues*

1. A: 为什么这么多人都想进北京大学呢？

   Why so many people want to enter Peking University?

   B: 他们认为一旦进了这所大学，就业就有了保证。

   They believe that once they are enrolled, they will surely be employed after graduation.

2. A: 要分别了，我心里真不舍得。

   We are going to say goodbye, but I hate to leave you.

   B: 大家朝夕相处这么久，一旦分别，怎能不难过呢？

   Having been together for so long, we cannot help missing each other once we are separated.

练习 *Exercises*

用"一旦 ~"完成句子。Complete the sentences with the pattern.

1. 这个学校对学生考试作弊管得很严，_____。

2. 当然要买保险啦，_____。

解释 *Explanation*

用于否定句，强调完全否定。"一点儿"后可加入名词再跟"都"搭配使用。

Used in a negative sentence to emphasize absolute negation. A noun can be used after 一点儿 and be followed by 都.

例句 *Examples*

1. 他们两兄弟虽是双胞胎，可性格一点儿都不像。

   Although they are twins, the two brothers are totally different in disposition.

2. 他对自己做的种种坏事儿，一点儿悔改的表示都没有。

   He even does not show the faintest sign of repentance about all the bad deeds he did.

3. 你现在再说什么也是白费唇舌，他一点儿也听不进去。

   Whatever you say now, you're only wasting your breath. He does not listen to you at all.

4. 一个人不可能一点儿缺点也没有，也不会一点儿优点也没有。

   It's impossible that a person is flawless or of no merits.

对话 *Dialogues*

1. A: 这次大地震前，难道一点儿征兆也没有？

   Was there no sign of the great earthquake before it occurred?

   B: 科学还不够发达吧。

   I think science is not advanced enough.

2. A: 他可能还认识不到，这样四处树敌对他一点儿好处都没有。

   He may not know that it's no good making enemies everywhere.

   B: 可不是嘛。

   It's true.

练习 *Exercises*

用"一点儿也/都 ~"改写句子。Rewrite the sentences with the pattern.

1. 这件事我完全不知道。→＿＿＿＿＿＿＿＿＿＿＿＿＿。

2. 今天天气真好，完全没有风。→＿＿＿＿＿＿＿＿＿＿＿＿＿。

解释 *Explanation*

用于列举事物，"一"、"二"中间一般有停顿；或是强调程度高，这时"一"、"二"分别放在双音节形容词的两个语素前，中间不停顿。

Used to list things, with pause betweven — ~ and 二 ~; or to emphasize degree, with each morpheme of the disyllabic adjectives used after — and 二 respectively without pause.

例句 *Examples*

1. 办个有实力的企业，一要钱，二要人，三要时间。
   To start a competent enterprise needs money, people and time.

2. 面对投资的巨大损失，你可不能像有的人那样，一急、二怨、三跳楼的。
   In face of the huge investment loss, you should not act like some people who are anxious at first, then start to complain and finally kill themselves by jumping off the building.

3. 今天我姐做的饭菜太香了，八菜一汤，大家吃得一干二净。
   My elder sister cooked delicious dishes today. We ate up all the eight dishes and one bowl of soup.

4. 我们的武会计可真是个好会计师，账目总是做得一清二楚的。
   Mr Wu is really a good accountant. He always makes the account very clear.

对话 *Dialogues*

1. A: 听说，他已经提前回国了？
   I heard that he had returned from abroad ahead of schedule. Is it true?

   B: 对，因为他一不会德语，二举目无亲，很难适应那里的环境。
   Yes. Because he can't speak German, and was totally a stranger there. He could hardly adapt to the environment there.

2. A: 上个世纪五六十年代你们过得怎么样？
   What's your life like in the 1950s and 1960s?

   B: 可以说是一穷二白。
   I would say we were very poor.

练习 *Exercises*

用"一 ~ (,) 二 ~"完成句子。Complete the sentences with the pattern.

1. A: 你不是去看演出了吗？怎么这么早就回来了？

   B: _____。

2. A: 你可以自己办个厂子啊。

   B: 现在_____，怎么办厂？

汉语常用格式330例

一方面~，一方面~

解释 *Explanation*

表示并列关系，从两个方面来说明某一件事情。后一个"一方面"前可加"另"，后面常用"又、也、却"。

Used to explain something from two coordinate aspects. 另 may be used before the latter one, often followed by 又, 也 or 却.

例句 *Examples*

1. 这座桥要大修，我们一方面设计方案，一方面筹集资金。
   This bridge needs thorough repairing. We will make a design on the one hand and raise fund on the other.

2. 任何事情都要做两种准备，一方面要积极争取，一方面也要做最坏的打算。
   You have to make two kinds of preparations for anything: actively work for it on the one hand, and prepare for the worst on the other.

3. 为了身体健康一方面我们要经常运动，另一方面也要注意不能过量运动。
   For the sake of health, we must do exercises regularly on the one hand, and avoid excessive exercises on the other.

4. 他一方面到处捐钱，好像热衷于慈善事业，另一方面却利用职权搜刮民脂民膏。
   On the one hand, he donated money everywhere, looking committed to charity; on the other, he abused his power to fleece the people.

对话 *Dialogues*

1. A: 听说他退休后过得很逍遥自在。
   I've heard that he's leading a carefree and comfortable life after retirement.

   B: 那当然，他现在一方面有钱，一方面又有时间。
   Certainly. He has money and time as well.

2. A: 小万试用期满了，现在怎么跟他谈呢？
   Xiao Wan has finished his probation. What shall I tell him?

   B: 一方面要肯定他的成绩，一方面也要指出年轻人的不足之处。
   You should acknowledge his achievements on the one hand, and point out his deficiencies as a young man on the other.

练习 *Exercises*

用"一方面~，一方面~"完成句子。Complete the sentences with the pattern.

1. A: 在中国为什么有那么多人买基金？

   B: _____。

2. A: 你也喜欢养宠物狗吗？

   B: _____。

一个 ~，一个 ~

解释 *Explanation*

常用来列举并列的两种不同事物。

Used often to list two kinds of coordinate but different things.

例句 *Examples*

1. 一个苹果，一个梨，都是我喜欢的水果。

   Apple and pear are both my favorite fruit.

2. 他有两样不离身的东西，一个是烟，一个是手机。

   He always carries two things with him: cigarette and cell phone.

3. 他们离得太远了，一个天南，一个海北的，怎么能交流感情啊。

   They are too far away, one in the south and the other in the north. How can they exchange feelings?

4. 你瞧我今天做的这两样菜，一个过咸，一个又太淡，凑合着吃吧。

   Well, I cooked two dishes today, but one is too salty while the other is too light. Just make do with them.

对话 *Dialogues*

1. A：你看这花篮一个大一个小，你要哪个？

   One of the flower baskets is big and the other is small. Which one do you want?

   B：你先挑吧。

   You choose first.

2. A：你今天精神怎么这么差，有什么心事吧？

   Why are you in low spirits today? What's on your mind?

   B：咳，一个是妈，一个是妻，她们吵得不可开交，你说我该怎么办？

   Well, one is my mother and the other is my wife. They two quarrel fiercely. What shall I do?

练习 *Exercises*

用"一个 ~，一个 ~"完成句子。Complete the sentences with the pattern.

1. 我有两个孩子，_____。

2. 你看这哥俩，_____ _____。

解释 *Explanation*

表示在不长的时间内两种情况交替发生。

Used to indicate alternating circumstances in a short time.

例句 *Examples*

1. 这天气真是的，一会儿出太阳，一会儿下雨。

   The weather is changeable. It shines one moment and rains the next.

2. 这么大的人，怎么跟孩子似的，一会儿哭，一会儿笑。

   How come you cry one moment and laugh the next, just as a child?

3. 你看他那忙劲儿，一会儿写，一会儿算的，连头都不抬。

   Look, how busy he is! Now writing, now calculating, he does not even raise his head.

4. 手机铃声怎么一会儿是我自己设置的，一会儿是默认的?

   Why does the ring tone of my cell phone change by itself? One moment it is what I have set, the next it shifts to default settings.

对话 *Dialogues*

1. A: 他们家的人今天怎么一会儿出一会儿进的?

   Why are their family members so busy, now coming out, now going in?

   B: 发生什么事了吧。

   I think something happened.

2. A: 现在他们夫妻俩的关系怎么样啦?

   How is the relationship between the husband and wife?

   B: 还是老样子，一会儿好，一会儿吵的。

   Same as usual. They are on good terms the moment, and quarrel the next.

练习 *Exercises*

用 "一会儿 ~ ，一会儿 ~" 完成句子。Complete the sentences with the pattern.

1. 这个热水器是不是出问题了? 怎么出的水_____?

2. 你好好开车，别_____的。

一 ~ 就 ~

解释 *Explanation*

表示两件事情紧接着发生。可以是同一主语，也可以是不同主语。

Used to indicate two things happen closely in sequence of time. The subjects of two clauses may be the same one or different ones.

例句 *Examples*

1. 小郝是不是对我有意见，怎么我一来他就走了？

   Does Xiao Hao have some problem with me? Why did he leave the moment I came in?

2. 小季和我真够交情，一到北京，就先来看我了。

   Xiao Ji is really good to me. He came to visit me as soon as he arrived in Beijing.

3. 这几天她一吃就吐，不会是怀孕了吧？

   These days she has vomited the moment she eats. Is it possible that she's pregnant?

4. 我听老师讲汉语语法，常是一听就懂，一用就错。

   When I listen to the teacher explaining Chinese grammars, it's often the case that I understand as soon as I hear them but make mistakes when putting them to use.

对话 *Dialogues*

1. A：他这样说是什么意思？

   What did he mean by saying so?

   B：你不懂吗？我可是一听就明白了。

   Didn't you understand? I understood as soon as I heard it.

2. A：我们明天什么时候出发？

   When will we start off tomorrow?

   B：天一亮就出发，那时路上绝不会堵车。

   We will start off at dawn, because there won't be any traffic jam at that time.

练习 *Exercises*

用 "一 ~ 就 ~" 完成句子。Complete the sentences with the pattern.

1. 你的声音我太熟悉了，＿＿＿＿＿＿＿＿＿＿＿＿＿＿＿＿。

2. 这些房子都是泥草房，＿＿＿＿＿＿＿＿＿＿＿＿＿＿ 。

解释 *Explanation*

列举出表示并列的几个原因或目的，还可以接着说"三来 ~，四来 ~"。

Used to list several coordinate reasons or purposes. 三来 ~，四来 ~ may be used after them.

例句 *Examples*

1. 用电子邮件联络一来快，二来方便，三来省钱。

   E-mail is used for communication because first, it is fast, second, it is convenient; and third, it saves money.

2. 不少企业家们到中国去，一来为了观光，二来为了考察投资环境。

   Many entrepreneurs visit China to go sightseeing on the one hand and explore the investment environment on the other.

3. 这部电影实在没看头，一来内容乏味，二来主角的表演太做作了。

   This movie is not worth seeing because for one thing, it's boring; and for another, the leading actor's performance is overdone.

4. 我想再找份工作干，一来可以退而不休，二来也能增加点儿收入。总之可以提高生活质量。

   I want to find another job, because first, I don't want to rest though I've retired, and second, I can have more income. In a nutshell, it can help improve my life.

对话 *Dialogues*

1. A：你喜欢穿布鞋？

   You like wearing cloth shoes, don't you?

   B：嗯，一来舒服，二来便宜。

   Yes, because for one thing they are comfortable and for another cheap.

2. A：你怎么对这个地方特别有感情？

   Why are you attached to this place?

   B：一来我在这里住过几年，二来这里真是山清水秀啊。

   Because first, I lived here for a few years; and second, the scenery is picturesque.

练习 *Exercises*

用"一来 ~，二来 ~"完成句子。Complete the sentences with the pattern.

1. A：我觉得大学生打工挺好的。

   B：是啊，＿＿＿＿＿＿＿＿＿＿＿。

2. A：你怎么没答应跟他一起出游？

   B：＿＿＿＿＿＿＿＿＿＿＿。

解释 *Explanation*

用于否定句，表示完全否定。"一"后用量词。

Used in a negative sentence to indicate absolute negation, with a measure word used after 一.

例句 *Examples*

1. 这次期末物理考试，小李一道题都没有做出来。

   Xiao Li failed to work out any problem in the final exam of physics.

2. 今天学校大扫除，结果一个学生也没有来，真不像话。

   There was a sweepup at school today, but no student came. What a shame!

3. 现在好电影越来越少了，这半年来，我一次电影都没看过。

   There are fewer and fewer good movies now. I have not seen a single movie in the past half year.

4. 在几位首长面前，这个年轻士兵紧张得一句话也说不出来。

   The young soldier was too nervous to say anything before a few senior officers.

对话 *Dialogues*

1. A: 你还经常去邮局寄信吗？

   Do you still often go to the post office to mail letters?

   B: 自从我装了宽带，老发电子邮件，一封信也没寄过。

   Since I have broadband installed at home, I always use e-mail, and have not mailed any letter.

2. A: 我不想再听你说什么，请出去吧。

   I don't want to listen to you anymore. Get out please.

   B: 难道连一个解释的机会也不给我吗？

   Don't you even give me a chance to explain?

练习 *Exercises*

用"一 ~ 也/都 ~"完成句子。Complete the sentences with the pattern.

1. 我今天忙得四脚朝天，_____。

2. 一年前我刚到这儿时，_____。

解释 *Explanation*

"一"分别用在两个名词前，表示整个或数量少；分别用在两个动词前，表示动作是连续的或两种动作交替进行；分别用在两个方位词、形容词前，表示相反的方位或情况。

Used respectively before two nouns to indicate the whole or a small amount; used respectively before two verbs to indicate the continuance of the action or the alternation of two actions; used respectively before two opposite nouns of direction or two opposite adjectives to indicate contrary positions or situations.

例句 *Examples*

1. 我对他可以说是一心一意，从来没有别的想法。
   I love him whole-heartedly, and never have other thoughts.
2. 我在这里住了大半辈子，对这里的一草一木都很有感情。
   I've lived here most of my life and thus feel attached to every tree and grass.
3. 一阵狂风过后，兄妹二人一前一后地往家赶。
   After a gush of wind, the brother and sister rushed home with one in front and the other following.
4. 这件衣服的两只袖子怎么一长一短，袖口也是一松一紧?
   What's wrong with the clothes? One sleeve is long while the other is short, and one cuff is loose while the other is tight.

对话 *Dialogues*

1. A: 最近工作很紧张，常常熬夜。
   Recently I've been working under high pressure and often have to stay up late.
   B: 工作再紧张也不能老开夜车啊，一张一弛，才能提高效率。
   No matter how gruelling your work is, you cannot frequently stay up late. Only with both tension and relaxation, will you enhance efficiency.

2. A: 你走路怎么一瘸一拐的?
   Why are you walking lamely?
   B: 咳，别提了，我昨天在足球场上摔了一跤。
   Well, I'm embarrassed to mention it. I fell down on the football field yesterday.

练习 *Exercises*

选词填空。Choose the right phrases to fill in the blanks.

一言一行   一生一世   一起一落   一上一下

1. 当老师的要为人师表，_____都要特别注意。

2. 在这场灾难中你失去了两条腿，但别怕，我_____都会照顾你的。

解释 *Explanation*

"一"和"再"分别用在同一个动词前,表示该动作多次重复。

Used respectively before the same verb to indicate the repetition of the action.

例句 *Examples*

1. 他早就该去看医生,但是因为忙而一拖再拖,结果病情恶化了。

   He should have seen a doctor earlier. But he made repeated delays due to busy work and consequently, his condition became worse.

2. 政策要有连续性,如果一变再变,就会令人无所适从。

   Policies should be consistent. If they change again and again, people won't know which one to follow.

3. 夏教授学风严谨,文章写完后总是一改再改才投稿。

   Professor Xia is strict in his style of academic study. He always makes repeated revisions before contributing his article.

4. 他咽不下这口气,想要报复,我一劝再劝,他才打消了这念头。

   He was unable to take the insult and wanted to revenge himself. I tried to persuade him again and again, and finally he gave up this idea.

对话 *Dialogues*

1. A: 今年手机话费一降再降,可是老百姓还是不满意。

   Cell phone charge keeps decreasing this year, but people are still unsatisfied.

   B: 漫游费、双向付费不合理嘛。

   Because roaming service charges and two-way charges are both unreasonable.

2. A: 这些事我们还是等一段时间再议吧。

   Let's discuss these matters some time later.

   B: 这些都是有关国计民生的大事,必须立即办理,不能一拖再拖了。

   These matters concern national economy and the people's livelihood and must be handled immediately. We cannot postpone them again and again.

练习 *Exercises*

用"一~再~"完成句子。Complete the sentences with the pattern.

1. 这只股票_____,已经跌破发行价了。

2. 犯了错误要及时改正,千万不能_____。

解释 *Explanation*

"以便"用于后半句的开头，表示目的。前半句提出应如何做，能使后半句提出的某个目的容易实现。

Used at the beginning of the second part of a sentence to indicate a purpose. The first part of the sentence talks about how to do something, to facilitate the fulfilment of the purpose mentioned in the second part.

例句 *Examples*

1. 你要多阅读一些中文翻译资料，以便写论文时参考。

   You should read more materials translated into Chinese for reference when writing your thesis.

2. 请提供一份你的简历，以便我们招聘人员时考虑。

   Please provide a copy of your resume so that we can take you into consideration for employment.

3. 请告诉我们贵公司的传真号码，以便及时联系。

   Please tell me the fax number of your company so that we can get in touch with you in time.

4. 这些文件请分类保管，以便易于查找。

   Please archive these files in category for easy reference.

对话 *Dialogues*

1. A: 你能否用简单的语言把文章概括一下，以便大家讨论。

   Would you please summarize the article in simple words so that we may discuss it conveniently.

   B: 好的。遵命！

   OK, I will do it.

2. A: 我们看不懂这篇文章，因为有太多的专业词汇。

   We cannot understand this article, because it has too many specialized terms.

   B: 那我会对这些词加以注释，以便你们阅读。

   I will annotate these terms for your reading.

练习 *Exercises*

用"~，以便 ~"完成句子。Complete the sentences with the pattern.

1. 我眼睛不好，得把字写大些，_____。

2. 现在的网速很慢，我要换个高速的，_____。

～，以免～

解释 *Explanation*

前句表示采取某种措施，后句表示目的：为了避免发生某种不希望发生的事情。多用于书面语。

Placed in the second half of the sentence to indicate the purpose of some measures stated in the first half of the sentence. It means to avoid or prevent certain undesirable condition and is mostly used in written Chinese.

例句 *Examples*

1. 中药煎煮前不需清洗，以免造成药材成分丢失。

   Don't wash Chinese medicine before decocting, lest medicinal ingredients will wash off.

2. 你要事先做好准备，以免到时候措手不及。

   You must make preparations in advance so as not to be caught unprepared.

3. 这些数字要多核对几遍，以免出现差错。

   You should check the figures for more times to avoid errors.

4. 专家建议月供最好不要超过收入的1/3，以免房屋贷款压力过大。

   According to experts' suggestion, it's better to make your monthly instalment less than one third of your income to avoid too much burden of repaying housing mortgage.

对话 *Dialogues*

1. A：沈书记，我们已调查清楚这次事故发生的原因了。

   Secretary Shen, we've made an investigation and found out the cause of the accident.

   B：要认真总结经验教训，以免再发生类似的问题。

   We must sum up experience and draw a lesson from it to avoid the recurrence of similar problems.

2. A：买卖房产一定要先仔细地阅读合同内容，再签合同。

   When buying or selling house property, you must carefully read the contract before signing it.

   B：是啊，以免日后发生纠纷。

   I agree. It's to avoid future dispute.

练习 *Exercises*

用"～，以免～"完成句子。Complete the sentences with the pattern.

1. 过马路要一慢二看三通过，_____。

2. 请你们说话小声点儿，_____。

274

解释 *Explanation*

表示"把~作为~"或"认为~是~"。

Used to indicate to take/regard … as… or to consider … to be ….

例句 *Examples*

1. 雷雷是个爱情英雄，为了他心爱的人，他宁愿以生命为代价。

   Lei Lei is a hero of love. For his beloved, he would rather sacrifice his life.

2. 政府正在加快推进以改善民生为重点的社会建设。

   The government is accelerating social construction with the focus on improving people's livelihood.

3. 他们推崇以客户为中心的设计思想，所设计的产品深受用户的欢迎。

   They value the design philosophy of putting customers first, and the products they designed are quite popular among users.

4. 青岛人以青岛啤酒为自豪。

   Qingdao people are proud of Tsingdao Beer.

对话 *Dialogues*

1. A: 你说做人的原则应该是什么？

   In your opinion, what principle does a man should follow?

   B: 每人有所不同，我是以诚信为本。

   It's different for everyone. I regard credibility as my principle.

2. A: 韩国这个世纪的经营战略是什么？

   What's the economic strategy of South Korea for this century?

   B: 韩国以资讯产业为经济命脉，全力发展这个领域。

   It takes the information industry as its economic artery and goes all out to develop the industry.

练习 *Exercises*

用"以 ~ 为 ~"完成句子。Complete the sentences with the pattern.

1. 这个人总是_____，从来不为他人考虑。

2. 这是一本_____为主的小说。

以为 ~，原来/没想到 ~

解释 *Explanation*

表示说话人发现实际情况与自己以前的想法、猜测完全不同。

Used to indicate that the speaker finds out that the reality is completely different from his previous thought or assumption.

例句 *Examples*

1. 我以为你在图书馆呢，原来在这儿。
   So you are here. I thought you were in the library.

2. 我还以为她是个文静的姑娘呢，原来她玩儿起来也会这么疯。
   I thought she was a gentle and quiet girl. I did not expect that she could enjoy herself without restraint.

3. 我以为我碰到了白马王子，没想到他是个大骗子。
   I thought I had found Prince Charming. But it turned out he was a big liar.

4. 刚看到这个网名的时候我还以为是个女的，没想到是个男的。
   When seeing this net name, I believed it belonged to a woman. But it turned out to be a man's.

对话 *Dialogues*

1. A: 我有一个儿子，一个女儿。
      I have a son and a daughter.

   B: 什么？我还以为你没结婚呢，没想到你孩子都有了！
      What? I thought you were unmarried. I didn't expect that you had had children.

2. A: 这份工作让我觉得压力好大！
      This job gives me much pressure.

   B: 我以为只有我觉得压力大呢，原来你也一样。
      I thought only I felt the pressure. So you have the same feeling as well.

练习 *Exercises*

用"以为 ~，原来/没想到 ~"完成句子。Complete the sentences with the pattern.

1. 我以为他对我没什么感觉，_____。

2. 初恋的时候我以为爱情会天长地久，_____。

汉语常用格式330例

解释 *Explanation*

用在下半句话的开头，表示下文是上文所述原因造成的结果。多为不好的结果。

Used at the beginning of the second half of a sentence to indicate that what follows is a consequence, mostly bad, of the fact stated in the first half of the sentence.

例句 *Examples*

1. 他的腿受了重伤，以致好几个月都下不了床。

   His leg was seriously injured so that he stayed in bed for several months.

2. 司机疲劳驾驶，以致酿成这起五人死亡的车祸。

   The traffic accident, with five people dead, happened as a result of fatigue driving.

3. 父母对他过分地溺爱，以致他变得目中无人，自以为是。

   His parents spoil him. And as a result, he looks down upon everyone else and regards himself as infallible.

4. 因为医生没有及时采取恰当的治疗措施，以致病人病情恶化。

   The doctor did not take proper measures in time. Consequently, the patient got worse.

对话 *Dialogues*

1. A: 昨天你大醉，后来回家了吗？

   Did you go home yesterday after you got drunk?

   B: 回了，不过没带钥匙，深夜叫门，以致惊醒了左邻右舍。

   Yes. But I did not take the key and had to knock on the door. As a result, my neighbors were awakened.

2. A: 听说他们俩真的要离婚了？

   I've heard that they are getting divorced. Is it true?

   B: 是啊，两个人平时缺乏沟通，以致感情破裂，无法弥补了。

   Yes. They lack communication so that they lose affection for each other and cannot make it up.

练习 *Exercises*

用 " ~ ，以致 ~ " 完成句子。Complete the sentences with the pattern.

1. 她太软弱了，_____。

2. 因为出门前忘了关窗，_____。

～，以至于～

解释 *Explanation*

用在下半句话的开头，表示由于上文所说的动作、情况的程度极高极深而形成某种结果。也说"以至"。

Used at the beginning of the second half of a sentence to indicate the action or situation stated in the first half of the sentence is such that a result is produced. And 于 may sometimes be omitted.

例句 *Examples*

1. 他的表演太好笑了，以至于大家笑得肚子都疼了。

   His performance was so funny that everyone laughed himself into convulsion.

2. 最近我常常感到眼皮沉，以至于有时候连眼睛也睁不开。

   Recently I often feel my eyelids are so heavy that sometimes I even cannot open my eyes.

3. 她一整天沉浸在那本小说的世界里，以至不知身在何处。

   She lost herself in the world of the novel for a whole day and even didn't know where she was.

4. 她太会骗人了，以至我们被告知真相后，几乎无法相信自己的耳朵。

   She is so good at lying that we could not believe what we heard when we were told the truth.

对话 *Dialogues*

1. A: 这几年来那个地方变化肯定挺大的吧？

   Great changes must have taken place there in recent years, right?

   B: 那儿发展变化十分迅速，以至于很多人都感到吃惊。

   That place has been developing so rapidly that many people are surprised.

2. A: 你的胳膊怎么了？摔伤了吗？

   How about your arm? Is it hurt?

   B: 不是，只是常常觉得无力，以至于有时候都抬不起来。

   No. I just often feel it's so weak that sometimes I even cannot raise it.

练习 *Exercises*

用"～，以至于～"完成句子。Complete the sentences with the pattern.

1. 这个地方风景太美了，_____。

2. 你看，我真是忙得晕头转向了，_____。

解释 *Explanation*

表示因果关系。

Used to indicate a cause-and-effect relationship.

例句 *Examples*

1. 因为时间的关系，今天的会议就到此结束。

   Due to time limitation, today's meeting is over now.

2. 因为我是独生子的关系，在家备受宠爱。

   As the only child, I am doted on at home.

4. 因为父亲的关系，她从小就受过不同年代、不同风格的音乐熏陶。

   Owing to her father, she has been surrounded by music of different periods and different styles since childhood.

3. 因为职业的关系，他经常要上夜班。

   Because of his profession, he often has to work the night shift.

对话 *Dialogues*

1. A: 因为北京是首都的关系，所以从四面八方来北京的人很多。

   Since Beijing is the capital, many people come to Beijing from far and near.

   B: 怪不得北京的交通这么拥堵呢。

   No wonder the traffic is so terrible.

2. A: 他学习那么差，怎么还能上这么有名气的学校?

   How could he enter such a prestigious school with such bad performance?

   B: 大概因为他爸爸是校长的关系吧。

   I think it's probably because his father is the principal of the school.

练习 *Exercises*

用"因为 ~ 的关系"完成句子。Complete the sentences with the pattern.

1. _____ ，他晚上常常有应酬。

2. _____ ，我这次不能去看你了。

应~的邀请

解释 *Explanation*

表示接受某人或某组织的邀请而做某事。多用于书面语。

Used mostly in written Chinese to indicate "at one's invitation".

例句 *Examples*

1. 应世界博览会举办方的邀请，张部长参加了开幕式。

   Invited by the host of the World Exposition, Minister Zhang attended the opening ceremony.

2. 我应小方的邀请去参加了她的婚礼。

   I went to Xiao Fang's wedding ceremony at her invitation.

3. 应中国政府的邀请，总统先生将于下月初对中国进行国事访问。

   Invited by the Chinese government, the president will make a state visit to China at the beginning of next month.

4. 应比赛组委会的邀请，范教授将担任本场比赛的评委。

   Invited by the Organizing Committee, Professor Fan will be a judge of this competition.

对话 *Dialogues*

1. A: 我昨天去你家吃了个闭门羹。

   I went to your home yesterday but the door was locked.

   B: 对不起，我应科学院的邀请，去那里作了个学术报告。

   Sorry for that. I was invited by the Academy of Sciences to make an academic report there.

2. A: 明天有足球赛，你知道吗?

   Do you know that there will be a football match tomorrow?

   B: 知道，韩国足球队应我们的邀请，到北京来进行友谊赛。

   Yes, I know. The South Korean football team will come to Beijing for a friendly match at our invitation.

练习 *Exercises*

用"应~的邀请"写两个句子。Make two sentences with the pattern.

1. ＿＿＿＿＿＿＿＿＿＿＿＿＿＿＿＿＿＿＿＿＿＿。

2. ＿＿＿＿＿＿＿＿＿＿＿＿＿＿＿＿＿＿＿＿＿＿。

解释 *Explanation*

表示原因。多用于书面语。

Used mostly in written Chinese to indicate the reason.

例句 *Examples*

1. 由于改革开放的缘故，中国城乡都发生了巨大的变化。

   Owing to the reform and opening up, great changes have taken place in urban and rural areas of China.

2. 由于水流得太急的缘故，堤坝被冲坏了。

   Due to turbulent currents, the dyke was burst.

3. 由于不接受联合国决议的缘故，他们受到了经济制裁。

   Since they did not accept the resolution of the United Nations, they suffered economic sanctions.

4. 由于工作生活压力大的缘故，我年纪轻轻的就生出了很多白发。

   Due to great pressure from work and life, I have had a lot of gray hair at a young age.

对话 *Dialogues*

1. A：为什么这里仍然这么贫困？

   Why is this place still so poor?

   B：是由于交通不方便的缘故。

   Because of poor transport facilities.

2. A：他这么大年纪，怎么身体还这么健壮？

   Why is he still so healthy and strong at such an old age?

   B：那是由于他长期坚持锻炼并注重营养的缘故。

   It's because he keeps exercising and pays attention to nutrition for a long time.

练习 *Exercises*

用"由于 ~ 的缘故"完成句子。Complete the sentences with the pattern.

1. _____，不少人不愿意吃中药。

2. _____，我开始对学习汉语感兴趣了。

解释 *Explanation*

表示某事物的组成结构。

Used to indicate the composition or structure of something.

例句 *Examples*

1. 学校代表团是由老师和学生共同组成的。

   The school delegation is composed of teachers and students.

2. 九三学社是中国的民主党派之一，主要由中高级知识分子组成。

   As one of democratic parties in China, the Jiu San Society comprises senior and middle-level intellectuals.

3. 中国的养老保险由基本养老保险、企业补充养老保险、个人储蓄性养老保险三部分组成。

   The endowment insurance in China is made up of three parts: basic endowment insurance, enterprise supplemental endowment insurance and individual endowment insurance in the form of personal savings.

4. 这个卫星发射中心承担卫星发射任务，由指挥、测试发射、测量控制、通信、气象、技术勤务6个分系统组成。

   This satellite launch center is composed of six sub-systems: command, launch test, measurement control, communication, meteorology and technical service.

对话 *Dialogues*

1. A：你知道水是由什么组成的吗？

   Do you know what water consists of?

   B：水分子是由氧原子和氢原子组成的。

   The water molecule consists of oxygen and hydrogen atoms.

2. A：求职简历一般应包括哪几部分？

   What does a resume include in general?

   B：一般由基本情况、教育背景、工作经历、特长爱好这四个部分组成。

   It's generally composed of four parts: basic information, education, work experience, and skills and interests.

练习 *Exercises*

用"由～组成"完成句子。Complete the sentences with the pattern.

1. 电脑_____。

2. 我们学校的乐团_____。

解释 *Explanation*

在此格式中间嵌入名词或数词短语，表示评价或指明事实，语气略带夸张。

Used in a slightly exaggerating tone to indicate an assessment or a reality, with a noun or numeral phrase between 有 and 呢.

例句 *Examples*

1. 中西部山区不少贫困户都有五六个孩子呢！

   In mountainous areas of central and western China, many poor families have five to six children.

2. 我表妹身材好，举止端庄，很有舞蹈家的气质呢！

   My cousin's good figure and dignified bearing endow her with a dancer's temperament.

3. 虽然股市有些利好消息，可今天大盘下跌了有一百多点呢！

   Although there is some good news about the stock market, the large-cap index dropped by more than 100 points today.

4. 那个新建的学校规模很大，光外国留学生就有一千多呢！

   That new school is very big. It has over 1,000 overseas students alone.

对话 *Dialogues*

1. A: 她喜欢她所学的专业吗？

   Does she like her major?

   B: 可以说很有兴趣呢！

   She is very interested in it, as it were.

2. A: 田处长是个模范丈夫，连做饭也有两下子呢！

   Director Tian is a good husband, and can even cook good dishes!

   B: 你才知道？

   You didn't know that?

练习 *Exercises*

用"有 ~ 呢"完成句子。Complete the sentences with the pattern.

1. A: 你的钱够用不够用？

   B: 足够了，_____！

2. A: 是不是有很多男生追田莉？

   B: 是啊，听说_____！

解释 *Explanation*

表示否定，常用来表示对对方的言行不以为然或不满。

Used to indicate negation, often to express disapproval of or dissatisfaction with the words or actions of the other person.

例句 *Examples*

1. 就是考上了名牌大学又有什么好吹嘘的。

   It's not worth boasting that you enter a prestigious university.

2. 刚到外国，人生地不熟，语言又不通，闹点儿笑话，这有什么奇怪的！

   It's not strange to make a fool of yourself sometimes as you just come to a foreign country as a stranger there and cannot speak the local language.

3. 跟这样不讲理的人还有什么好说的，只能通过法律途径来解决。

   Don't argue with such unreasonable person. Only by legal approaches can you solve it.

4. 你瞧他傲的！有什么值得炫耀的！不就是有个当官的爹吗？

   Look, how proud he is! There is nothing worth showing off! He just happens to be the son of an official.

对话 *Dialogues*

1. A: 我想搞风险投资，但又有点儿担心。

   I want to make risk investments but I'm a bit worried.

   B: 有什么担心的！不冒风险怎么能赚钱？

   What to worry about? How can you earn money without taking risks?

2. A: 我爱上一个小伙子，可又不好意思向他表示。

   I fall in love with a guy but I'm too shy to confess to him.

   B: 这有什么难为情的，都21世纪了。

   There is nothing to be embarassed of. It's already the 21st century.

练习 *Exercises*

用"有什么~的"完成句子。Complete the sentences with the pattern.

1. A: 在游乐园我最怕坐过山车和海盗船了！

   B: _____。

2. A: 明天有毕业论文答辩，我很紧张！

   B: _____。

汉语常用格式330例

解释 *Explanation*

表示有的时候这样，有的时候那样，不是固定不变的。

Used to indicate the situation changes at times.

例句 *Examples*

1. 我有时喜欢热闹，有时喜欢一个人静静地读点儿书。

   Sometimes I enjoy crowds, but sometimes I like to read books alone and peacefully.

2. 我有时觉得她很聪明，有时又觉得她真有点儿傻。

   Sometimes I find her smart, but sometimes I think she is a bit silly.

3. 股票价格总是在波动的，有时涨，有时跌。

   The stock price is always influctuating：sometimes rising, sometimes dropping.

4. 高原地区，温差极大。一天之内，有时热得像夏天，有时冷得像冬天。

   The temperature range is very wide in plateau areas. In one day, it's sometimes as hot as in summer but sometimes as cold as in winter.

对话 *Dialogues*

1. A：你周末都怎么过呢?

   How do you usually spend your weekends?

   B：有时出去爬山，有时待在家里搞卫生。

   I sometimes go to climb mountains, and sometimes stay at home and do some cleaning.

2. A：他的态度真让人捉摸不透。

   His attitude is really unpredictable.

   B：是啊，有时对人非常热情，有时又冷得像块儿冰。

   It's true. He is sometimes warm but sometimes cold as ice.

练习 *Exercises*

用"有时 ~ ，有时 ~"完成句子。Complete the sentences with the pattern.

1. A：你说你不想做饭，也不会做饭，那你吃什么?

   B：_____。

2. A：你上网常看些什么?

   B：_____。

有～无～

解释 *Explanation*

表示有前者，没有后者；或表示有了前者就可以没有后者。

Used to indicate that there is the former but not the latter, or that with the former there is no need for the latter.

例句 *Examples*

1. 这些年外地人在京购房有增无减，所以房价也大幅上升。

   In recent years, the number of flats purchased by outcomers in Beijing has seen all increase but no decrease, and thus the housing price rises sharply.

2. 我真是有眼无珠啊，没看出来沉默寡言的老孟学问竟如此高深。

   I'm as blind as a bat; I have not found that Lao Meng, who is always silent, is so knowledgeable.

3. 虽然现在房价节节攀升，但有价无市，很多人都在观望。

   Although its price is soaring now, housing has no big market because many people take a wait-and-see attitude.

4. 修水库，雨天可以蓄水，旱天可以灌溉，可以说是有备无患。

   Reservoirs are built to retain rain water and irrigate dry land. Preparedness averts peril.

对话 *Dialogues*

1. A：她怎么这么说话呢？真气人！

   How could she speak this way? I'm angry!

   B：她是有口无心，你别计较了。

   She's sharp-tongued but not malicious. Don't argue with her.

2. A：昨天我开车出去差点儿跟人撞车。

   I almost crashed with another car yesterday.

   B：啊，老天爷保佑，有惊无险。以后一定要小心。

   God bless you. It's a near miss. You must be careful in the future.

练习 *Exercises*

选词填空。Choose the right phrases to fill in the blanks.

> 有名无实　　有勇无谋　　有始无终　　有气无力

1. 我只是名义上的经理，什么事都不能做主，真是_____。

2. 她整天病病歪歪的，总是一副_____的样子。

解释 *Explanation*

表示两方面兼而有之，两个"有"分别用在意思相反或相对的词前；或表示强调，这时两个"有"分别用在意思相同或相近的词（或语素）前。

Used separately before two words of opposite or contrastive meanings to indicate that both are involved; or used separately before two words or morphemes with the same or similar meaning for the purpose of emphasis.

例句 *Examples*

1. 这篇报道写得生动具体，有血有肉。

   This report was vivid and true to life.

2. 任何事情都是有利有弊的，所以让人有时候很难取舍。

   Everything has both advantages and disadvantages, and therefore sometimes it's hard to make a choice.

3. 这小伙子在当地是个有头有脸的人，他未来的丈母娘一眼就相中了。

   This young man is quite a personage there and thus has gained approval from by his future mother-in-law at first sight.

4. 别看新来的秘书很年轻，做起事情来却有板有眼、有条有理的。

   Although the new secretary is very young, he handles things in a systematic and organized way.

对话 *Dialogues*

1. A: 小江两口子结婚有十年了，还是恩恩爱爱的。

   It has been ten years since Xiao Jiang got married. The couple remains very affectionate.

   B: 是啊，两个人总是有说有笑的，真让人羡慕！

   It's true. The two always talk and laugh merrily. They are indeed enviable.

2. A: 这事太麻烦了，我不想继续干了。

   This is too troublesome and I don't want to continue.

   B: 那怎么行呢？做事情要有头有尾。

   You shouldn't quit halfway. You have to do it from beginning to end.

练习 *Exercises*

选词填空。Choose the right phrases to fill in the blanks.

| 有凭有据 | 有鼻子有眼儿 | 有多有少 | 有赏有罚 |

1. 我绝对不是瞎说，我是＿＿＿＿＿＿＿＿＿＿的，你们看看这些发票就知道了。

2. 作为管理层，对员工一定要＿＿＿＿＿＿＿＿＿＿，赏罚分明。

有~，有~，还有~

解释 *Explanation*

表示并列的几部分。"还"有进一层的意思，表示项目、数量增加或范围扩大。

Used to indicate parallel parts. 还 indicates the increase in number or expansion in scope.

例句 *Examples*

1. 我家有父母，有姐姐，还有弟弟。

   There are my parents, my elder sister and my younger brother in my family.

2. 一望无边的牧场上有牛群，有羊群，还有牧童和猎狗。

   In the vast pasture there are herds of cattle and sheep, as well as cowboys and hounds.

3. 这里有花草树木，有小桥流水，还有一座寺庙，真像画儿一样。

   The place is picturesque with the flowers, grass, trees, a small bridge over flowing water, and a temple.

4. 如泣如诉的乐曲里有悲伤，有哀怨，还有那剪不断理还乱的缠绵。

   The pathetic and touching music embodies sadness, plaintiveness and abiding affection.

对话 *Dialogues*

1. A: 他们现在日子过得怎么样？

   How is their life now?

   B: 他们现在有钱、有地位，还有很多朋友，过得挺不错的。

   With money, status and many friends, they are living a fairly good life.

2. A: 这地方真是自然美和艺术美的结合。

   This place is really a combination of natural and artistic beauty.

   B: 是啊，有山，有水，还有不少古代建筑。

   I agree. There are mountains, water and many ancient buildings.

练习 *Exercises*

用"有~，有~，还有~"完成句子。Complete the sentences with the pattern.

1. 晚会上好吃的东西多着呢，＿＿＿＿＿＿＿＿＿＿＿＿＿＿＿＿＿。

2. 酒柜里放着各种各样的酒，＿＿＿＿＿＿＿＿＿＿＿＿＿＿＿＿。

解释 *Explanation*

用反问语气表示对再次发生的情况略有不满或指责，有时也用来表示自己的估计是对的。

Used in a rhetorical mood to indicate slight dissatisfaction with or criticism for something's recurrence, and sometimes to express the speaker's estimation is right.

例句 *Examples*

1. 让你多穿点儿你不听，又感冒了不是?

   I told you to wear more, but you didn't listen. So you've caught a cold again!

2. 叫你少喝点儿，你不听，又喝多了不是?

   I told you to drink less but you did not listen. So you get drunk again!

3. 瞧这小子的英文，又现眼了不是?

   Because of his poor English, he made himself a fool again.

4. 你看股市又跌了不是? 幸亏没买。

   Look, the stock market dropped again. Luckily I did not buy.

对话 *Dialogues*

1. A: 你帮我整理一下行李吧。

   Help me to pack, please.

   B: 又来不及了不是? 应该早些准备。

   You're in such a hurry again! You should prepare earlier.

2. A: 我想现在还是不跟他见面好。

   I think I'd better not meet him now.

   B: 你看又变了不是?

   You've changed your mind again!

练习 *Exercises*

根据所给语境用 "又 ~ 了不是" 完成句子。Complete the sentences with the pattern according to the context.

1. 妈妈回家，看到儿子站在门口，知道他又是因为忘带钥匙进不了门。妈妈会说：

   _____?

2. 老师检查晓强的作业，又发现了错字。他会对晓强说：

   _____?

又是～，又是～

解释 *Explanation*

表示几种动作、情况、事物同时存在。

Used to indicate the coexistence of several actions, situations or things.

例句 *Examples*

1. 他酒喝多了，又是哭，又是笑。

   He drank too much, crying while laughing.

2. 看着他那一脸无奈的样子，我又是好气，又是好笑。

   Seeing his helpless expression, I felt angry and found it amusing at the same time.

3. 你瞧你，又是鼻涕又是眼泪的，让人看见了像什么样！

   Look at yourself, a running nose and tears. What a scene you will make if seen by others!

4. 他女朋友真的生气了，他又是哄，又是劝，总算让她露出了笑脸。

   His girlfriend was really angry. He coaxed and tried to persuade her, and finally made her smile.

对话 *Dialogues*

1. A: 餐桌上又是鱼，又是肉，又是新鲜蔬菜，真丰盛！

   There are fish, meat and fresh vegetable dishes on the dining table. It's really sumptuous!

   B: 可以饱餐一顿啦！

   So we can eat to our hearts' content.

2. A: 我从国外给你带了些礼物，快来看看！

   I brought you some gifts from abroad. Come and have a look!

   B: 呀，这又是穿的，又是戴的！真不好意思。

   Wow! There are clothes and accessories! Thank you very much.

练习 *Exercises*

用"又是～，又是～"完成句子。Complete the sentences with the pattern.

1. 同学们聚在一起，＿＿＿＿＿＿＿＿＿＿＿＿＿＿＿，高兴极了。

2. 最近我常常觉得累，决定多补充营养，于是＿＿＿＿＿＿＿＿＿＿，每天吃好多。

解释 *Explanation*

表示对两种情况比较之后进行取舍，说话人认为应放弃前者选择后者。

Used to indicate that the speaker chooses the former rather than the latter after comparison.

例句 *Examples*

1. 与其在这里受气，不如回家种地。

   Better go home for farming than suffer here.

2. 与其在家待着，不如出去找点儿事情做做。

   Better go out and find something to do than stay at home.

3. 面对节节攀升的房价，有些人认为与其买房，不如租房。

   As housing price soars, some people think it is better to rent than to buy a flat.

4. 男孩子总是顽皮的，与其限制他，不如给他空间。

   Boys are always naughty. Better give him room than restrict him.

对话 *Dialogues*

1. A：我们坐公交车去吧。

   Let's go there by bus.

   B：排队的人这么多，与其坐车去，不如走着去。

   There are so many people queuing. Better walk there than take a bus.

2. A：你现在有什么打算？

   What's your plan now?

   B：我觉得与其这样生活，还不如回学校继续深造。

   I would rather pursue further education than live in this way.

练习 *Exercises*

用"与其 ~，不如 ~"完成句子。Complete the sentences with the pattern.

1. A：走，我请你去外面吃。

   B：_____。

2. A：我们买辆二手车吧。

   B：_____。

与其说 ~ , 不如说 ~

汉语常用格式330例

解释 *Explanation*

表示对不同情况或事物进行判断后的选择, 认为后一种说法、看法较恰当。

Used to indicate a choice of the latter one after comparing two different conditions or things.

例句 *Examples*

1. 与其说那是一首诗, 不如说那是一幅画。

   It's more of a painting than a poem.

2. 太极拳与其说是一种肢体运动, 不如说是一种意志的锻炼。

   Taiji Boxing is more of a training of willpower than a kind of body movement.

3. 与其说她是他的太太, 不如说她是他的保姆。

   She is not so much his wife as his nanny.

4. 我对这部电影的评价是: 与其说它是部电影, 不如说这就是现实生活。

   In my opinion, this movie is real life rather than a movie.

对话 *Dialogues*

1. A: 新来的贾秘书对目前的工作不感兴趣, 要辞职。

   Mr. Jia, the new secretary, is not interested in his work and wants to quit.

   B: 与其说他对工作不感兴趣, 不如说他嫌工资及福利待遇太低。

   I would rather put it that he is unsatisfied with the salary and welfare benefits.

2. A: 你看, 我又挨批评了。

   I was criticized again.

   B: 与其说是批评, 不如说是鼓励。

   It's not so much criticism as encouragement.

练习 *Exercises*

用 "与其说 ~ , 不如说 ~" 完成句子。Complete the sentences with the pattern.

1. A: 他说是因为工作忙, 所以很少去看她。

   B: _____。

2. A: 这些学生学习真是不努力, 考得这么差。

   B: 我倒觉得_____。

解释 *Explanation*

表示后事由前事所引起，也可以说"于是乎"。

Used to indicate that the former thing leads to the latter one. 于是乎 can also be used.

例句 *Examples*

1. 为了了解这次重大事故发生的原因，于是成立了调查小组。

   An investigation group was set up to find out the cause of this grave accident.

2. 她觉得自己是好心没好报，越想越委屈，于是大哭了起来。

   She thought she got no thanks for her good intentions and felt hurt, and thus she cried.

3. 他看到自己确实有进步了，于是就觉得学习有意思了。

   He has found himself making progress and thus feels study is interesting.

4. 屋子里太闷，我想出去呼吸点儿新鲜空气，于是就走出了家门。

   It's so stuffy in the room and I want to have a breath of some fresh air. So I walk out.

对话 *Dialogues*

1. A: 你最近精神好像好点儿了。

   It seems that you're more cheerful recently.

   B: 朋友们一直鼓励我，于是我又恢复了信心。

   My friends keep encouraging me and I has regained my confidence.

2. A: 他为什么离开干了十几年的单位？

   Why did he leave the place where he has worked for a dozen years?

   B: 他觉得在原来的单位没什么大发展，于是就决定跳槽了。

   He thought that he had no good prospects there, and therefore decided to leave the job for another.

练习 *Exercises*

用"~，于是 ~"完成句子。Complete the sentences with the pattern.

1. 我想一个人静一静，_____。

2. 他想哄女朋友开心，_____。

汉语常用格式330例

解释 *Explanation*

表示两种事物有关联、有关系。常用来说明某种情况发生的原因。

Used to indicate that two things are linked, related. Often used to explain the cause of something.

例句 *Examples*

1. 他突然感冒、发高烧，肯定与昨晚淋雨有关。

   He suddenly caught a cold and had a high fever. It was certainly because he was caught in the rain last night.

2. 他体重不断增加，与长期缺乏锻炼有关。

   His growing weight is a result of his lack of exercises for a long time.

3. 他这么快就提升为副厂长，与他的组织才能与业务能力有关。

   He was promoted to vice-president of the factory in such a short time because of his organizing ability and professional skills.

4. 严局长很后悔，他明白妻子得肺癌与她长期吸二手烟有关。

   Director Yan is regretful and knows that his wife's lung cancer is a result of long-term passive smoking.

对话 *Dialogues*

1. A: 乔部长对这方面的问题特别敏感。

   Minister Qiao is especially sensitive to such issues.

   B: 这与他的职业有关。

   It's because of his profession.

2. A: 我总是腰酸背痛的。

   My back always aches.

   B: 会不会与床的软硬度不合适有关？

   Is it because that the bed is too soft or too hard?

练习 *Exercises*

用"与 ~ 有关"完成句子。Complete the sentences with the pattern.

1. A: 你未来想从事什么工作呢？

   B: 我想做_____的工作。

2. A: 你为什么要跟我说这件事？

   B: _____。

越(是)~，越(是)~

解释 *Explanation*

表示两个行为、状态的关系，后者随前者的变化而变化。书面语常用"愈（是）～，愈（是）～"。

Used to indicate the relationship between two actions or states：the latter changes with the former. In the written Chinese, 愈（是）～，愈（是）～ is often used.

例句 *Examples*

1. 朋友之间沟通得越多，关系越好。

   The more communication between friends, the better the relationship becomes.

2. 他是个犟脾气，你越劝，他就越不听。

   He is stubborn. The more you try to persuade him, the more impervious he is.

3. 越是年纪大的人，越是要注意锻炼身体。

   The older a person becomes, the more attention he must pay to exercises.

4. 愈是情况紧急，愈是要沉着冷静。

   The more urgent the situation is, the calmer you should be.

对话 *Dialogues*

1. A: 真是的，越忙越出错。

   Shit! The busier I am, the more mistakes I make.

   B: 别慌，别急。

   Don't panic! Take it easy.

2. A: 我说你怎么干得这么慢？别人都等着呢。

   Hey! Why are you working so slowly? Others are waiting.

   B: 咳，越是心急，手脚越是不听话。

   Well, the more anxious I am, the clumsier I become.

练习 *Exercises*

用"越(是)~，越(是)~"完成句子。Complete the sentences with the pattern.

1. 孩子越大，_____。

2. 越是紧张，_____。

解释 *Explanation*

表示某人的观点和看法如何。

Used to indicate one's opinion or viewpoint.

例句 *Examples*

1. 在他看来，发生这种事实在太荒唐、太令人无法理解了。

   In his opinion, it's too ridiculous and incomprehensible that such a thing has happened.

2. 在不少亚洲人看来，儒家学说博大精深。

   Many Asians believe that Confucianism is rich and profound.

3. 在很多企业家看来，产品打入国际市场是最理想的。

   Many entrepreneurs think it's optimal to promote their products into the world market.

4. 在父母看来，甭管自己的孩子多大，永远是孩子。

   In parents' eyes, their children are always children no matter how old they are.

对话 *Dialogues*

1. A: 我想知道您对这件事的意见。

   I want to know your opinion on this.

   B: 在我看来，这件事处理得太急了一点儿。

   In my opinion, it's handled too rashly.

2. A: 冬天到哪儿去旅行好？

   Where shall we travel in winter?

   B: 在我看来，去西双版纳或海南岛最好。

   I think Xishuangbanna or Hainan Island would be the best place.

练习 *Exercises*

用"在 ~ 看来"完成句子。Complete the sentences with the pattern.

1. A: 你觉得在哪里养老好，农村还是城市？

   B: _____。

2. A: 老李，你看这个紧急任务交给谁比较合适？

   B: _____。

解释 *Explanation*

补充另外的或更深层的原因。

Used to add an additional or a deeper reason.

例句 *Examples*

1. 太晚了，我不去了，再说家里人都等着我呢。

   I will not go, because it's too late, and moreover, my family is waiting for me.

2. 别回去了，已经没有公共汽车了，再说你一个人走我也不放心。

   Don't go back. There is no bus now; besides, I will worry about you if you go by yourself.

3. 教练这次没派 17 号运动员上场，因他精神状态不佳，再说教练也想培养锻炼一下新手。

   The coach did not let No. 17 play because he was out of form. Moreover, the coach wanted to train new members.

4. 这事我可帮不了他，再说我也不想帮他。

   I cannot help him with it. Besides, I don't want to.

对话 *Dialogues*

1. A: 明天的谈判要不要叫王秘书也去？

   Shall I ask Secretary Wang to go with us for tomorrow's negotiation?

   B: 别叫他了，他明天有事，再说这些天他也够累的。

   No. He has work to do tomorrow. Moreover, he has been so tired these days.

2. A: 听说你毕业后还打算继续读博士？

   I heard that you wanted to study for doctorate after graduation? Is it true?

   B: 是啊，这里的科研环境好，再说我也没找到合适的工作。

   Yes. The environment here is good for scientific research. Besides, I have not found a proper job.

练习 *Exercises*

用"~，再说~"完成句子。Complete the sentences with the pattern.

1. A: 你说这次老邵怎么没能升职加薪？

   B: _____。

2. A: 最近你老垂头丧气的，怎么了？

   B: _____。

汉语常用格式330例

297

解释 *Explanation*

表示无论在怎样的情况下结果也不会改变。

Used often in an assumption to indicate the outcome won't change under whatever circumstances.

例句 *Examples*

1. 你到了北京，时间再紧也要去看老师。

   When you arrive in Beijing, however tight your schedule is, you must go to visit your teacher.

2. 质量差的产品再便宜也别买。

   Don't buy low quality products no matter how cheap they are.

3. 妈妈为了孩子，再苦再累也心甘情愿。

   For the sake of children, mothers are willing to suffer pain and tiredness.

4. 如果他真的变了心，那你就是付出再多，他也很难回心转意。

   If he really jilts you, he will not change his mind whatever you do for him.

对话 *Dialogues*

1. A: 他家里现在生活的确有困难。

   His family is really in difficulty now.

   B: 再困难也不能偷别人的东西呀。

   No matter how hard his life is, he should not steal.

2. A: 都这么晚了，你就别来了。

   It's so late. You don't have to come.

   B: 不，我想见你，再晚我也要去。

   But I want to see you. However late it is, I will go to your place.

练习 *Exercises*

用"再~也~"改写句子。Rewrite the sentences with the pattern.

1. 不管多么困，我也要做完今天的事情。

   →_____ 。

2. 无论条件多么艰苦，他也不会放弃当个地质学家的梦想。

   →_____ 。

解释 *Explanation*

表示从某个时候起，某种动作行为或情况永远不会发生或一直没有发生过。

Used to indicate that some action or situation would never take place or has not taken place since a certain time.

例句 *Examples*

1. 这个人真差劲儿，我再也不和他交往了。

   This man is no good. I won't deal with him any more.

2. 请你原谅我，以后我再也不会这么粗心大意了。

   Please excuse me. I won't be so careless again.

3. 分手以后，我再也没看见过他。

   After we separated, I haven't seen him any more.

4. 吃了几副这位老中医的药后，我的病再也没复发过。

   After taking the medicine prescribed by this old practitioner of traditional Chinese medicine several times, my illness hasn't recurred any more.

对话 *Dialogues*

1. A: 这家餐馆的菜实在没味道，服务又差。

   The dishes at this restaurant are tasteless, and the service is bad.

   B: 以后再也不来了。

   We won't come again.

2. A: 小李现在是名扬天下了，你最近见过他吗?

   Xiao Li is famous around the world now. Have you seen him recently?

   B: 没有，毕业后我再也没见过他。

   No. I haven't seen him since graduation.

练习 *Exercises*

用"再也不/没 ~"改写句子。Rewrite the sentences with the pattern.

1. 这里小偷真多，我的钱包、相机都被偷走了。以后我永远不会来这儿了。

   →_____。

2. 高中毕业以后，我一直没再学过英语。

   →_____。

解释 *Explanation*

强调事物已达到最高程度。也说"再～不过了"。

Used to indicate the highest degree. 再～不过了 can also be used.

例句 *Examples*

1. 我去过空巢老人的家，真是再冷清也没有了。

   I have been to an empty nest family of the aged. It couldn't be more desolate.

2. 我认为这本书的内容再好也没有了，为什么会被列为禁书呢？

   I think the book couldn't be better. Why is it among the banned books?

3. 你要学会用 MSN，互相联系起来再方便不过了。

   You should learn to use MSN Messenger. It couldn't be more convenient for communication.

4. 他女朋友对他再温顺不过了，他还不知足。

   His girlfriend couldn't be meeker to him, but he is still discontented.

对话 *Dialogues*

1. A：诗人把杭州西湖比作美女西施。

   Poets compare the West Lake of Hangzhou to Xi Shi, a beauty.

   B：这个比喻真是再恰当也没有了。

   This metaphor couldn't be more proper.

2. A：我这件毛衣怎么样？

   What do you think of my sweater?

   B：再漂亮也没有了。

   It couldn't be prettier.

练习 *Exercises*

用"再～也没有了"改写句子。Rewrite the sentences with the pattern.

1. 这次的考试是最容易的。　→＿＿＿＿＿＿＿＿＿＿＿＿＿＿＿。

2. 他们这一对儿是最般配的。→＿＿＿＿＿＿＿＿＿＿＿＿＿＿＿。

解释 *Explanation*

表示事情、情况、动作、行为发生的时间不合适，不受说话人的欢迎。也说"早也不 ~ ，晚也不 ~ ，偏 ~"。

Used to indicate a thing, situation or action takes place at an inconvenient time, which is thus unwelcome. 早也不 ~ ，晚也不 ~ ，偏 ~ can also be used.

例句 *Examples*

1. 你早不到，晚不到，偏在我最忙的时候到！

   You come just at the time when I'm terribly busy!

2. 我怎么早不病，晚不病，偏在这节骨眼上病了？

   Why am I sick at this critical moment?

3. 你看这孩子，早不上厕所，晚不上厕所，偏在我快排到售票窗口的时候，他要上厕所。

   My boy wants to go to the toilet just when it's almost my turn to buy tickets at the wicket.

4. 他这腿早也不伤，晚也不伤，偏在这场最重要的比赛前伤了。

   His leg was hurt just before the most important competition.

对话 *Dialogues*

1. A: 你昨天买的那套高档西服今天降价了。

   The high-end suit you bought yesterday is cheaper today.

   B: 早不降价，晚不降价，偏在我买的第二天降价，真气人。

   Why does the shop reduce price on the second day after I bought it? It makes me crazy!

2. A: 小王，赶快来接电话。

   Xiao Wang, come to answer the phone.

   B: 这电话早也不来，晚也不来，偏在我刚要睡着时来。

   It rings just at the very moment when I almost fall asleep.

练习 *Exercises*

用"早不 ~ ，晚不 ~ ，偏 ~"完成句子。Complete the sentences with the pattern.

1. 这股票＿＿＿＿＿＿＿＿＿＿＿＿＿＿＿＿＿，偏我刚卖就涨。

2. 你看这雨＿＿＿＿＿＿＿＿＿＿＿＿＿＿＿＿＿，偏在我出门时下。

解释 *Explanation*

表示强调很早就发生了某种行为、情况，离现在已经有一段时间。

Used to emphasize that it has been quite a while since some action or situation has taken place.

例句 *Examples*

1. 这孩子很聪明，早就能写一笔好字了。

   This child is very smart and could write well a long time ago.

2. 我和大林已经断了联系，说不定他早就成家立业了。

   I have no contact with Da Lin. Perhaps he has been married and working successfully for a long time.

3. 这件事情发生的经过以及前因后果我们早就调查清楚了。

   We found out the cause, process and result of this event through investigation a long time ago.

4. 其实他们俩早就开始恋爱了，只不过保密工作做得好，大家都不知道。

   Actually they fell in love with each other a long time ago. But they keep it a secret, and we're not aware of it.

对话 *Dialogues*

1. A: 你为什么不告诉我这件事情的真相？

   Why didn't you tell me the truth?

   B: 说真的，我早就该告诉你了，可是一直没有勇气说。

   To be frank, I should have told you earlier, but I didn't have the guts to tell you.

2. A: 嘻嘻，这道数学难题我做出来啦，比你早吧？

   Aha, I have worked out this difficult maths problem. Am I quicker than you?

   B: 我早就做完了，怕打击你才没说。

   I worked it out a long time ago. But I didn't speak out for fear of disheartening you.

练习 *Exercises*

用"早就 ~ 了"完成句子。Complete the sentences with the pattern.

1. A: 她有孩子了吗？

   B: ＿＿＿＿＿＿＿＿＿，都上小学了。

2. A: 你看过这本小说吗？

   B: ＿＿＿＿＿＿＿＿＿。

解释 *Explanation*

表示后面的按照前面的做法去做。

Used to indicate that the latter is based on the former.

例句 *Examples*

1. 领导怎么安排，我们就得怎么做，没商量。

   We should do as our leader arranges. No argument.

2. 我们是双职工，所以平时做饭就是怎么简单、方便怎么做。

   We both have to work. And thus we cook in a simple and convenient way.

3. 你看我怎么做，你就怎么做。很容易掌握。

   Follow me and do as I do. It's easy to master.

4. 怎么有利于国家的发展，有利于人民，咱们就怎么做。

   We should handle the matter in a way that is good for national development and the people.

对话 *Dialogues*

1. A: 范工程师，这活儿怎么干呢？

   Engineer Fan, how shall we do it?

   B: 上次怎么干的，这次还怎么干。

   Do as you did last time.

2. A: 他这个人老是上边怎么说，他就怎么说。

   He always echoes what his superior says.

   B: 怪不得大家管他叫"应声虫"呢。

   No wonder people call him "yesman".

练习 *Exercises*

用"怎么 ~，怎么 ~"完成句子。Complete the sentences with the pattern.

1. 我都听你的，＿＿＿＿＿＿＿＿＿＿＿＿＿＿＿＿。

2. 人和人之间的交往是相互的，＿＿＿＿＿＿＿＿＿＿＿＿＿＿。

怎么能 ~（呢）

解释 *Explanation*

用反问句式表示否定，强调不可能如此，或不应该如此。也说"哪能~呢"。

Used in a rhetorical question to emphasize negation: "it couldn't/shouldn't be like this". It can be replaced by 哪能 ~ 呢.

例句 *Examples*

1. 这么重要的事情，我怎么能忘呢？

   How could I forget such an important thing?

2. 你怎么能这样对老师说话呢？要尊重师长，懂吗？

   How can you speak to your teacher like this? You should respect teachers. Understand?

3. 他哪能做出这样伤天害理的事情呢？

   He can't have done such unhuman things, right?

4. 牵扯到这么多人的事，领导哪能这么草率地处理呢？

   How could the leader handle it so rashly? It involves so many people!

对话 *Dialogues*

1. A: 我不跟你说了，我们有代沟。

   I don't want to talk to you. There is a generation gap between us.

   B: 你怎么能这样跟爸爸说话呢？

   How can you talk to Dad like this way?

2. A: 这日子简直没法过，我们干脆离婚算了。

   I cannot tolerate such a life. Let's simply get a divorce.

   B: 你怎么能说出这么不负责任的话，孩子怎么办？

   How could you say such irresponsible words? How about our child?

练习 *Exercises*

用"怎么能 ~（呢）"完成句子。Complete the sentences with the pattern.

1. A: 这款手机现在不流行了，我要换部新的。

   B: _____。

2. A: 我昨天没刷牙就睡觉了，早上醒来嘴里可不舒服了。

   B: _____，太不卫生了！

解释 *Explanation*

"无论怎么"的意思。"怎么"前面也可用"不管"、"不论"。

Used to indicate "however/no matter how". 不管 or 不论 can also be used before 怎么.

例句 *Examples*

1. 我怎么听也听不出来这两个音有什么不同。

   No matter how hard I listened, I could not find out the difference between the two pronunciations.

2. 这孩子刚睡醒，迷迷糊糊的，怎么逗她也不笑。

   The baby is dazed as she's just waked up. She won't smile no matter how you tease her.

3. 衣服上不知沾了什么，不管我怎么洗都洗不掉。

   There is something on the clothes and I cannot wash it off no matter how hard I try.

4. 他一直跑在我前边，不论我怎么追也追不上他，只好甘拜下风。

   He always runs before me and I cannot catch up with him no matter how hard I try to run. So I have to admit defeat.

对话 *Dialogues*

1. A: 他这样混下去不行，你可得好好劝劝他。

   He should not always fool around like this. You'd better urge him to work hard.

   B: 怎么劝他也不听，我把嘴皮都快磨破了，对他已经没辙了。

   He won't accept my advice whatever I say. I'm at my wit's end.

2. A: 大雪天的，多穿点儿，别感冒了。

   It's snowing. Wear more clothes, or you may catch a cold.

   B: 放心，我身体棒着呢，不管天气怎么冷都没事儿。

   Set your mind at rest. I'm very healthy. I won't get sick however cold it is.

练习 *Exercises*

用"怎么~也/都不~"完成句子。Complete the sentences with the pattern.

1. 不管我怎么解释，_____。

2. 小金的隐形眼镜掉地上了，_____。

汉语常用格式330例

解释 *Explanation*

表示不管条件、情况、规定有什么变化，还是照样做某事，不会因此而改变。多和单音节动词一起用。

Used often with a monosyllabic verb to indicate that something will be done and will not change in spite of changing conditions, situation or regulations.

例句 *Examples*

1. 我真佩服你，这么吵，你也能照睡不误。
   I really admire you. You can sleep in spite of the noise.
2. 有的学校高昂学费照收不误，把教育部的规定当成了一纸空文。
   Some schools continue to charge high tuition fees, regarding the regulation of the Ministry of Education as a mere scrap of paper.
3. 说是公共场所禁止吸烟，可是有不少人还是照抽不误。
   Smoking is forbidden in public places, but some people still smoke regardless of the regulation.
4. 有些市场，没有食品安全意识，过期食品也照卖不误。
   People in some markets have no sense of food safety and continue to sell expired food.

对话 *Dialogues*

1. A: 国家对房价进行宏观调控，效果怎么样?
   The government has exercised macro-control over the housing price. What's the effect?
   B: 我看房价还是照涨不误。
   I think the price is still rising anyway.

2. A: 这种产品，环保部门不是已经亮了红灯了吗?
   Didn't department of environmental protection ban this kind of products?
   B: 是啊，可是他们还是照生产不误。
   Yes. But they continue to produce them.

练习 *Exercises*

用"照 ~ 不误"和所给动词写两个句子。Make two sentences with the pattern and verbs in parentheses.

1. _____。（看）

2. _____。（罚）

解释 *Explanation*

"着呢"用在形容词后，表示程度深，并有夸张的意味。多用于口语。

Often used in oral Chinese after an adjective to indicate a high degree, embodying exaggeration.

例句 *Examples*

1. 那条路坑坑洼洼的，难走着呢。

   That rough road is hard to walk.

2. 你可别招惹他，这个人厉害着呢，常常是无理搅三分。

   Don't provoke that man. He often quibbles even without reason.

3. 你问我什么时候能当教授? 还早着呢。

   You asked me when I could be a professor. It's a long way off.

4. 你可不知道，他的知识面宽着呢，上知天文，下知地理。

   You don't know how wide his range of knowledge is. He knows from astronomy to geography.

对话 *Dialogues*

1. A: 你去过北京长安街吗?

   Have you been to the Chang'an Avenue of Beijing?

   B: 去过，两边的建筑物漂亮着呢。

   Yes, I have. Buildings on the two sides are very beautiful.

2. A: 才几年不见，你女儿都长成亭亭玉立的大姑娘了。

   I haven't seen your daughter for only a few years, and now she is already a pretty girl.

   B: 是啊，女孩子家，变起来快着呢。

   Well, girls grow and change fast.

练习 *Exercises*

用"～着呢"完成句子。Complete the sentences with the pattern.

1. A: 你爷爷奶奶身体都好吧?

   B: 托您的福，他们身体都_____。

2. A: 我来帮你拎着这个箱子吧。

   B: 你可拎不动，_____。

~着玩儿的

解释 *Explanation*

表示对某事不是用严肃、认真的态度去对待，而是以开玩笑的态度去做或只是作为一种业余爱好。

Used to indicate to do something in a joking manner or take it as hobby instead of with a serious attitude.

例句 *Examples*

1. 我刚才是说着玩儿的，你可别当真。

   I was joking just now. Don't take it seriously.

2. 别担心，他们俩是打着玩儿的，伤不着。

   Don't worry. They're fighting for fun, and won't get hurt.

3. 我是个医生，不是作家，小说嘛，只是写着玩儿的。

   I'm a doctor, not a writer. I write novels just for fun.

4. 这吉他我是学着玩儿的，并不想当什么专业演奏家。

   I play the guitar just for fun, and I don't want to be a professional player.

对话 *Dialogues*

1. A: 哇，你拍的照片好漂亮啊，够得上专业水平了。

   Wow! The pictures you took are so beautiful. You can be a professional photographer!

   B: 哪里，哪里，我只是拍着玩儿的。

   Thank you. I take pictures just for fun.

2. A: 听说你演电影了？改行了吗？

   I heard you appeared in a movie. Have you changed your profession?

   B: 那是临时被拉去充数，演着玩儿的，我还是干老本行。

   I was asked to act for the occasion, and I did it for fun. I'm still in my previous profession.

练习 *Exercises*

用"~着玩儿的"和所给动词写两个句子。Make two sentences with the pattern and verbs in parentheses.

1. _____。（唱）

2. _____。（画）

解释 *Explanation*

表示某动作进行中出现了新的情况。"着"前多用单音节动词。

Used to indicate that a new situation occurs in the process of an action. Mostly a monosyllabic verb is used before 着.

例句 *Examples*

1. 他开夜车赶稿子，写着写着睡着了。

   He worked late into the night to dash off a manuscript, but fell asleep.

2. 他刚开始发言时还很平静，可说着说着就激动起来了。

   He was calm at the start of his speech, but became excited then.

3. 你看前面那个小女孩儿刚学会走路，走着走着就摔倒了。

   Look, the little girl just learned to walk, but she fell down while walking.

4. 我们在操场上跑着跑着，忽然下起了倾盆大雨。

   We were running on the playground when it suddenly rained cats and dogs.

对话 *Dialogues*

1. A：她怎么看着看着电影就哭了起来？

   Why did she suddenly cry while watching the movie?

   B：大概是故事触动了她的心事吧。

   Probably because the story touched her.

2. A：我昨晚在邻居家玩儿牌，玩儿着玩儿着天已经大亮了。

   I played cards at my neighbor's home last night. We played and played, and didn't notice it was already the daytime.

   B：这么说你们一夜没睡？

   So you stayed up all night?

练习 *Exercises*

用"~着~着"完成句子。Complete the sentences with the pattern.

1. 那天在舞会上跳华尔兹时，我转着转着，突然_____。

2. 他喝着喝着，_____。

这就 ~

解释 *Explanation*

指马上会发生某种行为或情况。多用于口语。

Used often in oral Chinese to indicate that some action or situation will soon take place.

例句 *Examples*

1. 不要着急，我这就写完，别再催了。

   Don't worry. I will soon finish writing. Don't push me again.

2. 你别慌，我这就来，你千万别走开。

   Don't panic. I will arrive right away. Don't walk away.

3. 阿姨，我这就走，你别给我做饭了。

   I'm going, Auntie. Don't cook for me.

4. 不就这么几个碗碟嘛，我这就去刷，你就别啰嗦了。

   There are only several bowls and dishes. I will wash them immediately. Don't be fussy.

对话 *Dialogues*

1. A: 你怎么还不起床？班车马上就来了。

   Why haven't you got up? The shuttle bus will arrive at once.

   B: 我这就起！

   I'm getting up!

2. A: 小文，饭菜都凉啦，快来吃饭！

   Xiaowen, dishes are becoming cold. Come and eat, quickly!

   B: 好，好，这就来。

   OK! OK! I'm coming.

练习 *Exercises*

用"这就～"完成句子。Complete the sentences with the pattern.

1. 你要的文件，我_____。

2. 不好意思，请稍等一下，_____。

解释 *Explanation*

表示明白了某种情况发生的原因。

Used to indicate that the speaker understands the reason for something.

例句 *Examples*

1. 他家的小狗这么可爱，怪不得人见人爱。

   His puppy is so cute. No wonder everyone likes it.

2. 你最近这么忙啊，怪不得那天秋游没见你去呢。

   You're so busy recently. So that's why I didn't see you in the autumn outing.

3. 这么简单的游戏，票价却这么贵，怪不得没人玩儿。

   Such a simple game charges so much. That explains why nobody comes to play it.

4. 小董的体重增加了这么多，怪不得他说要节食呢。

   Xiao Dong puts on so much weight. That's why he said he would go on a diet.

对话 *Dialogues*

1. A: 这个饭馆一个鱼香肉丝就要30块。

   This restaurant charges 30 yuan for a dish of fish-flavored shredded pork.

   B: 这么贵，怪不得没几个顾客呢。

   So expensive! That's why there are few customers.

2. A: 我最近准备毕业考试，同时还忙着找工作。

   I'm preparing for the graduation examination and busy looking for a job at the same time.

   B: 这么忙啊，怪不得大家都说见不到你的人影儿呢。

   How busy you are! That explains why we haven't seen you recently.

练习 *Exercises*

根据所给语境，用"这么~，怪不得~"完成句子。Complete the sentences with the pattern according to the context.

1. 郝欣今天去听了韩老师的课，说特别有意思，现在他明白了韩老师的课为什么那么受欢迎。他会说：＿＿＿＿＿＿＿＿＿＿＿＿＿＿＿＿。

2. 小陈看大家都不怎么吃"麻婆豆腐"这个菜，觉得奇怪，于是他尝了一口，发现这个菜太辣了。他会说：＿＿＿＿＿＿＿＿＿＿＿＿＿＿。

解释 *Explanation*

表示根据对方提供的情况做出某种推断。

Used to indicate a judgment is made based on what the other provides.

例句 *Examples*

1. 这么说，你们跟他也并不熟悉？

   So, you are not familiar with him either, are you?

2. 这么说，你早就在考虑上这个项目了？

   So, you considered carrying out this project a long time ago, didn't you?

3. 这么说，出事故那天，你根本没在现场？

   So, you were not on the spot the day the accident occurred, were you?

4. 这么说，咱们申请的科研经费可能已经批了？

   So, the funds we applied for scientific research may have already been approved. Is it true?

对话 *Dialogues*

1. A: 我们业务上有联系，但我不太了解他。

   We have business contact. But I don't know much of him.

   B: 这么说，你们接触并不多？

   So, you don't have much contact, do you?

2. A: 这个周末我要和女友去看个新楼盘。

   This weekend, I will go to see a new residential building with my girlfriend.

   B: 这么说，你们打算结婚了？

   So, you're going to get married, aren't you?

练习 *Exercises*

用"这么说，~"完成句子。Complete the sentences with the pattern.

1. A: 我觉得自己可能永远也学不好汉语了。

   B: _____?

2. A: 我吃了一段时间的中药，现在身体好多了。

   B: _____?

解释 *Explanation*

"一"后加动词，整个句子表示经过这个动作，马上就发生了后句所说的情况。

— is followed by a verb and the pattern is often used to indicate that the latter situation takes place soon after the action of the verb.

例句 *Examples*

1. 孩子这么一哭，当妈的就心软了。

   Mother instantly relented when her child burst into tears.

2. 半夜里他这么一喊，把全楼都惊动了。

   All people living in this building were immediately waked up when he shouted at midnight.

3. 他这么一骂，一挥拳头，彻底把对方给惹火了。

   Cursing and shaking his fist, he has provoked the other.

4. 没想到老师拿话这么一激，把学生的好胜心给激起来了。

   It has never occurred to us that the teacher's words have aroused students' ambition to win.

对话 *Dialogues*

1. A：你不觉得这里静得有些反常吗?

   Don't you think it's abnormally quiet here?

   B：你这么一说，我也注意到了。

   I realized it after you've told me.

2. A：下周一我们是不是该交读书心得了?

   Shall we hand in our book reports next Monday?

   B：对，对，你这么一提醒，我想起来了。

   Yes. I remembered after your reminding.

练习 *Exercises*

用"这么一~，~"完成句子。Complete the sentences with the pattern.

1. 你这么一打扮，_____。

2. 他父亲把眼睛这么一瞪，_____。

这么~，这么~

解释 *Explanation*

表示两个方面程度都很高，起加强语气的作用。

Used for emphasis to indicate a high degree in two aspects.

例句 *Examples*

1. 像他这么勤奋，这么老实的人很难得。

   It's hard to find such a diligent and frank man as him.

2. 她这么活泼，又这么善良，没人不喜欢她。

   She is so lively and kind that everyone likes her.

3. 房间里这么闷，这么热，不开空调哪儿受得了。

   It's so stuffy and hot in the room that no one can stand it without turning on the air-conditioner.

4. 这药丸这么大，这么苦，我怎么咽得下去呢？

   This pill is so big and bitter that I cannot swallow it.

对话 *Dialogues*

1. A: 这就是你们的房间。

   This is your room.

   B: 哎呀，这么脏，这么乱，服务员还没打扫呢，怎么住啊？

   Well. It's so dirty and disorderly and has not been cleaned. How can we live in it?

2. A: 这小伙子这么能干，脾气又这么好，哪儿找去呀？

   This young man is so capable and good-tempered that you can hardly find another.

   B: 我说也是。

   I agree.

练习 *Exercises*

用"这么～，这么～"完成句子。Complete the sentences with the pattern.

1. 作业＿＿＿＿＿＿＿＿＿＿＿＿＿＿＿＿＿＿，我做了一晚上才做完。

2. 这部电视剧里的男主角＿＿＿＿＿＿＿＿＿＿＿＿＿＿＿＿＿，我太喜欢他了！

~这~那(的)

解释 *Explanation*

"这"和"那"用来代替动作的多个对象，前面分别用同一动词，表示某动作行为反复多次发生，涉及多个对象。

Used with the same verb to indicate repetition of the same action. 这 and 那 are used to refer to several objects of the same verb.

例句 *Examples*

1. 事情没那么复杂，你别想这想那的了。

   It's not so complex. Don't think too much of it.

2. 想干什么你就大胆地去干，怕这怕那的什么也干不成。

   Do boldly whatever you want to do. You will achieve nothing as a timid person.

3. 爷爷疼孙子，每次见面都要给孙子买这买那。

   Grandpa loves his grandson. Every time he goes to see his grandson, he will buy gifts for him.

4. 他刚出国回来，朋友们围着他问这问那，他也滔滔不绝地讲着所见所闻。

   He just returned from abroad. His friends surrounded him and asked him about this and that, and he kept talking about what he saw and heard.

对话 *Dialogues*

1. A: 我儿子小潘一个人在外地工作，不知过得怎么样，真让我不放心。

   My son Xiao Pan works in another place. I really worry about his life.

   B: 你别总是担心这担心那的，二十几岁的人了，该有独立生活能力了。

   Don't worry too much about him. He is in his twenties and should be able to live a life independently.

2. A: 郑大妈真是个闲不住的人。

   Aunt Zheng is really an active person.

   B: 是啊，整天为别人跑东跑西，忙这忙那的，没见她有停的时候。

   Yes. She runs about and is busy helping other people all day long, and I seldom see her stop and rest.

练习 *Exercises*

用"~这~那（的）"完成句子。Complete the sentences with the pattern.

1. 我每次回家，妈妈总要忙活半天，＿＿＿＿＿＿＿＿＿＿，都是我最爱吃的菜。

2. 他在家什么都要别人伺候，还老＿＿＿＿＿＿＿＿＿＿，一百个不满意。

解释 *Explanation*

表示说话人经过考虑，提出解决问题的办法。

Used to indicate that the speaker proposes a solution after thinking it over.

例句 *Examples*

1. 这样吧，你先回去，到时候我再通知你。

   OK. You go back first and I will notify you in time.

2. 这样吧，你在这儿等一下，我去试试说服她。

   Then, you wait here for a while and I try to persuade her.

3. 我今天实在太忙了，这样吧，我们以后再找时间细谈。

   I'm too busy today. How about talking later in details?

4. 这样吧，你先在我这儿凑合住两天，慢慢再找房子。

   How about this? You manage to stay in my place for a couple of days and take your time to find a house.

对话 *Dialogues*

1. A: 那我现在该怎么办？

   What shall I do now?

   B: 这样吧，你先参加考试，等成绩出来再说。

   Let's do it this way. You take the exam first and we will discuss it after knowing your marks.

2. A: 哎呀，可能赶不上末班车了。

   Well, I may not be able to catch the last bus.

   B: 这样吧，我开车送你回去。

   Let me drive you home.

练习 *Exercises*

用"这样吧，~"完成句子。Complete the sentences with the pattern.

1. A: 明天我五点就要到机场，可首班公交车是五点半。

   B: _____。

2. A: 卢主任，今天该我值夜班，可是我家有急事得回去。

   B: _____。

解释 *Explanation*

表示做了某件事以后，便产生某种结果。

Used to indicate that a certain result comes out because something has been done.

例句 *Examples*

1. 这样一来，全家人就可以在一起生活了。

   So, all the family members can live under one roof.

2. 这样一来，很多人都会知道你的网站了。

   In this way, many people will know your website.

3. 那样一来，你就变被动为主动了。

   In that way, you will transform passivity into initiative.

4. 那样一来，所有的问题就都迎刃而解了。

   In that way, all the problems will be solved.

对话 *Dialogues*

1. A: 你干脆去登一则征婚广告，挑选范围就宽多了。

   You can just put a lonely heart advertisement, and you will have more candidates to choose from.

   B: 这样一来，不是会有很多人骚扰我吗？

   Then many people will disturb me.

2. A: 你要是觉得实在吃不消，就别学了。

   Stopping learning it if you are really unable to stand the hardship.

   B: 那样一来，我不就前功尽弃了吗？

   Then all my previous efforts are wasted.

练习 *Exercises*

用"这/那样一来，～"完成句子。Complete the sentences with the pattern.

1. A: 今天早上我跟我们组长大吵了一架。

   B: 哎呀，这样一来，_____。

2. A: 现在股市行情很好，我看我们把存款都取出来投资吧？

   B: 不行，那样一来，_____。

这也不~，那也不~

解释 *Explanation*

指出某人的否定性行为太多，说话人带有不满的语气。

Used to indicate that the speaker is discontented with the negative actions of another person.

例句 *Examples*

1. 你这也不吃，那也不吃，身体能好吗？

   You eat neither this nor that. How could you be healthy?

2. 这也不满意，那也不满意，我伺候不了你了！

   You're unsatisfied with all. I cannot please you!

3. 你胆子太小了，这也不敢说，那也不敢做，那怎么行。

   You're so cowardly that you dare say nothing. You cannot be that way!

4. 他对我横挑鼻子竖挑眼，这也不行，那也不对，真是欺人太甚！

   He is always finding fault with me and unsatisfied with whatever I do. He really pushes me too hard.

对话 *Dialogues*

1. A: 你给他买着衣服了吗？

   Did you buy clothes for him?

   B: 没买成，他这也说不好，那也说不好，太挑剔了！

   No. He's too picky, unsatisfied with all that we saw.

2. A: 哎，小心，别动我这个花瓶。

   Well, be careful. Don't touch my vase.

   B: 这也不准动，那也不准动，我怎么打扫卫生？

   How can I do the cleaning without touching anything?

练习 *Exercises*

用"这也不~，那也不~"完成句子。Complete the sentences with the pattern.

1. _____，以后一个人怎么生活？

2. _____，你到底喜欢什么？

解释 *Explanation*

对某种情况认为不严重，没什么，不必大惊小怪，也表示无关紧要，无所谓。

Used to indicate that the speaker doesn't think something is serious and asks others not to make a fuss over trifles, or used to indicate something is insignificant.

例句 *Examples*

1. 35 摄氏度，这有什么，北京比这里热多了。

   It's only 35 degree centigrade. No big deal. Beijing is much hotter.

2. 不就是损失了些钱吗？这有什么！只要人没事就行。

   You just lost some money. It's nothing serious, as long as you're safe.

3. 谁说得对，就听谁的。这有什么！

   We'll listen to whoever is right. That's it.

4. 优柔寡断让你吃了点儿亏，这有什么，以后果断一些就是了。

   You suffered from indecision. Take it easy. Be decisive in the future.

对话 *Dialogues*

1. A: 你今天穿的这套衣服太显眼了吧？

   Isn't your dress today too showy?

   B: 这有什么？现在就流行这种款式。

   What's wrong with it? This style is in vogue.

2. A: 你怎么在别人面前这么说他，一点儿面子也不给他留呢？

   Why did you criticize him before others? Why didn't you save face for him?

   B: 这有什么？我说的是事实。

   What's wrong with it? I was telling the truth.

练习 *Exercises*

用"这有什么"完成句子。Complete the sentences with the pattern.

1. A: 他会说两国语言，真了不起！

   B: _____。

2. A: 唉！今天又被老板骂了一通。

   B: _____。

解释 *Explanation*

表示不满、抱怨。

Used to express discontent or complaint.

例句 *Examples*

1. 真是的，我刚睡着，你就把我吵醒了。

   Well, you waked me up just after I fell asleep.

2. 你这人，真是的，跟你开个玩笑你也这么认真。

   Why do you take a joke so seriously?

3. 真是的，这些文件我刚整理好，你又弄乱了。

   Well, I just sorted out these files and you tumbled them again.

4. 真是的，刚回来没几天，你又要走！

   Well, you just came back several days ago, and now you're going again.

对话 *Dialogues*

1. A: 我明天要跟朋友去郊游。

   I'm going for an outing with friends tomorrow.

   B: 真是的，整天不学习，就知道玩儿。

   Well, you don't study but play all day.

2. A: 我的书你带来了吗？我要查些资料。

   Did you bring my book? I want to look something up in it.

   B: 真是的，我又忘了。

   Gosh! I forgot again.

练习 *Exercises*

用"真是的，~"完成句子。Complete the sentences with the pattern.

1. A: 我的电脑又死机了。

   B: _____ 。

2. A: 哎呀，坏了，护照忘带了。

   B: _____ 。

解释 *Explanation*

表示动作正在进行中或某种状态正在持续。如用单音节动词，后面常加"着"。

Used to indicate that an action is going on or to be in a certain state. When a monosyllabic verb is used, 着 often follows it.

例句 *Examples*

1. 刘科长正在大会上发言呢，现在不能接电话。

   Director Liu is giving a speech at the meeting and he cannot answer the call now.

2. 部长打电话来时，局长正吃着饭呢，他撂下碗筷就走了。

   When the minister called, the director was having a meal, but he immediately put down his bowl and chopsticks, and left.

3. 你要请我吃饭？那太好了，我正发愁做什么饭吃呢。

   You invite me to dinner? Great! I was thinking what to cook just now.

4. 突然发生了特大地震灾害，损失惨重，各级领导正忙着救灾呢。

   A strong earthquake occurred suddenly and caused great losses. Leaders at all levels are busy with disaster relief.

对话 *Dialogues*

1. A: 下午的辩论会取消了。

   The debate this afternoon has been canceled.

   B: 太好了，我正想着不去呢。

   Great news! I was considering skipping it.

2. A: 你刚才去他那里，怎么没跟他谈呢？

   Why didn't you talk with him when you were there just now?

   B: 我去的时候他正开会呢。

   He was at a meeting at that time.

练习 *Exercises*

用"正 ~ 呢"完成句子。Complete the sentences with the pattern.

1. A: 邱先生在吗？

   B: 在，请进吧，他＿＿＿＿＿＿＿＿＿＿＿＿＿＿＿＿＿。

2. A: 我买了些点心，过来一起吃吧。

   B: 你买得太及时了，＿＿＿＿＿＿＿＿＿＿＿＿＿＿＿。

正因为～，才～

解释 *Explanation*

强调正是由于所说的原因，才产生某种结果。

Used to emphasize that the fact mentioned leads to a certain result.

例句 *Examples*

1. 正因为我昨天喝得太多，才误了今天的大事。

   It is because I drank too much yesterday that I caused delay in today's business.

2. 正因为有人袒护着他，他才这么放肆。

   He's so impudent just because he is shielded.

3. 正因为他们平时刻苦训练，在赛场上才能大显身手。

   Owing to their painstaking practice, they could show their abilities on the court.

4. 正因为我们是好朋友，我才对你直言不讳。

   I'm frank with you because we are good friends.

对话 *Dialogues*

1. A：听说他爸爸是大企业的老板。

   I heard his father was the boss of a big company.

   B：是啊，正因为有个有钱的爸爸，他才那样目中无人。

   Yes. It is because he has a rich father that he looks down upon everyone else.

2. A：明天就要高考了，你怎么还出去玩儿啊？

   You will take the college entrance exam tomorrow. Why are you going out to play?

   B：正因为要面临几天的考试，我才要出去放松放松。

   Because the exam will last several days, I need to relax myself.

练习 *Exercises*

用"正因为～，才～"完成句子。Complete the sentences with the pattern.

1. A：四川菜这么辣，你怎么吃得下去？

   B：＿＿＿＿＿＿＿＿＿＿＿＿＿＿＿＿＿，不辣我还不爱吃呢！

2. A：夫妻不是最亲近的人吗？为什么常争吵得很厉害？

   B：＿＿＿＿＿＿＿＿＿＿＿＿＿＿＿＿＿＿＿＿。

解释 *Explanation*

表示某件事情的原因和结果，结果在前，原因在后。强调原因。

Used to indicate the reason and result of something, with the result before the reason and the emphasis is on the reason.

例句 *Examples*

1. 我之所以急于见校长，是因为有要事请示。

   I'm eager to meet the president because I have something important to ask him for instructions.

2. 世界之所以精彩，是因为它的多元性。

   The world is splendid because of its diversity.

3. 他之所以有现在的成就，是因为他父母在他幼儿时期就注意培养和教育。

   It is because his parents paid much attention to his education in his childhood that he has the current achievements.

4. 伟人之所以伟大，是因为他与别人同处逆境时，别人失去了信心，他却下决心实现自己的理想。

   A great man is great because in adversity he's determined to realize his ideal while others have lost their confidence.

对话 *Dialogues*

1. A: 他怎么生那么大的气?

   Why is he so angry?

   B: 他之所以生气，是因为事前没和他打招呼。

   He is angry because we did not tell him beforehand.

2. A: 他为何要赞助这所大学?

   Why did he sponsor this university?

   B: 他之所以捐款，是因为想让其子女能免试进入这所学校。

   He donated money because he wanted his children to enter this university without taking exams.

练习 *Exercises*

用 "之所以 ~，是因为 ~" 完成句子。Complete the sentences with the pattern.

1. A: 他今天为什么请我们吃饭呢?

   B: _____。

2. A: 我们两国贸易为什么能发展得这么快?

   B: _____。

直到~，才~

解释 *Explanation*

表示事情发生得晚，多用于已发生的事件。

Used to indicate that something happens late, mostly referring to something that has already taken place.

例句 *Examples*

1. 直到分手以后，我才知道他在我心目中的分量。

   I didn't know how important he was in my heart until after we broke up.

2. 直到回到了家，我才发现手提包丢在车上了。

   I didn't notice that I left my handbag on the bus until I arrived home.

3. 直到我自己当了妈妈，才真正体会到做母亲的心。

   I didn't understand maternal love until I became a mother myself.

4. 直到酿成大错，他才认识到自己粗枝大叶的危害。

   He didn't know the harm of his carelessness until he made a serious mistake.

对话 *Dialogues*

1. A: 听说他有些后悔离开了那家公司？

   I heard he was a bit regretful for leaving that company?

   B: 是的，直到经历过这些事情之后，他才知道还是原来的单位好。

   It's true. He didn't realize the advantages of the previous employer until he has experienced all these.

2. A: 昨天你下班后怎么又回办公室了？

   Why did you go back to office after work?

   B: 别提了，直到爬上了十层，才想起钥匙忘在办公室了。

   Well, it didn't occur to me that I left the key at office until I climbed up to the tenth floor.

练习 *Exercises*

用"直到~，才~"完成句子。Complete the sentences with the pattern.

1. A: 你很早就开始学汉语了吗？

   B: 不，_____。

2. A: 这两天天气怎么这么闷热！

   B: 是啊，热得我昨天_____。

解释 *Explanation*

"仅仅是"的意思，表示不太重要或数量不多。句子末尾可跟"罢了"或"而已"搭配。

Used to indicate something is not very important or the quantity of something is not great. It can be followed by 罢了 or 而已 at the end of the sentence.

例句 *Examples*

1. 大家只不过不想多给你添麻烦罢了，没别的意思。

   We just don't want to bring trouble to you. No disrespect.

2. 赵总只不过损失了上千块钱，对她来说没什么大不了的。

   Manager Zhao only lost a few thousand yuan. It's no big deal for her.

3. 在人生的道路上这只不过是微不足道的困难，何必垂头丧气。

   This is only a trivial difficulty in your life. You don't have to be down-hearted.

4. 他只不过是个小职员而已，哪来那么多钱老去泡夜总会？

   He's just a junior clerk. Where does he get so much money to frequent night clubs?

对话 *Dialogues*

1. A: 你只不过丢了一支钢笔，就急成这样子呀。

   You only lost a pen, and are so worried.

   B: 那可是我爷爷的遗物，对我来说是无价之宝。

   The pen is priceless for me because it was left behind by my late grandpa.

2. A: 哟，这古董可真是天价呀，你要买？

   Oh! This antique is really expensive. Are you going to buy it?

   B: 不，只不过问问价钱罢了。

   No, I just asked about the price.

练习 *Exercises*

用"只不过~"完成句子。Complete the sentences with the pattern.

1. A: 这么大的项目你都敢接下来，真佩服你的勇气。

   B: 我_____。

2. A: 你脸色苍白，不舒服吗？

   B: 没事儿，_____。

只要 ~ ，就 ~

解释 *Explanation*

表示具备某种条件，就有相应的结果。

Used to indicate that a result will come out under a certain condition.

例句 *Examples*

1. 只要大家齐心协力，就没有办不到的事情。

   As long as we make concerted efforts, there is nothing we cannot do.

2. 只要有勇气、有信心，就一定能克服困难。

   With courage and confidence, we can surely overcome difficulties.

3. 只要我还有一口饭吃，就不会让你饿肚子。

   As long as I have a piece of bread, I won't let you get hungry.

4. 只要大家出谋划策，设法降低成本，就能增加利润。

   As long as all contribute ideas to cut down cost, we can have more profits.

对话 *Dialogues*

1. A: 不管遇到多大的困难，我们都不要灰心，只要有毅力，就能达到目的。

   Whatever hardships we meet, we can achieve our goal so long as we don't lose heart and persevere in it.

   B: 对，我们应该继续干下去。

   I agree. We should continue.

2. A: 你目前有没有告别舞台的打算？

   Do you have plans to leave the stage now?

   B: 没有，只要观众需要，我就会一直干下去。

   No. As long as audience needs me, I will always be on the stage.

练习 *Exercises*

用 "只要 ~ ，就 ~" 完成句子。Complete the sentences with the pattern.

1. ＿＿＿＿＿＿＿＿＿＿＿＿＿＿＿，就行。

2. 只要能跟你在一起，＿＿＿＿＿＿＿＿＿＿＿＿＿。

解释 *Explanation*

表示只有具备某种条件，才有某种结果。

Used to indicate some result will come out only under a certain condition.

例句 *Examples*

1. 我们只有深入社会，才能了解真实情况。

   Only when we go deep into society, can we know the true situation.

2. 这个问题我看只有你亲自来，才有可能解决。

   I think this problem won't be solved unless you handle it personally.

3. 只有登上长城，才能体会到"不到长城非好汉"。

   Only when you climb to the top of the Great Wall, can you understand the saying "He who has never been to the Great Wall is not a true man."

4. 只有让人们都认识到"善待地球——从身边小事做起"，才能保护我们的地球。

   Only when people all understand the importance of "Be kind to the earth and start from small things" can the earth be protected.

对话 *Dialogues*

1. A: 说真的，只有跟你在一起，我才感受到真正的幸福。

   To tell you the truth, I'm really happy only with you.

   B: 我也是。

   So am I.

2. A: 章先生不爱说话，别人不容易接近他、了解他。

   Mr. Zhang is not talkative, and thus others find it not easy to approach and understand him.

   B: 只有多跟他接触，才能知道他这人有多好。

   Only when you have more contact with him, will you know what a good man he is.

练习 *Exercises*

用"只有 ~，才"完成对话。Fill the blanks with the expression.

1. A: 怎么才能学好外语呢？

   B: _____。

2. A: 中国经济怎么才能发展得更快？

   B: _____。

~，至于~

解释 *Explanation*

"至于"用在与前一个话题相关的后一个话题前，起转换话题的作用。

Used between two related topics for a change from one topic to another.

例句 *Examples*

1. 我只想把汉语口语学好，至于汉字写得好坏我就不管了。

   I only want to learn oral Chinese well, but I don't care my handwriting.

2. 给伯父看好病要紧，至于钱我来想办法。

   The most important thing is to get uncle cured. I will try to get the money.

3. 暑假我要出国转转，至于去哪儿还没最后定。

   I will travel abroad during the summer vacation, but I haven't decided my destination.

4. 我保证我一定支持你们，至于老黄嘛，我就没那么大的把握了。

   I promise I will support you. As for Lao Huang, I'm not so sure.

对话 *Dialogues*

1. A: 魏总，这么大的项目，咱们的经费可能不够。

   Manager Wei, we may not have sufficient fund for such a big project.

   B: 你就尽全力搞好设计，至于经费，我会解决的。

   You just focus to do your best in design. As to the fund, I'll see to it.

2. A: 你认为今天股市还会继续下跌吗?

   Do you think the stock market index will go on dropping today?

   B: 今天肯定要反弹，至于反弹的力度我就说不好了。

   I'm sure it will rebound today, but I'm not so sure how many points.

练习 *Exercises*

用"~，至于~"完成句子。Complete the sentences with the pattern.

1. 这几个菜中，咕咾肉做得非常地道，_____ 。

2. 这个小区的位置是没的说，_____。

解释 *Explanation*

表示重视一个方面，轻视另一个方面。

Used to indicate to value one aspect and belittle the other.

例句 *Examples*

1. 企业要发展就不能对产品重数量轻质量。

   Valuing quantity over quality of products is not a way to develop enterprises.

2. 不少单位招聘人员时重学历轻实践能力。

   Many companies attach importance to educational background instead of practical abilities when recruiting employees.

3. 投资专家建议，未来投资操作应重个股轻指数。

   Some investment experts suggest that shareholders should pay more attention to individual shares instead of index in future operations.

4. 现在家庭装修工程出现了重装饰轻装修的新风潮。

   Now a new wave of decoration rather than home improvement has come to vogue for home refurbishing.

对话 *Dialogues*

1. A: 我最近交了个女朋友，搞雕刻艺术的。

   I'm dating a girl recently, and she is a carving artist.

   B: 怪不得不来找我们玩儿了，呵呵，重色轻友。

   That's why you didn't come to play with us. Aha, you put your girlfriend before your buddies.

2. A: 为什么中国在技术方面落后于西方？

   Why does China lag behind the West in terms of technology?

   B: 因为中国历来重知识轻实践。

   It's because Chinese people always regard knowledge superior to practice.

练习 *Exercises*

选词填空。Choose the right phrases to fill in the blanks.

| 重男轻女 | 重理轻文 | 重钱轻德 | 重爱情轻友情 |

1. 现在很多地方仍然有＿＿＿＿＿＿＿＿的封建思想，只有生了男孩儿父母才高兴。

2. 中国的学生有＿＿＿＿＿＿＿＿的倾向，很多人不重视语文、历史等课程。

解释 *Explanation*

强调同类行为、动作或某种情况的多次反复。后面可用动词性词语；也可以用"一 +
量词"，量词后有时可以加名词。

Used to emphasize the repetition of the same action or the recurrence of similar situations. After 左 and 右, a verbal word or 一 + measure word (sometimes followed by a
noun) can be used.

例句 *Examples*

1. 左也不是，右也不是，你让我怎么办？

   I have tried a hundred and one ways. What shall I do? You tell me.

2. 左一个元宵节，右一个端午节，中国节日可真不少哇。

   China has quite a few festivals, from the Lantern Festival to the Dragon Boat Festival.

3. 这孩子嘴真甜，左一声"叔叔"，右一声"叔叔"，叫得我心里乐开了花。

   The child is honey-lipped and keeps calling me uncle, making me so happy.

4. 田大嫂凭着三寸不烂之舌，左说右说，终于把那姑娘给说动心了。

   Aunt Tian kept persuading the girl with her glib tongue and finally succeeded.

对话 *Dialogues*

1. A: 你找到辛会计报销了吗？

   Did you find Accountant Xin for reimbursement?

   B: 找是找到了，不过我左一趟右一趟，跑了好几趟才找到的。

   Yes, I did. But I went there several times before I finally found him.

2. A: 他怎么到现在还没有女朋友？

   Why does he still have no girlfriend now?

   B: 他呀，左挑鼻子右挑眼的，很难找哇。

   Well, he is too picky to find one.

练习 *Exercises*

用"左 ~ 右 ~"完成句子。Complete the sentences with the pattern.

1. 他说不喝酒，可今天_____，喝起来没完了。

2. 我_____，还是决定不去了。

图 书 推 荐
Highlights

HSK核心词汇天天学（上、中、下）
One Hour Per Day to a Powerful HSK Vocabulary (3 volumes)
210×285 mm
▲ 汉英 Chinese-English edition
  Vol Ⅰ: ISBN 9787802005945，214pp，¥49.00
  Vol Ⅱ: ISBN 9787802005952，214pp，¥49.00
  Vol Ⅲ: ISBN 9787802005969，214pp，¥49.00

HSK语法精讲精练
Practising HSK Grammar
▲ 汉英 Chinese-English edition
ISBN 9787802004511
210×285mm，252pp
¥58.00

汉语病句辨析九百例
Error Analysis of 900 Sample Sentences
▲ 汉英 Chinese-English edition
ISBN 9787800525155
140×200mm，332pp
¥35.00

简明汉语语法
A Concise Chinese Grammar
▲ 汉英 Chinese-English edition
ISBN 9787800525483
138×200mm，244pp
¥22.80

汉语语法难点释疑
Difficult Points in Chinese Grammar
▲ 汉英 Chinese-English
ISBN 9787800522024
140×200mm，245pp
¥29.00

汉语语法新通路
New Path Getting over Chinese Grammar
▲ 汉英 Chinese-English edition
ISBN 9787802006133
185×260mm，176pp
¥29.00

一百句式汉语通（附MP3）
Learn Chinese Through 100 Sentence Frames（with MP3）
▲ 汉英 Chinese-English
ISBN 9787802004054
210×145mm，220pp
¥58.00

责任编辑：任　蕾
英文编辑：韩芙芸
封面设计：黄金支点
印刷监制：佟汉冬

图书在版编目（CIP）数据

汉语常用格式 330 例：汉英对照／陈如，朱晓亚编著.
—北京：华语教学出版社，2009
ISBN 978-7-80200-647-8

I. 汉… II. ①陈… ②朱… III. 汉语—对外汉语教学—自学参考资料 Ⅳ.H195.4

中国版本图书馆 CIP 数据核字（2009）第 149382 号

汉语常用格式 330 例

陈如　朱晓亚　编著
＊

© 华语教学出版社
华语教学出版社出版
（中国北京百万庄大街 24 号　邮政编码 100037）
电话：(86)10-68320585, 68997826
传真：(86)10-68997826, 68326333
网址：www.sinolingua.com.cn
电子信箱：hyjx@sinolingua.com.cn
北京密兴印刷有限公司印刷
2010 年（16 开）第 1 版
2012 年第 1 版第 2 次印刷
（汉英）
ISBN 978-7-80200-647-8
定价：79.00 元